# ON ISLAND
# TIME

# ON ISLAND

## KAYAKING THE CARIBBEAN

# TIME

## SCOTT B. WILLIAMS

UNIVERSITY PRESS OF MISSISSIPPI / JACKSON

www.upress.state.ms.us

The University Press of Mississippi is a member of the
Association of American University Presses.

All photographs by Scott B. Williams unless otherwise credited

13 12 11 10 09 08 07 06 05   4 3 2 1

Library of Congress Cataloging-in-Publication Data

Williams, Scott B.
  On island time : kayaking the Caribbean / Scott B. Williams.
    p. cm.
  ISBN 1-57806-746-4 (cloth : alk. paper)—ISBN 1-57806-747-2 (pbk. : alk. paper)
  1. West Indies—Description and travel. 2. Key West (Fla.)—Description and travel.
3. Sea kayaking—West Indies. 4. Sea kayaking—Florida— Key West. 5. Williams,
Scott B.—Travel. 6. Caribbean Area—Description and travel. I. Title.
  F1613.W55   2005
  917.29053—dc22

                                                            2004020803

British Library Cataloging-in-Publication Data available

FOR MICHELLE, WHO EVERY DAY
MAKES ME GLAD I FOUND
MY WAY BACK TO MISSISSIPPI

# CONTENTS

# FOREWORD

I met Scott Williams in 1985 when my wife signed up for his kenpo karate course in McComb, Mississippi. When Scott found out I liked to canoe, he suggested we make a float together. Soon we were embarked on a three-day trip down Red Creek and the Pascagoula River in flood conditions, a real swamp adventure.

On that trip I learned that Scott has the first trait necessary to be a good adventurer: a sense of humor. We kept up a stream of ridiculous stories, puns, and jokes, meanwhile enjoying the fabulous scenery of giant cypress trees, redbuds, cottonmouth snakes, herons, and beavers.

Later we tackled a more challenging trip, a week's paddle in the Florida Everglades. On the fourth day we forced our canoe up a narrow channel in the grass until it would go no farther. Then Scott pointed to a distant clump of trees and said, "Want to hike over there?" Hiking in this environment meant wallowing up to our knees in snake- and alligator-infested marsh. That's when I knew he possessed the second quality necessary for a good adventurer: a love of exploring.

Scott and I kept paddling over the years. Meanwhile he discovered and fell in love with sea kayaks and eventually set off on the trip described in this book. He kept me posted on his exploits, and I ran excerpts from his journal in the *McComb Enterprise-Journal* newspaper where I work.

When the journey was over, Scott and I met on the banks of Bowie Creek, where he regaled me with his experiences. I saw then (and other times) that he had the third characteristic necessary for a good

[ ix ]

adventurer: humility. Despite his incredible accomplishments, Scott did not—and still doesn't—believe he's done anything extraordinary. I'm sure you will agree with me how wrong he is in that regard.

As I've read his journals and later magazine articles and other writing, I discovered Scott has another attribute that, though perhaps not necessary for a good adventurer, is mighty helpful: a talent for writing. As you will see, Scott is a top-notch writer—as good a writer as he is an adventurer, in fact, and that's saying a lot!

—ERNEST HERNDON

# ACKNOWLEDGMENTS

I would like to thank Craig Gill, editor-in-chief of the University Press of Mississippi, for support and suggestions regarding the preparation of the manuscript, and also outdoor author and fellow adventurer Johnny Molloy for advice that helped improve the narrative. This book would likely not exist if not for Michelle Calvert, to whom it is dedicated, who insisted that I should submit the manuscript for publication, despite the time that has passed since I returned from the journey described in these pages. I must also thank Christopher Cunningham, editor of *Sea Kayaker* magazine, who was the first to publish a short description of the journey. That article and others I wrote for this excellent magazine led to writing of this and other books.

Once again I must thank Ernest Herndon, my longtime canoeing partner and faithful friend, who was one of the few who did not doubt me or try to discourage me when I announced my intentions to attempt this trip. Ernest's adventures in the wilds of New Guinea and elsewhere were an inspiration to a young man who grew up in a place where such travel was unheard of. Ernest also encouraged me to keep a daily journal, and his regular newspaper stories kept friends and family informed of my whereabouts and inspired me to begin writing myself.

The journey would not have been possible without the support of my father, Frank Williams Jr., who has always been there for me, even though he might have questioned the logic of some of my undertakings over the years. My mother, Barbara Burgin Williams, has since passed on, but always inspired me to travel, explore, and learn, and even in her long and difficult illness set an example to all by smiling in the face of pain and adversity.

I am indebted to many other family members and close friends who in various ways helped make this trip possible, either at the beginning or end, or by sending letters or accepting my collect phone calls: my brothers; Frank and Jeff, and my sister Jenny and sister-in-law, Cathy; and Jeff Hudson, Martha Daley, Charlie Mayes, Dr. Steve Ross, Donna Rowland, Sara Szot, Rick Venturini, John Herman, Dennis Lawson, Robert Whiteside, Christopher Carter, Dek Terrell, Jenny Geraci, Elaine and Zeida Solis, Brianne Krupshaw, and Gary Delancy.

Those who helped with the equipment needed for the trip include Patrick Milton of Olde Sarge's Outdoor Center in Pensacola, Florida; the Gulf Coast Outdoor Club; world-renowned sea kayaking author John Dowd; Mike Neckar of Necky Kayaks; Bill Wildprett of Johnson Camping/Eureka Tents; Bill Masters of Aquaterra/Perception; and Mary Skinner of Recovery Engineering, Inc.

And I would especially like to thank all those wonderful people I met along the way who befriended and assisted me and enriched my solo journey far beyond what I ever envisioned when I set out: Ben, Sylvia, Sky, and Grant Olsen of *Whisper,* Pete Hill and Marty Zinn, Mike Williams, Lisa Roell, Frank Holzmacher and Josephine Adams of *Celebration,* Laura and Lawrence Pitcairn of *Heron I,* Lis Basballe and Mark of *Elske,* Dennis and Dee Catanzaro, and Charlie Leach of *Destiny,* Fred Long and Mary Eldergill of *Estrelita,* Charlotte Sirutus, Christine Thompson of *Foxglove,* George Bouillon and Millie of *Winning Edge,* John and Mary Gookin, Geoff Gordan, Bill and Maryanne of *Stay Up,* Jack and Veronica of *English Jack,* Viola Paulopski, Fred and Katy Ballou of *Cat Ballou,* Roy and Jane of *Magic,* and countless others whose names I either don't recall or never learned.

And finally, I want to thank Jimmy Buffett, a fellow Mississippi native who wrote the songs about the islands that made me have to go.

# ON ISLAND TIME

# ONE

# LEAVING

I went to the woods because I wished to live deliberately, to front only the essential facts of life, and see if I could not learn what it had to teach, and not, when I came to die, discover that I had not lived.

—HENRY DAVID THOREAU, *WALDEN*

There was never a question as to where I would begin my journey south. I was not sure if I would ever return, or even if I would survive what I was about to undertake. I wanted this time on the river so that I could indelibly imprint the sights, smells, and sounds of a favorite place into memory and carry a part of it with me. I wanted perfection for the first week of my travels, and I knew I would find it there, as I always had.

The color of well-aged whiskey, tannin-stained but clear, Black Creek flows over a bed of pure white sand as it meanders through cathedral forests of old-growth pine and southern hardwoods. Days of paddling this stream would be days of stillness and peace, punctuated by the quiet music of the gentle current and birdsong from the walls of green surrounding the way. I knew that wind and rough water waited beyond this ribbon of tranquility, but that would not intrude into my thoughts yet.

I would begin on Black Creek, because it was the beginning of everything that led me to the first step of this odyssey. My first overnight canoe trip had been there, and later my first experience of multiple days alone in the woods, camping and paddling and becoming comfortable with solitude.

This was to be a journey of solitude beyond anything I had ever known, but it would not start that way. I would have company for this first week, an escort downstream to the Gulf of Mexico. My canoeing partner Ernest Herndon and I had already paddled many waters together. We had explored the wilder reaches of the Everglades in south Florida, and there I got my first taste of the tropics. Ernest was not among the doubters when I began announcing my intentions to friends and family. He would take this week to paddle Black Creek with me and see me off, but he was not enamored of the sea. And being married and gainfully employed, he was not free to travel for the many months I expected to be gone.

We waited until late afternoon on a Sunday to arrive at the launching site near the community of Brooklyn, so that the weekend day-paddlers would be thinning out and thinking about getting back to work on Monday. A small mountain of gear began growing on the sandbar under the bridge as we unloaded the vehicles. Ernest had arrived with his wife, Angelyn. My ex-girlfriend had graciously agreed to bring me to the river in her car, since I no longer owned one. A few other friends had come along to witness my departure as well.

A couple of curious canoeists came over to look at our unusual boats. Sea kayaks were not often seen on Black Creek. Ernest was paddling the first one that I'd acquired, a yellow sixteen-foot Aquaterra Chinook, and I had an identical model in white, brand-new and provided for the trip by Perception Kayaks. I had insisted on the neutral color after reading somewhere that the bright shade of yellow of my first kayak had been dubbed "yum-yum yellow" by shark researchers trying to determine which colors might be most likely to provoke attacks. The kayaks were equipped with waterproof bulkheads and hatches for gear storage fore and aft of the cockpit. Each had a stern-mounted rudder

Ernest Herndon paddling a sea kayak past the forested banks of Black Creek

connected to foot pedals in the cockpit so that the paddler could focus on forward motion rather than steering strokes.

I told the canoeists we were paddling to the coast, a trip of about 150 miles with all the bends, most of it on Black Creek and the last stretch on the much larger Pascagoula River. The afternoon was almost gone and we still had to pack the boats and paddle down to a more secluded campsite. I didn't have time to explain myself and answer lots of questions, so I didn't mention where I was headed after I reached the coast. How could they comprehend that my destination was in the West Indies—and that I planned to paddle this twenty-four-inch-wide boat down the coast of Florida, then island-hop along the chain of the Bahamas and Antilles all the way to Trinidad, just off the coast of South America? Would anybody other than Ernest believe it was possible? I wasn't sure what he *really* thought, but at least he didn't try to talk me out of it like so many others did, and for that I was grateful.

Ernest had packed for a canoe trip, with all his gear carefully arranged in two large duffel bags. He dumped the contents of the bags on the sand in disgust when he saw how I was carefully pushing each item one at a time through the small hatches of the kayak's storage compartments. If we were canoeing, he could simply place his bags in the bottom of the canoe, tie them to a thwart for security, and paddle away.

Sea kayaks are much more complicated to pack and just as aggravating to unload at the campsite each evening after a long day of paddling. Even though the gear would be inside watertight compartments, I knew from experience that it was also wise to seal things that mustn't get wet inside waterproof bags before putting them in the kayak. I had lots of Ziploc freezer bags as well as specialized waterproof gear bags for this purpose.

Ernest was not prepared for this kind of packing. Some of the larger items he was used to carrying in the canoe had to go back in Angelyn's car. He found room in the kayak for his groceries, campfire sipping whiskey, coffee pot, propane stove, sleeping bag, camera, and a hammock and novel, as if he expected to spend a lot of time lounging around camp on this trip.

I sorted though my gear, looking for those least-likely-to-be-needed items that would be stuffed into the far extremities of the bow and stern of my kayak. These included my tool kit, spare rudder parts, and the snorkeling gear that I didn't expect to use until I reached clear tropical waters. Everything had a designated place in the boat. I had test-packed the kayak numerous times in the previous weeks of the gear selection process.

I marked every item off my three-page checklist as it went into its respective home in the boat. There was the usual wilderness camping gear: expedition-quality tent, sleeping bag, Coleman stove, cookware, hammock, machete, various knives, matches, candles, and two waterproof flashlights. There was gear specialized to sea kayaking: life jacket, bilge pumps, spare paddle, spare sprayskirt, large waterproof lantern with rechargeable Ni-Cad batteries, handheld VHF radio, a radio direction finder, a marine compass mounted on the deck of the kayak, emergency flares, and carefully waterproofed nautical charts.

Because of the anticipated length of my trip I had other items that would never be taken on weekend getaways. These included the usual camping and beach clothing but also some nice casual shirts and slacks presentable enough for the occasional civilized stopover. I had an extensive stock of first aid supplies. Also in the emergency category was an expensive hand-operated reverse-osmosis desalinator, capable of converting seawater to drinking water, in case I was lost at sea or stranded on some waterless island. I had means of procuring food as well: an assortment of fishhooks and lures, rod and reel, pole spear for underwater hunting with the mask and snorkel, and a compact .22 caliber survival rifle that could be taken apart; the barrel and receiver stowing inside the hollow plastic stock. I also had the means to defend myself against sharks in the low-riding kayak; a .223 caliber "bang stick" that would be carried right on deck in tropical waters, as advised by another kayaker who had paddled extensively in the Caribbean. A compact .22 caliber Beretta pistol would be kept beside me in the tent on all those foreign beaches where I knew I would feel lonely and vulnerable.

My library included: *How to Survive on Land and Sea, Fundamentals of Kayak Navigation, A Cruising Guide to the Caribbean,* a booklet about the Everglades' Wilderness Waterway, a guide to blues harmonica playing, French and Spanish phrasebooks, and a few novels.

There was a large assortment of gear in the miscellaneous category, including a waterproof 35 MM camera, notebook, harmonica, and a small solar panel to recharge my flashlight and VHF radio batteries. I had a Sony Walkman cassette player and about a dozen favorite tapes for entertainment. Several of these tapes were of Jimmy Buffett, whose music was largely to blame for my desire to go to the islands.

Somehow, all of this fit into the kayak, along with more than a week's supply of groceries. The total value of this stuff was about $4,000, excluding the kayak. I had another $3,500 in cash and traveler's checks. This was all that was left after I sold everything I had that would not fit into a kayak or the new life I was about to embark on. I had paid debts and gotten rid of my car and everything else that came with a monthly note. I was determined not to let money, or the lack of it, enter my thoughts for a long time. I could travel this way on a few dollars a day. I had reduced my needs to a level place to pitch a tent each night and a good meal to give me the strength to paddle the next morning.

Because I now had no possessions that were not with me in the kayak, I had no keys to any locks. Not a car key, a house key, or an office key. I viewed keys as a sign of responsibility, and a definite impediment to the freedom I was seeking. I could find this freedom only in a sea kayak.

This degree of personal freedom might seem extreme to many people, but my need to seek it could not be denied. Though I was only twenty-five at the time, I was already disillusioned with the pursuit of money and the material things it could buy. It seemed that no matter how much I earned, there was always something else that must be purchased that was just beyond my reach. I had graduated from junior college with a technical degree, working on computers for a couple of years before returning to a university to work on an engineering degree. In the meantime I operated a business, which, though successful, still left me wondering what I was missing by tying myself down to everybody's else's idea of the American dream.

I spent what little free time I had in the woods, camping and canoeing, or sometimes just walking for an hour or so to get away from the concrete and the buildings and the rush. I read and reread *Walden* and began seeing in my surroundings the same things that led Thoreau to his solitary retreat in the woods. I began to dislike the comfort and security of modern life and longed for a challenge and a chance to experience nature in its raw and untamed state.

My fascination with nature was not limited to the woods and rivers, and though I grew up in inland Mississippi with little experience of the sea, I knew that the open water promised boundless opportunities for adventure. I enrolled in scuba classes and got an advanced diver's certification. Almost every weekend I drove to Destin or Pensacola to catch a dive boat headed offshore. I dove on wrecks and artificial reefs, and especially enjoyed night dives, moving weightlessly through a black void of nothingness, every minute feeling an intensity of being alive that can only be experienced in an environment of uncertainty and, sometimes, fear. But my time underwater was always limited by the depth and by the capacity of the eighty-cubic-inch air tank strapped to my back. Diving also turned out to be an expensive way to explore since I did not own my own boat or live near enough to the Gulf to pursue it to the level I would have liked.

My fascination with deep woods and the sea was closely related to other dreams I had of tropical islands and jungles, fueled by countless adventure novels and explorers' journals I had devoured since first learning to read. I thought the only way to go to such places was with one of the "adventure travel" tour groups that led clients into the Amazon rainforest or the African bush. It was only after meeting Ernest Herndon that it occurred to me that many of the best places, though already "discovered," were still there and available for anyone adventurous enough simply to go. Ernest had captivated me with his tales of two expeditions into the highlands of New Guinea and a road trip to Belize. He advised me just to go wherever I wanted to go.

I decided to do just that, but I wanted an independent means of travel, not dependant upon airplanes, buses, or trains to get me where I was going. I knew that a boat was the answer—there is no greater freedom than being the captain of one's own boat—but boats are expensive and complicated. I already had a canoe, but it could not take me where I wanted to go. I had been reading more and more about a different kind of personal, human-powered watercraft in my canoeing and camping magazines, and was amazed at some of the expeditions that had been successfully undertaken in these skinny craft. The more I looked into the matter, the more it seemed that a sea kayak was the answer and would provide me a means of travel that would take me to the limits of my imagination. I began my search for one and soon found the yellow Chinook that Ernest would paddle down Black Creek for sale by an owner in New Orleans. The kayak was well used but in good condition, and for just six hundred dollars. I acquired it complete with a paddle and PFD.

It was not long after this discovery of sea kayaking and the personal freedom it could give me that the idea for a prolonged trip began to take shape in my mind. I paddled every weekend, and kayaking dominated my thoughts. I went to the beaches of Florida to learn techniques for paddling in surf, and I paddled to the barrier islands of Mississippi to experience camping from a kayak. I was amazed at the kayak's ability to handle rough water and at how easily and rapidly I could travel with all my camping gear, especially when compared to my canoe, the only other boat I had ever owned.

When I could not paddle I stared at maps and traced imaginary routes along exotic coasts I planned to explore. Although sea kayaking is more popular in northern wilderness areas such as coastal Alaska, I focused on the southern latitudes. I was thinking in terms of palm trees, bikinis, and piña coladas. I wanted to paddle in the kind of laid-back places Jimmy Buffett sang about and spend my days in the sunshine working on my tan.

A mere vacation would not be enough. I could not experience what I was looking for in a week, two weeks, or even a month. I wanted to savor the experience, to absorb the places I longed to visit at the average speed of three miles per hour. I could not do this and have a job. I could not pull this off with car notes, electric bills, or monthly rent to pay. Even a month would be stretching my budget if I remained tethered to society's demands. I would have to cut the lines and cash in and check out if I wanted to do this. And since I would have to go to such extreme measures, I knew I might as well get the most of it. Why not paddle for a year . . . or two years? How far could I get? I read accounts of other kayak expeditions, and I calculated my speed based on my weekend tours. It seemed reasonable to average one hundred miles per week, this leaving plenty of time for exploring ashore and taking a couple days a week off from paddling if I was tired or wanted to linger in a particularly good place.

From Mississippi, there are two coastal routes for a sea kayaker desiring to head south. The first is to turn west along the Gulf coast and follow the coastline of Louisiana and Texas down to Mexico and beyond. This route would allow one to stay close to land all the way. But I would be a lone gringo with no command of Spanish, and at the time some of the countries south of Mexico, such as Nicaragua, were considered risky for solo travelers.

I looked the other way, to the Florida peninsula, reaching farther to the south than Texas, with islands beyond. Just to the east of Miami, less than an inch away on my map, were the Bimini Islands, and then the rest of the Bahamas spilled away across the Atlantic to the southeast, like stepping stones to the Caribbean. The Turks and Caicos had been conveniently placed for a weary kayaker halfway between the last of the Bahamas and the island of Hispaniola, occupied by Haiti and the Dominican Republic. I was intrigued. I checked the scale of miles and made some measurements of the blue spaces in between the scattered islands. I saw no passages of more than a hundred miles. I made some quick calculations. At a sustained paddling speed of three miles an hour, even a full hundred miles would take only thirty-three hours or so, and most of the passages were much shorter than that. I had no doubt that my kayak could handle the conditions of the open ocean. Recent expeditions had proven that. Ed Gillet had survived an unprecedented ocean crossing in a kayak when he paddled from California to Hawaii. He spent sixty-three days at sea. I had no intention of spending days away from land, but I could train myself to paddle a hundred miles if I had to, and sleep when I got to the other side.

Further study of the map revealed that Puerto Rico was only a hop away from the eastern end of the Dominican Republic, and the Virgin Islands awaited east of there. A long jump from the British Virgin Islands to St. Martin would put me in the Lesser Antilles, and from there the islands had been thoughtfully spaced at intervals of ten to thirty-five miles apart clear down to Grenada. There was another nearly one-hundred-mile jump to Trinidad, which was just a stone's throw from Venezuela. It was theoretically possible to paddle all the way to South America. My route was decided.

From that point on, preparations for the trip involved collecting the gear that I would need and reading all I could find about the islands along my route. I began tying up loose ends and extricating myself from the web of commitments and obligations everyone in modern society is a part of. I told the people closest to me of my plans and prepared for difficult goodbyes.

I had watched with a sense of hopelessness as my mother grew weaker and more helpless in the grip of multiple sclerosis. She had been robbed of her independence in her early fifties by this crippling disease for which there was no cure. She could not walk without falling, and then one day a fall broke her hip and she never walked again. Her world had been reduced to her bed and her wheelchair, but her spirit remained as strong and positive as ever. There was no time in her life for self-pity, and though it was impossible, she always planned to recover and walk again. She encouraged me to travel and follow my heart. It was unspeakably difficult to see her confined like that, but at the same time I felt that living every day to the fullest was the best thing I could do for her. She had my father, who took care of her with selfless devotion, and I would spend time with her again before her condition got much worse.

Her illness convinced me to begin living my life for now rather than some vague and uncertain future. I set a departure date nine months in advance and planned to stick to it. When spring came, I gave away all my winter clothes. I had carefully planned my journey south to stay ahead of the cold until I got to a latitude winter could not reach. Like the birds, I was migrating south, and my plan was to skip the next two winters entirely. Leaving in late September, I would have time to paddle to the southern tip of Florida by the end of November, and from that point south, T-shirts and shorts would be my standard attire.

Ernest at last managed to get all his stuff hidden away in his kayak and was ready to go. He said goodbye to Angelyn, and my friends and well-wishers that had come to see me off waved good-bye from the bank. We pushed the loaded kayaks into the current and climbed in. Already, without dipping a paddle, Black Creek was taking us with it on its inexorable course to the Gulf.

Ernest struggled to keep his unfamiliar kayak from sliding sideways when we hit a stretch of swift water under the bridge, and in a moment we were around the first bend and surrounded by forest, visual signs of mankind out of sight. Ernest's thoughts, I'm sure, were on the physical aspects of learning to wield the double-bladed paddle and to coordinate his strokes with slight steering corrections of the foot-controlled rudder. My thoughts were far from the mechanics of paddling and even the beauty of the verdant vegetation that pressed in on the narrow stream and hung over both banks. I had a hopeless, sinking feeling and a boundless elation at once, each fighting for domination as that bridge slipped astern and with it my previous way of life. I wondered if I would ever go back to that life . . . and if I would ever be *able* to go back to it.

It was after 5 P.M. when we got under way, and the late afternoon sun was filtering through a mist that hung over the creek, splitting into pale yellow rays that reflected off the dark water. Entranced by this mystical setting, I daydreamed about what might lie ahead as I paddled. Ernest, who perceived the light with a photographer's eye, snapped me out of my musings with unreasonable requests:

"Scott!" He called, just as I rounded a bend a hundred yards downstream from where he had pulled over to the bank to dig out his Nikon. "You think you can paddle back up here so I can get a shot as you drift through that mist?"

This went on for the remainder of the afternoon. At every serpentine bend of the creek, I would have to break my downstream momentum, turn the long kayak with great difficulty in the narrow stream, and fight the current to get in place for his "perfect" shot. An outdoor writer for a newspaper, Ernest planned to cover the progress of my trip at regular intervals. This first week would give him a chance to experience a part of it and provide lots of photo opportunities. I was grateful for the publicity that might help me get support for my trip, but I was getting tired of turning my boat around and fighting the current. When we came to a suitable sandbar, I suggested we make an early camp.

It took almost an hour to unpack and set up camp. We cooked a concoction of sweet potatoes, onions, and other fresh vegetables in the coals of the fire and washed it down with some Myer's Jamaican rum. Later, Ernest played the blues on his harmonica as we stretched out on the sandbar and stared up into an infinity of stars in a cloudless sky. The rum and the song of nighttime insects, combined with the exhaustion of a long day of preparation, began to take effect, so we retired to the tent early that first night. Tomorrow afternoon, my older brother, Jeff, would meet us at the next bridge crossing with his canoe and travel with us for a few miles.

I woke Monday morning as the first light of dawn filtered through the nylon of the tent. When I crawled out on the sandbar and glanced in the direction of the creek, I stopped and stared for a moment, not believing my eyes. The kayaks were *gone*. I ran to the edge where we had pulled them up the night before. The water had risen a couple of feet and swept the boats away with it. I couldn't believe my stupidity. After months of meticulous planning and preparation for the challenges of paddling in the open ocean, a simple rainstorm somewhere far upstream robbed me of my kayaks and most of my gear on the first night I made camp! I was furious and distraught at the same time. Yelling for Ernest to wake up, I raced downstream along the bank in an adrenalin-fueled panic. From the end of the sandbar I could see his kayak snagged on something under the bushes a hundred yards down.

"We've lost the boats!" I answered when he rushed out of the tent in confusion, asking what was wrong. He followed as I jumped in the creek and we swam with the swift current to his boat. Miraculously, it was hung up by a drop hook he dangled beneath the bushes the night before in hopes of catching a catfish for breakfast. I didn't set any hooks myself, and it looked like I was out of luck, but upon swimming around the next bend, I spotted my kayak, stopped by some deadfalls that choked the river. We were lucky. It was an inexcusable mistake not to tie the boats up. Even though the skies were clear when we made camp, a storm somewhere far upstream had caused the sudden rise in water level. Ernest and I had both spent enough time on rivers to know better than to leave our boats untied, but for some reason, perhaps an apathy induced by one too many shots of rum, we did it anyway. I would have to be a lot more careful if I expected to paddle to the West Indies.

We resumed our downstream journey in the cool of the early morning after a quick breakfast, drifting with the current and soaking in the sounds of unseen birds and squirrels busily feeding in the surrounding trees. By noon, we reached the bridge crossing at Janice, and Jeff arrived shortly with his seventeen-foot aluminum canoe. He could only get off work for two days, so he would float with us just a few miles to the next landing at Cypress Creek. This was our favorite part of Black Creek, a designated federal wilderness area within the much larger Desoto National Forest. The 5,000-acre Black Creek Wilderness Area is home to the biggest trees and free of the patches of cutover land found scattered throughout the rest of the national forest. Motorized vehicles are prohibited. Silence and solitude can be found in abundance.

We wanted to camp about halfway between the two landings, to be as far from any road as possible, so we spent the afternoon drifting slowly. We stopped often for a bit of unsuccessful fishing in likely-looking holes. We swapped boats so Jeff could try paddling a loaded kayak. Along the upper reaches of Black Creek, there is no shortage of idyllic campsites. Broad, high beaches of sugar-white sand are found in almost every sharp bend, providing an open buffer zone between the creek and the dark tangle of forest on both sides of the waterway. These sandy beaches make ideal campsites, free from swarms of mosquitoes that are active day and night in the woods and clear of underbrush and leaf litter that might conceal a rattlesnake or cottonmouth. This is an important consideration if you stumble sleepily out of the tent at night to answer Nature's call. The piney woods of Mississippi's coastal plain are home to some of the largest eastern diamondback rattlers to be found anywhere, and there are always copperheads and cottonmouths hanging around a Mississippi stream.

Later that afternoon, we chose one of these sandbars, the biggest we'd seen, and set up camp on the top, where we had a commanding view of the creek. Ernest started a fire and Jeff produced an ice chest from his canoe.

"Check out what I've got in here for supper tonight," he said, as he opened the cooler and held up one of three inch-thick rib-eye steaks.

"Wow! You went all out, huh?" I commented as he handed Ernest and me cold Coronas and opened one for himself.

"Well, I figured this would be the last time I would ever see you, since you're determined to paddle that kayak off into the ocean and get yourself drowned. You better enjoy this meal; you'll be eating a lot of rice from now on—if you *do* survive."

We wrapped the steaks in foil, along with potatoes and onions, and buried them in the coals. No restaurant could have competed with the results or the setting. I knew Jeff was right about the rice though. I wouldn't be eating like this often. I would have to live cheaply to stretch my funds far enough to take me where I wanted to go. There would be rice and more rice, as well as pasta, pancakes, canned soups and tuna. Not just because it was cheap, but also because I could only carry those things that would keep without ice.

Unwittingly, Jeff had planted a seed for this trip in my mind a few years before when we canoed and camped on this same stream. We talked about the mountain men and other explorers from frontier times and what it would be like to wander in the wilds for days, weeks, and months. As our short trip came to an end at a bridge and we loaded the canoe on the truck and faced going back to traffic and jobs, Jeff had wondered aloud, "What would it be like to just keep going?" He had meant going on wherever the river went, following it to the end.

The idea stuck in my mind and remained all that time. It seemed so logical, and the thought of doing it was so compelling. Now I was about to find out what it would be like.

We sat around the fire and finished off the last of the beer, Jeff and Ernest talking about their jobs and the day-to-day problems of ordinary life. To them, I was embarking on an endless vacation with no worries of work or anything else. I mentioned the problems I would surely have; finding places to camp, keeping my gear and kayak maintained, and living with beach sand in every conceivable nook and cranny of every piece of equipment and clothing I had for the next year or more. They had little sympathy for my problems.

"*Sand* in my underwear! I wish that's all I had to worry about for the next year," Jeff told Ernest.

They joked about my seemingly insignificant worries and saw my departure from the *real* world as a great indulgence in the luxury of time off. And it would be. But it would not all be perfect campsites like this and with cold beer and steaks. Ernest knew this. He had suffered enough on his various adventures to know there would be hard times indeed. He would not have traded places with me, and in reality, I doubt if Jeff would have either.

The next morning we reached Cypress Creek landing, and Jeff pulled his canoe from the water and wished me luck as Ernest and I paddled away. Black Creek was growing wider as more tributaries like Cypress Creek added their flow. We were moving away from the sandy hills of the pine country and toward the river bottom swamps of the coastal plain.

We paddled under towering oak and beech trees festooned with wild grapevines, and drifted past steep clay banks that seeped cold spring water. Often, as we rounded a bend, a water snake would slip off a stump or branch and disappear beneath the surface. Occasionally, we would hear a sudden crashing in the undergrowth near the bank and look up to catch a glimpse of a startled deer. The only sound of man was the faraway thunder of artillery shells exploding on the practice range at Camp

Shelby, an Army National Guard base miles to the north. We made camp that night below the next landing at Fairley Bridge, and though we were now out of the national forest, there was no indication in the seemingly endless woods that still hid Black Creek from the rest of the world.

By Wednesday afternoon, we came to a bridge that we calculated to be about halfway between Brooklyn and the coast. Concerned that we might not get to the coast in time for him to drive home on Saturday, Ernest suggested that we paddle on into the night to make up some mileage. The moon would be full, so we could probably reach the confluence of Black Creek and the Pascagoula River before our next camp. Already the terrain was becoming swampy, and numerous cypress trees at the water's edge suggested that we were nearing the big river and its vast bottomlands.

We stopped after sunset to refill our water containers from a clear spring on the bank, and in the dark shadows of the trees, swarms of mosquitoes emerged to torment us. I saw this as the perfect opportunity to test a new repellant I hoped would work for me in the tropics. It was not really a repellent at all, but rather a bath oil by Avon that had become the rage among outdoorsmen after someone accidentally discovered that it had the side effect of discouraging mosquitoes. Ernest stubbornly refused to try it, being too manly to use such a product, and stuck to his DEET chemical spray, while I applied liberal amounts of the strong-scented bath oil to the exposed parts of my body.

"Hey, this stuff works!" I proclaimed in triumph as the mosquitoes vanished. "And it's not poisonous like that chemical junk you're using."

"Maybe so," he muttered in contempt as he paddled quickly to get upwind of me, making some crack about me "smelling like a floating house of ill repute."

I didn't care what he thought. Nor did I care how I smelled. Mosquitoes and other biting insects would be a constant part of my life for the duration of the trip. I would use anything that would keep them at bay, and after this success I paddled smugly on, convinced that I had found the answer. Little did I know that these docile Black Creek mosquitoes had nothing in common with those I would later encounter in the tropical mangrove swamps along my route. The Avon product would prove to be worthless, as would even the most toxic chemical repellants.

We continued cautiously downstream in the gathering darkness, straining to see and avoid the numerous stumps and deadfalls obstructing the twisting waterway. The last of the light faded within thirty minutes, and the forest swallowed us in blackness, forcing us to guide our kayaks by sound and intuition. We knew that navigation would again be easy after 10 P.M., when the full moon would rise.

Rounding a bend, we were startled by a terrific splash as a frightened beaver dove to escape the kayaks bearing down on him. Through the gloom, Ernest saw a large alligator sink like a lifeless log just as he was about to run over it. Snakes were ever in our minds as we brushed under overhanging branches and were sometimes pushed by the current into the matted weeds and reed brakes near the banks. Ernest slammed into the tangled branches of a large oak that had fallen across the creek, and his boat was quickly pinned to the debris by the current. With difficulty, he managed to extricate himself from the mess after I checked for snakes with my flashlight.

The river grew in width as we moved downstream, and soon we came to a floating fish camp tethered to the bank. The camp was a houseboat of sorts, really just a shack built of salvaged lumber and tin, fastened down to a barge of empty oil drums that floated it just high enough to keep the floor clear of the river. I knew from a previous trip that such floating camps were endemic along the backwaters of the Pascagoula River. Some were permanent residences, but most were used as camps for extended hunting and fishing trips in these wild reaches of bottomland forests and swamps. Its presence was a good indication that there was navigable water the rest of the way to the Gulf, as most of these camps are built in the towns downriver and towed upstream by outboard-powered johnboats. Since there was no sign anyone had been around lately, we decided to stop for a meal on the deck of the dilapidated houseboat while waiting on the moonrise.

The maniacal laughter of barred owls and the eerie screams of screech owls permeated the blackness as we ate cheese, tuna, and crackers while under siege by mosquitoes. My bath oil and Ernest's chemical repellant was already wearing off, so we applied more and managed to keep the pests at bay. When the moon finally emerged over the treetops, its soft light illuminated our winding path through the jungle-like forest, so we slipped back into the kayaks and paddled on.

We reached the mouth of Black Creek by midnight and drifted into the lazy current of the broad Pascagoula, eager to find a campsite and call it a night. There was an occupied houseboat near the confluence, and two men on the porch talked under the glow of a Coleman lantern, unaware of the stealthy kayaks that slipped past just outside their circle of lamplight. Without a houseboat of our own, stopping here was not an option, because the banks of the lower Pascagoula are not inviting to campers, either being steep bluffs or swampy tangles of snake-infested woods growing right to the water's edge. We paddled on in search of a spot, getting sleepy with the hypnotic dipping of the paddles like drivers trying to stay awake all night on an interstate highway. I nearly capsized once when I dozed off and woke with a start, forgetting where I was. At two in the morning, we came to a low sandbar, and casting aside good judgment in favor of sleep, we set up camp. Heavy rains brought a rise in the water before dawn, and we awoke to find the river at the door of our tent.

We broke camp in the rain and paddled all day through intermittent showers. Cypress was the predominant tree species here, and gray curtains of Spanish moss hung from the branches and blended with the gray skies that surrounded us. Dense thickets of palmettos on the forest floor lent a tropical touch to the scene, however, and reminded me that sunnier islands were my destination.

On Friday morning, we reached an open area of marshland where the river lost definition in a maze of channels and bayous. This broad expanse of river delta that meant we were near the Gulf. We stuck to the westernmost channel and by noon reached the public boat ramp where Ernest had left his truck. Our night paddling had turned out to be unnecessary. We had arrived a day early. Ernest could spend one more night camping, but now we had run out of river and the only dry land was near the boat ramp and the highway bridge.

I suggested that he accompany me out into the Mississippi Sound to Round Island, my next planned stop on my route to Alabama and Florida. Ernest had never paddled in the sea before, but I assured him we could make the easy 4½-mile crossing with no worries, despite the strong wind that was blowing out of the south. He expressed some doubts when we stopped near the railroad bridge at the mouth of the river and looked out across the choppy waters of the sound at our destination, which appeared as a hazy hump of blue, too far away for its pines and beaches to be discernable. I reminded him that the kayaks were seaworthy, and besides, the Mississippi Sound is protected by the string of barrier islands farther offshore. The waves would not be big enough to threaten us.

After this brief discussion, we sealed ourselves back into the kayaks and set out through the outlying marsh islands at the river mouth. Ernest had never learned any kayak self-rescue techniques and had never experienced a "wet exit," which is the kayaker's term for getting out of an upside-down boat without panicking. I didn't think he would need any of this knowledge, but an hour later, I was to find out how wrong I was.

We passed the last stretch of marsh grass and entered the open sound. I was surprised at how rough the chop was in the 20-to-25-knot headwinds.

"Nothing to worry about," I told Ernest, "just enough wave action to make it a fun ride."

He thought it was great. He quickly pulled ahead, delighted with the experience of paddling a kayak in the sea for the first time. I knew the exhilaration he was feeling, and watching him reminded me of the first time I took my kayak out to sea not all that long ago . . .

I remembered carrying the boat across a crowded beach in Florida, climbing in at the water's edge, and plunging out through the breakers to the calmer swells beyond the surf zone. What a feeling of freedom that had been, out there far from the reach and sounds of the masses of sunbathers, beachcombers, and swimmers as the kayak silently carried me out to sea. It was a feeling of utter peace, so different than the busy shore, dancing on waves that shimmered under my hull in the summer sun. A dolphin had joined me for a time, leaping and playing just out of reach. I was soon a mile from land in my tiny plastic boat, but felt strangely secure, the benevolent blue ocean beckoning to be explored . . .

I was snapped back to the reality of the present by a large wave that washed over my deck and forced me to brace with the paddle for balance. This was not the peaceful blue dreamscape of that other day but rather an ominous gray cauldron of churning waves that made me feel insignificant in my kayak. Wave after wave washed over the low decks of the overloaded craft, and I noticed that I was taking on more water around my sprayskirt than normal. When I stopped to pump out the excess, I was surprised that the pool of water inside the cockpit was getting deeper still and creeping up around my waist. The stern of the boat was completely awash, and now I realized that the entire rear compartment behind the seat was flooded. Sea kayaks are incredibly seaworthy small boats for two reasons: One is the watertight deck and sprayskirt arrangement that is supposed to keep all the water out of the boat regardless of conditions, and the other is the segmentation of the hull interior into three separate compartments by watertight bulkheads, which keep the boat afloat even if the cockpit is full of water. Both of my kayak's defenses had been breached by this nasty chop. I was taking on gallons of water through a failing sprayskirt seal, and the water was filling not only the cockpit but the entire stern compartment as it was somehow getting past the rear bulkhead. With the bulkhead compromised, the boat was in real danger of sinking if enough water got inside.

I yelled for Ernest, but he was probably two hundred yards upwind of me, blissfully paddling into the 3-to-4-foot breakers and oblivious to my predicament. I pumped as fast as I could with the hand-operated bilge pump I carried on deck. I remembered the loud emergency whistle attached to my life vest, as required by the Coast Guard, and blew sharp blasts on it as I pumped. Whether Ernest heard the whistle or just looked back to see where I was I don't know, but when he looked I waved frantically and motioned for him to come back.

He slowly made his way to my position while I continued to pump as fast as I could. Since the stern compartment was crammed completely full of gear, which although heavy, was still lighter than water, the kayak did not take on enough water to sink.

Ernest was having a tough time negotiating the breaking waves. Thanks to me, here he was more than two miles from the nearest land in rough conditions with no knowledge of bracing strokes or kayak handling. And the only person that could help him was in a sinking boat. I watched him struggle as I pumped; then a particularly large wave caught him broadside as he tried to maneuver close to me. The next thing I saw was the upturned yellow hull of his kayak. It seemed like forever before he finally broke the surface, coughing and spitting seawater. He clung to the inverted kayak with one hand and his paddle with the other, a surprised and betrayed look on his face.

Reentering a capsized and flooded kayak requires a precise and practiced technique, even in calm conditions. Ernest didn't know where to start, and he was being pummeled by breaking waves and had lost his glasses in the capsize. This situation was rapidly deteriorating. If he didn't get back into his boat, and if my boat *did* sink, we would be miles from land in nothing but our life jackets.

I managed to maneuver my half-sunken kayak alongside him and instructed him to turn his upright. I then handed him the pump and he began pumping his cockpit out while treading water and nervously wondering what might be swimming around beneath him in the murky waters of the sound. When he had most of the water out, I held his boat tightly against mine, and, by climbing up onto my stern, he was able to slide back into his seat without capsizing. He quickly pumped out the rest of the water and sealed his sprayskirt to keep the waves from refilling it.

There was nothing I could do about the water in the stern of my boat. I would have to try and paddle it to shore swamped. We stayed close together, fighting a headwind and the breaking waves. I frequently had to stop and pump, and paddling with the stern submerged required all the remaining endurance I could muster. Late in the afternoon, we finally reached the lee of the island and paddled until we ran the bows of our boats up on the sand.

Ernest collapsed on the beach, seasick from the motion and from swallowing seawater. I was exhausted but immediately emptied the wet gear from my boat and began inspecting the hull to see what damage there was. As it turned out there was no hole or structural damage. The hull was simply too flexible to withstand rough seas when so heavy-laden. The flexing had caused the rear bulkhead to break loose and lose its watertight integrity. The hull was plastic—a type of polyethylene formed into a kayak by a manufacturing process called roto-molding. It is a low-cost way of mass-producing kayaks, but the inherent problem with plastic is its lack of stiffness, when compared to other boat-building materials, such as wood, fiberglass, or Kevlar. I was to find out later that stiffness is everything when it comes to kayaks, not only to withstand breaking waves, but also to allow the energy put out by the paddler to be transformed into forward motion. A flexible boat absorbs some of this energy and is less efficient.

The other problem with the plastic used in this molding process is difficulty of gluing anything to it. Epoxy and most adhesives will not bond to it. The bulkheads in my kayak were made of stiff, closed-cell foam, sealed with a marine sealant. Under stress the seams had easily let go of the smooth surface inside the hull. I could reseal it with the marine goop I had brought for repairs, but it was obvious that if this happened so soon in the trip, it would happen again and again. This time I had been lucky. The waves were nothing compared to what they would be in the Atlantic and the Caribbean, and I had been only a couple of miles from land. I realized with dismay that I had the wrong kayak for the trip I had embarked upon. I would need a more seaworthy model, made of rigid material such as fiberglass. I had a sinking feeling of defeat as I stood on the beach and looked southeast to the horizon I could not reach. Only one week into the journey I had planned for so long, and now an impasse. I didn't even make it out of Mississippi. I would have to dip deeply into my limited travel funds to shuck out the cash for a better boat.

I pitched the tent and cooked some rice while Ernest remained stretched out on the sand, trying to recover from nausea. There was nothing we could do that night, and no great urgency anyway. The wind still whipped across the island from the south, and with rough seas, it would be out of the question to return to the mainland. The capsize had undermined Ernest's faith in sea kayaks, so he was not in favor of paddling back.

We ate dinner and discussed my predicament as we sat on the north side of the island that evening and looked at the distant lights of Pascagoula, on the mainland. Ernest agreed with my assessment of the plastic kayak, and thought I would be wise to replace it before going on. After his experience, he thought it would be wiser not to go on at all, but that was never an option for me.

Sometime after we went to sleep, the wind abated, and when we awoke in the morning, the surface of the Mississippi Sound was mirrorlike. There was not much danger of my kayak taking on water with no waves breaking, so I felt sure we could make it back to the mainland. We quickly loaded and launched the kayaks. The crossing was easy and without incident. Two hours of paddling gave me time to think of solutions to my problem, and by the time we reached Ernest's truck, I had a plan for obtaining a better kayak.

TWO

# SOUTHBOUND

A boat is freedom, not just a way to reach a goal

**—BERNARD MOITESSIER, *A SEA VAGABOND'S WORLD***

Feeling out the sleek new kayak and testing its response with a full load, I paddled slowly past the expensive homes and private yachts lining the canals of Apollo Beach. With each stroke the turquoise and white craft surged forward, moving easily despite the two hundred pounds of gear, food, and water stashed below the decks. In just a few minutes I left this pricey waterfront community behind and cruised through the cut into the open waters of Tampa Bay. Far across the wide bay to the west, I could see the skyline of St. Petersburg glinting in the morning sun. I pointed my kayak south and fell into a steady paddling rhythm, slipping past the man-made beach at the Holiday Inn.

After the incident off Round Island, I didn't intend to let anything stop me this time. Perhaps it was because I was already far from home, and I could smell the salt of the Gulf and see the palm trees and circling gulls, but I had no doubts now that I was going places in my kayak.

A month had passed since Ernest and I had paddled back to the mainland from Round Island. It was the month that I had planned to be working my way along the Gulf coast to reach this part of central Florida. Instead, it had been a month of making phone calls and then

South Seas Plantation Resort, Florida Gulf Coast

waiting for a new kayak to be built and delivered from British Colombia to Savannah, Georgia, where I had arranged to rendezvous with the builder to pick it up.

Immediately after accepting the certainty that the plastic kayak in which I'd begun the journey was unfit for the task, I called John Dowd, a New Zealander famous among sea kayakers for his epic voyages and for the magazine *Sea Kayaker*, of which he was then the editor. He was also the author of the definitive book on the techniques of long-distance kayak touring. I had met John earlier that same year at a sea kayaking symposium, where he had patiently answered my barrage of questions about the Caribbean kayak expedition he had done with three companions ten years before. If anyone knew expedition sea kayaking, and knew what kind of kayak I would need for my voyage, it was John Dowd.

John understood my dilemma and promised to do all he could. He put me in touch with Mike Neckar, the designer and builder of Necky Kayaks, in British Colombia. Mike built the kayak that Ed Gillette paddled from California to Hawaii. He knew what I needed to make the trip I envisioned, and he said he could build me one of his Tesla designs in Kevlar—the toughest and lightest boat-building material available. The Tesla is a seventeen-foot kayak with a twenty-four-inch beam, providing more interior volume and load-carrying capability than most sea kayaks. Mike said he would build it extra-strong, laminated with epoxy resin, and fully equipped with bulkheads, hatches, and a foot-controlled rudder. He would do all this for only the cost of materials, which was about a third the retail price of the boat. I was elated at the prospect of getting a kayak of that quality at a price I could afford. The only catch was that I would have to pick it up in Savannah, Georgia, where Mike was going to personally deliver a dozen or so of his kayaks to a dealer. There would be a three-week wait while he built the boat and made the road trip from Canada.

I studied my charts and the dates I had marked off on my carefully planned itinerary. It would be November before I could get under way again. If I resumed the trip at Round Island, cold fronts would overtake me before I could get to tropical latitudes. I decided to move my departure point farther south, to where I expected to be around the first of November anyway. I didn't want to have to find room in the kayak for warm clothing. My oldest brother, Frank, lived in Apollo Beach, on Tampa Bay, and his waterfront home conveniently featured a dock in the backyard.

When my kayak was ready, I arranged to have a friend drive me to Savannah to pick it up. When we got there, I was surprised at how beautiful it was with its sleek, sweeping curves and brilliant Gelcoat finish. The white hull was mated to a teal-green deck the color of tropical seawater. This boat was a sports car of sea kayaks compared to what I had been paddling. I felt a renewed sense of confidence that I could achieve my paddling goals with such an excellent craft. We loaded the kayak on the roof racks and drove to Tampa. I left the boat at Frank's house and then helped my friend drive her car back to Mississippi, where I quickly got my gear together and bought a Greyhound ticket to get back to

Tampa. By the time all this was accomplished, November had arrived and my travel funds were reduced by $1,500.

Conditions were choppy on the wide-open waters of Tampa Bay, but the wind was from astern and I made good progress as I paralleled the eastern shoreline from about a mile out. Before dark I passed under the massive span of the Sunshine Skyway bridge that connects St. Petersburg with the east side of the bay and paddled to a deserted-looking shore about a mile farther south. The coast here consists of mangrove swamp and small islands, a pocket of wild land in the midst of one of Florida's largest urban areas. I landed on an island identified on my chart as Rattlesnake Key. There was a small beach among the mangroves, piled high with debris washed in by the sea and backed by a grove of cabbage palms and sea grape trees. Mosquitoes swarmed out to greet me as soon as I stepped onto shore, so I quickly changed from swimming shorts to jungle fatigues and a long-sleeved cotton shirt before pitching my tent.

Driftwood was available, so rather than unpack the stove, I built a small fire and boiled some fresh squash, onions, and potatoes. A scorpion crawled out of the burning palm frond I used to start the fire. I didn't know there were scorpions in Florida; seeing this one made me glad I had a tent to sleep in at night. I would be more careful in the future about where I put my hands and bare feet when gathering materials to build fires.

I left Rattlesnake Key early the next morning and headed southwest across the mouth of Tampa Bay. Midway through the crossing, with the emptiness of the open Gulf to starboard, I intercepted a pod of perhaps twelve dolphins that changed course and fell in beside me. They stayed with me for almost a mile, leaping out of the water, racing ahead, and circling back to pass me again. I felt it was a good omen to be joined by these friends from the sea. They seemed to be encouraging me to keep going south, and seemed to know that they lifted my spirits and inspired me to paddle on. With this job done they disappeared to take care of whatever other business dolphins have to take care of on a sunny

Thursday morning. I paddled on to Anna Maria Island, a barrier island on the south side of the entrance to the bay. When I reached its shelter I stayed on the inside and entered the Intracoastal Waterway.

I would have the option of following this protected route down most of the west coast of Florida to the Keys. My kayak could handle the conditions of the outside coastal route, but staying in the waterway would allow me to travel in any weather and would offer more possibilities for finding campsites than on the developed beaches of the Gulf. In addition to the shoreline on each side of the waterway, there are numerous spoil islands created by channel dredging, and some of these might offer a secluded spot for an overnight bivouac.

The disadvantage of traveling the Intracoastal Waterway is that it is a highway for powerboats of every description. In places where the channel was narrow, they were a threat to me, but I found that more often than not they slowed when they saw me, probably thinking their wake would capsize my frail-looking craft.

In some areas waterfront homes lined the shore on both sides of the channel, but I was always able to find places to camp on the manmade islands. Each evening I waited until dark to land, then concealed my kayak in the mangroves and pitched my tent out of sight of the houses. I was not the only one to do this, as evidenced by the remains of campfires and small clearings in the woods on almost all the islands.

Four days after leaving Tampa, I passed through Englewood, and camped on a Gulf-front beach on the north end of Don Pedro Island. The scenery was changing somewhat as I moved south, with signs of the tropics becoming more evident. Though absent in the Tampa area, coconut palms were abundant here. In some places, the water under my hull was so clear that it felt as though my kayak was suspended in air above the extensive grass flats that covered the bottom. Mangrove forests dominated the shoreline in all but the developed areas. The insect populations I encountered each night as I made camp were getting more aggressive and more diverse the farther south I went. I kept them at bay with repellent and smoky fires but usually retreated to the tent shortly after dark.

One hundred miles south of my departure point I came upon an idyllic setting and for the first time felt the desire to spend more than one night in the same camp. Cayo Costa is a wilderness island, protected as a Florida state park and inaccessible except to those who visit in their own boats. I left the Intracoastal Waterway at Boca Grande Pass, at the north end of this island, and paddled a couple of miles down the pristine Gulf beaches of this subtropical key.

I needed a campsite where I could relax and not have to worry about moving out at daylight, so I pitched my tent among a grove of tall cabbage palms and slung my hammock for some daytime reading. I spent time walking the deserted beaches in the morning and evening and experimented with living off the land and sea.

By digging in the sand just above the reach of the surf, I soon collected a cooking pot full of tiny clams, which I boiled in the shells until they opened and I could pick out the meat. They were tasty but too small to be worth the trouble unless I got really hungry. With my rod and reel, I tried fishing in a brackish lagoon behind the beach, but had no luck other than a close-up encounter with two bold alligators six or seven feet in length. I almost stepped on the first one before I noticed it stretched out on the sand near the lagoon. Both of them reluctantly retreated into the water, where they floated on the surface, eyeing me as if to say: "We dare you to come into *our* element."

Wild plant food was abundant on Cayo Costa. I sampled the seaside purslane, a low-growing herb that is good eaten raw, and, using my machete, I cut a palm heart out of a small cabbage palm growing in the dense grove behind my camp. The palm heart was tender and delicious, if a bit difficult to get at. It was good to know this, since palms were so abundant here and I was sure they would be along most of my route. I intended to sample every tropical plant food I encountered on the trip, mainly as a way to extend my stay on remote islands with the limited amount of supplies I could carry in the kayak. I could also save money by supplementing my store-bought food with hunting, fishing, and gathering.

Leaving Cayo Costa to go south, I left solitude behind and landed on an idyllic but ritzy beach at the South Seas Plantation Resort. This beach had the look to fit its name, with tall coconut palms leaning out over the shallows and shading the ship's store and yacht basin that harbored dozens of gleaming motor yachts. I bought postcards in the store and sat down to write to folks back home while enjoying my first cold soda in days. A look at my charts told me that the next 20 or so miles were heavily developed. Sanibel Island and Ft. Myers Beach lay ahead, and it was already mid-afternoon when I was ready to get under way again. I resolved to paddle into the night—as long as it would take to get past the Ft. Myers area and find an unoccupied beach.

After sunset it was easy to navigate on open water with only the scant starlight and distant city lights to guide me. The bow of my kayak sliced through big schools of fish that evidently thought it was some huge predator. Panicked fish leapt out of the water in all directions in an attempt to escape, one even slamming painfully into the side of my face with a stinging slap. All this splashing made me nervous as I scanned the dark waters for the dorsal fins of *real* predators.

By midnight I was paddling past the condos and beach hotels of Ft. Myers Beach. I skirted the beach from just a few yards out, looking up at the line of buildings that were crammed into every available space. There were rows of wooden beach chairs between the buildings and the water, empty except for one, occupied by a passionate young couple thinking they were getting away with making love on a public beach, but oblivious to my silent passing on the dark waters just a stone's throw away. Farther south, live music blared from a row of rowdy waterfront bars. By two in the morning, I was getting cold, sleepy, and miserable. The magic of being out on the Gulf at night was wearing off, and I was ready to find a place to sleep. In the dark I couldn't see a long sandbar that extended hundreds of feet in front of me, exposed by the low tide and blocking my route completely. Soon I found myself boxed in and surrounded by sandbars that were covered with hundreds, if not thousands, of roosting sea gulls. The stench of accumulated guano was overwhelming. I was forced to laboriously drag the loaded kayak over the sandbars. My movements and muttered profanities woke the resting gulls, and they took to the sky in every direction, filling the night with a din of panicked squawking and dropping of more stinking excrement. I'd had about all I could take by the time I was clear of the sandbars. It was 5:30 A.M. by this time. I found a narrow beach backed by woods, dragged the kayak ashore, and threw my sleeping bag on the sand.

Sunlight in my eyes woke me at 7 A.M., and I looked around to see several people milling about looking for seashells. This beach was not as deserted as it had appeared in the dark. I quickly put away my sleeping bag and was preparing to leave when a man in uniform drove up in a Jeep and told me that the beach was part of a state park.

"Did you camp here last night?" he asked in an accusatory tone.

I told him that I had paddled all night and merely stopped here to eat breakfast for a few minutes. The ranger looked around for evidence of a campfire, and when he found nothing he glanced at my kayak, noticing the bang-stick in the cockpit, which he told me was illegal in Florida state parks. I was expecting a citation or worse, but when I explained the nature of my trip his attitude changed and the conversation turned friendly. He understood my need for the bang-stick, but warned me to keep it well hidden when I reached Everglades National Park.

Despite the lack of sleep, I put in a hard morning of traveling and reached the condominiums and resort hotels of Naples shortly after noon. Paddling a straight coastline like this far from land is relatively boring, but if the surf is heavy, it is necessary to stay well out to avoid the breakers. This day there was little if any surf, so I was able to cruise just a few yards from the crowded beaches. There was an endless display of bikini-clad sun worshippers here, and being so close in allowed me to have passing conversations with some and to wave at others while weaving between those who ventured out for a swim. I stopped often to swim myself, as the downside of a windless day was the suffocating heat.

I found my next campsite in the early afternoon south of all the development of Naples. It was a mostly deserted area of Australian pine forest with a narrow beach facing the Gulf. A woman walking the beach told me that the land was private and that police patrolled this section of coast by boat and by air because it was a favored spot for drug runners trying to slip their cargo ashore. Following her advice, I hid my camp well in the shadows of the pines and camouflaged everything with brush. Sure enough, a patrol boat cruised slowly by an hour later, but the officer carefully studying the shoreline did not see me crouching next to my tent. It seemed that there was no way I could travel this coast without trespassing or breaking someone's rules. It was inconvenient to have to hide everything and to not be able to build a campfire openly, but to get to where I was going, I had to travel through populated areas, and in those areas, this sort of guerilla camping was going to become a way of life. I looked forward to a brief respite from this when I reached Everglades National Park. Beach camping is legal in the park, so long as you have the necessary backcountry permits and camp in the designated wilderness campsites.

Not being able to build a fire turned out to be especially inconvenient that evening when my thoughts turned to preparing dinner. I set up my multi-fuel backpacker stove and began pumping it to build pressure for burning. The seal on the pump failed, spraying white gas in my face and eyes. I used a gallon of my water supply flushing my eyes. The stove sputtered and flared up in huge flames when I attempted to light it again, and in a fit of rage I tossed it clear past the beach and into the waves of the Gulf. With no stove and no option to build a fire, I ate cold beans from a can for dinner.

The next morning after leaving my wooded hideaway, I stopped on the beach at Marco Island to buy groceries. From the sea I had no way of knowing where the nearest supermarket was, and as it turned out I had landed miles south of the only one and ended up spending half the day walking there and back, carrying plastic bags heavy with groceries back to the kayak. On Marco Island the November sun beat down with summer-like intensity, making this resupply effort more difficult than a half day of paddling. I carefully selected my groceries, knowing that Marco Island was my last chance to buy supplies before I reached the Everglades, where I would have more than 100 miles of wilderness coastline to traverse. I knew what to expect there from a weeklong trip two years before with Ernest. We had been traveling in an open canoe, so we avoided the coast and instead explored the mangrove swamps and the open savannas the Indians called Pa-hay-oh-kee—The River of Grass. Swarms of mosquitoes tormented us in the mangroves, so my intention this time was to skirt the edge and camp on the open beaches of the barrier islands. I would be more exposed if the weather should turn bad, but I hoped that the Gulf breezes would help keep the insects at bay. I could always change my mind if I needed to and take the alternate route of the Wilderness Waterway, a hundred-mile marked water trail that leads to the southern tip of Florida by way of the swamps.

I entered insect hell the same day I left Marco Island, when I set up camp on a deserted beach just east of Cape Romano. Clouds of vicious salt-marsh mosquitoes filled the air and forced me into my tent as soon as it was erected. In the morning I tried to cook pancakes for breakfast but mosquitoes flew into the batter by the dozens and clung to the protective head net I was wearing in such numbers that I could hardly see. I shoved my half-packed gear into the kayak and hastily paddled for open water, the only place I could get any relief. That day I worked my way south through the mangrove archipelago known as the Ten Thousand Islands and reached the national park boundary at Indian Key by nightfall. Though I had no permit, I camped there anyway. In the morning I would have to make a six-mile side trip to Everglades City to visit the ranger station and get the necessary permits to continue south.

After paddling to the ranger station the next day, I returned to Indian Key to camp there one more night before pushing on. I had permits for six nights in the park, with each campsite spaced close enough to reach in an easy day's paddle.

I would not be alone on Indian Key the second night. The park service had also issued a permit to a couple traveling in a canoe, or at least what had begun as a canoe. The man in the stern introduced himself as Pete Hill. He and his girlfriend, Mary Zinn, had driven from Ohio, and were planning an adventurous week's vacation in the Everglades. Pete had lived in Micronesia for a time, and his stock fiberglass canoe was modified to emulate the native dugouts he'd seen there. Two slim bamboo outriggers protruded a few feet out from either side, and a wooden bowsprit extended the length of the seventeen-foot craft another three feet or so. A wooden mast was stepped amidships and stayed with rope. Twin leeboards clamped to the gunwales extended into the water to port and starboard. The sails were handmade, and in case the wind didn't cooperate, there was an auxiliary outboard hanging off to one side of the stern on a makeshift bracket. A huge pile of gear rose above the gunwales, barely leaving room for Pete and Marty to sit.

They set up folding chairs and a table complete with tablecloth and invited me for dinner. We talked about my trip and Pete's experiences in the south Pacific over a bottle of wine. As we talked into the night, a cruising sailboat arrived and dropped anchor nearby. When the sun came up the next morning, the sailboat was heeled-over at a 45-degree angle, left hard aground by the ebbing tide. The couple on board invited us over for coffee, despite the awkward position of their boat, and afterwards we all tried to help them pull and shove the vessel into deep water. It was no use. They weren't going anywhere until the next high tide.

I left for Pavilion Key, my next campsite, ten and a half miles to the south. Pete and Marty would be joining me there later. After I had set up my camp that evening, I saw them sailing toward me across a wide bay, the canoe gliding along on a beam reach. Pete's design worked, and his method of travel didn't look as tiring as kayaking, but his boat did look complicated and cumbersome, and such a craft would not have been easy to conceal when camping in the populated areas I had passed through.

The campsite on Pavilion Key was located on a spit of sand that extended far out from the mangroves and was exposed to the wind. Mosquitoes were not much of a problem. When Pete and Marty had set up their tent nearby, we pooled our resources to have a big dinner and sat up late again talking. Pete's tales of Micronesia fired me up for the journey ahead, making me anxious to reach the real tropics. I parted with them early the next morning, as they weren't going any farther south and I was bound for Lostman's River, my next assigned campsite sixteen miles to the south. On the way I stopped at another of the endless mangrove islands for lunch, attracted by the waving fronds of a lone coconut palm that thrust its crown far above the other vegetation. I had to use my machete to cut my way through the thicket to the base of the palm. A tantalizing clump of fat green coconuts hung just beneath the fronds. This was both water and food, free for the taking; all I had to do was climb nearly thirty feet of smooth trunk to get it.

Barefoot, I managed to walk up the slightly leaning palm native-style, pulling with my hands to keep pressure on my feet and provide enough friction to hang on. I was exhausted when I reached the top, but managed to pull four of the nuts off their stems. By this time, the mangrove mosquitoes were swarming over me and I quickly slid down the rough trunk, painfully scraping my bare arms and chest. I was bleeding from the cuts and slapping madly at my insect tormentors as I gathered up the fallen nuts and raced out of the thicket for the open beach. The only way I could elude the mosquitoes was to dive into the Gulf and stay submerged for as long as I could hold my breath. The coconuts had been free, but I paid for them in blood. I opened one with the machete and drank the delicious water. The water found in green coconuts is completely different than that of the ripe nuts sold in North American supermarkets. "Drinking nuts" as they are referred to in the tropics, are completely full, so that there is no sound when the nut is shaken. The water inside is pure and cool, even on a hot day, with only a hint of sweetness and coconut flavor. I would rely on green coconuts often to supplement my precious water supply on the arid islands along my route.

The campsite at Lostman's River was on an island in the mouth of the river, surrounded by mangroves and cut off from Gulf breezes. The mosquitoes were upon me as soon as the bow of my kayak touched the sand. I put on my long-sleeved shirt and fatigues despite stifling heat and quickly cooked, opened another of the coconuts for a beverage, and retreated to the tent. During the night the incessant buzzing around my tent was frequently punctuated by terrific splashes in the nearby water. Whether these sounds were made by some kind of huge fish, alligators, or some other swamp inhabitant, I could not tell. Raccoons swarmed over the campsite all night, picking over the coconut scraps I'd scattered around and sniffing and scratching at the kayak.

I woke to find my tent almost completely covered with mosquitoes. The only way to leave was to put on the heavy clothes, spray myself from head to toe with DEET, and dash outside. Even in desperation it took a half hour to get everything stowed and make the kayak ready for sea. Getting hundreds of mosquito bites was unavoidable in a situation like this. In addition to the mosquitoes, tiny no-see-ums that seemed immune to all repellants flew into my eyes, ears, nose, and hair, their bites driving me mad in my frenzy to get out on the water. The insects here were as bad or worse as I remembered from the Everglades trip of two years before. I began to wonder if I would encounter these conditions throughout the tropics, as I made my way farther south into the West Indies. If the insects were as bad as here, I would have to question whether the trip was worth doing after all.

From Lostman's River I made my way south to a campsite at Graveyard Creek, and from there another day of paddling brought me to the beaches of Cape Sable. The beaches of this cape stretch in two great curving crescents for twenty miles, making it the longest stretch of undeveloped beach in the state of Florida. I stopped at the point called Northwest Cape and got out to walk. Beyond the 20-to-30-yard-wide strip of sand, the dry land of the cape was covered in impenetrable thickets of scrub brush and cactus. Dozens of coconut palms grew well back from the beach in the tangle, but getting to them through the interwoven branches of thorn bushes defied my best efforts, and my crashing around drew out the mosquitoes. I returned to the kayak empty-handed, bleeding, and slapping mosquitoes. Despite the difficulty of moving through it, though, the subtropical forest of Cape Sable was beautiful and untrammeled. The narrow beach that separated this green wilderness from the clear Gulf waters was as pristine as any beach I'd ever walked upon. There was a loneliness there and a great silence the likes of which I had only experienced in the fastness of mountain forests such as those of the Appalachians and the Rockies.

I paddled on for miles along this desolate beach to the designated campsite at Middle Cape, another point that juts out to seaward midway between the north and south ends of the cape. The thorn forest there also prevented me from exploring inland, but I was able to walk for miles on the beach. Not a soul was in sight, and a decent breeze kept me bug free, making this the most pleasant camp I'd had in the park. This breeze increased during the night, however, and the next day a moderate surf was rolling into the beach. I paddled on south to the end of Cape Sable, and pitched my tent at the East Cape campsite that was the last site I had a permit for. My solitude ended when two powerboats arrived and the three guys in them set up their camp nearby, complete with loud music from a boom box. I missed the silence, but I looked forward to reaching the ranger station at Flamingo, where I would check out of the park and prepare to cross Florida Bay to the Keys. I had heard there was a campground at Flamingo, and I looked forward to a day or two of relaxing hot showers, cold drinks, and rest. More than anything else, I wanted to get away from the mosquitoes. I had been bitten so many times in the last week that I felt sick. I turned in early at the East Cape campsite, ignoring the blaring music coming from the camp down the beach.

I paddled the ten miles to Flamingo the next morning. There was a small marina enclosed by a concrete seawall, but no place to beach a kayak. Racks of aluminum rental canoes stood behind a row of floating docks on one side of the basin, and I tied up there and went into the rental office to inquire about camping. The woman behind the desk said the campground was two miles down the road. There was no access by boat. There was no way I was going to pay for the privilege of lugging my gear two miles overland. She informed me that I could not even leave my kayak where it was long enough to check in to the ranger station and buy groceries at the marina store. Instead, I would have to pay a five-dollar slip fee and move it to the designated dock. My visions of hot showers faded as I confronted the reality that such places were not set up to accommodate people traveling by such lowly means as kayaks. I paddled to the assigned slip and tied off to the guano-splattered dock.

Since it was Sunday, the ranger station was closed, so there was really no need to check out. I had not seen a ranger during the entire trip through the park anyway. Here in Flamingo, even in the daytime, the mosquitoes swarmed just as fiercely as in the mangrove jungles I'd been through. I watched with amusement as a handful of tourists drove up and stepped out of their cars only to instantly dive back in and slam the doors. Those who braved the onslaught were spraying themselves with the Deep Woods Off that the swindlers in the gift shop were selling for double the retail price. I studied the map displayed outside the ranger station as I tried to decide what to do next. I would have to move on, but there were no nearby alternatives for camping. Landless mangrove swamp extended for miles in all directions from Flamingo, and the distance across Florida Bay to the Keys was more than thirty miles.

I bought overpriced canned goods and snacks in the marina store and made some phone calls. I decided to leave for the Keys immediately. It was 3 P.M., and a thirty-mile crossing would take at least ten hours, but it seemed the best alternative. There were numerous mangrove islands dotting the bay along my intended route. Most would have no dry land, and all but two were off-limits to boats by park regulations. But at least if I got too tired to go on, I thought I might find a place to tie up in the mangroves and get some rest slumped down in the cockpit.

The memory of Flamingo faded quickly as I paddled out into Florida Bay, navigating on a compass course through the maze of islets that stretched to the horizon as far as I could see. The water was aquarium-clear, and I soon forgot my earlier miseries as I watched with fascination the marine life visible beneath my hull. I saw five sharks within the first hour of paddling, all of them about six feet long. By sunset, I still had not seen a patch of dry land among the mangrove islands that were nothing but clumps of these weird trees growing out of the shallow water on stilts. The water near these tree islands was about two feet deep, and when I stepped out of the kayak to stretch my legs and dig a snack out of the storage compartment, I sank another foot into the mud bottom. My options were to keep paddling or sleep in the boat, so I continued south, knowing the moon would be full that night.

Two hours later, I could see a distant glow from the south and knew it had to be from the towns along the upper Keys, still twenty miles away. I decided to make for that light, even if it took all night to reach land. The muddy bottom of Florida Bay would be mostly just two or three feet below my hull, so I could climb out of the kayak occasionally to take a break. There would be no hot supper tonight, so I stuffed myself with cheese, crackers, and other ready-to-eat snacks to maintain the energy to paddle.

When at last I could see individual lights on the horizon ahead after another two hours, I thought I was close, but as I paddled they seemed to be moving away at the same speed I was approaching. I ran aground on mud flats three to four inches deep, and often had to get out and drag my kayak. With each step I sank up to my knees in oozing mud, so even pulling a short distance over a narrow bar was exhausting work. Some of them were more than a hundred yards across.

By midnight I broke free of the flats found myself in an area of deep water at last. But now I was fighting a strong headwind out of the south and bracing to keep the boat upright in breaking waves. I was focusing on a long row of lights that appeared to be less than two miles away on the horizon. It seemed strange that such large swells could be coming towards me out of the south when I should be in the lee of the land where those lights were. As I drew nearer, the swells did not diminish, and I realized that I was looking at bridge lights on a long expanse of the Overseas Highway and that there was no land ahead of me, only the empty Atlantic Ocean. I made a right turn to parallel the bridge, knowing that I would soon reach the next key down the chain, though I had no way of knowing which one that would be. I thought I was somewhere in the vicinity of Key Largo, since I maintained a course slightly east of south throughout the crossing.

Ahead to the west now were more lights, and the variety and number of them convinced me that I was looking at land. I continued west until I was adjacent to the island, then turned to paddle toward shore. As I drew within a half mile I could clearly see buildings illuminated by streetlights and looked forward to stepping ashore in a few minutes.

Over an hour later though, I was still struggling to find a way across a line of mud bars that cut me off from the island only a quarter mile from shore. This mud was so soft that it was impossible to walk across. I sank to my thighs in it each time I got out of the boat. The only way to cross the bars was to lie across the stern deck of the kayak so I wouldn't sink, and push and swim with my feet to propel it forward. Stingrays scattered in every direction as I plowed across the flats, cursing the low tide that stranded me when I was so close to land and the rest I needed. By 3:30 A.M. I managed to get the loaded kayak across the mud and climbed back in to paddle across a stretch of deep water that separated me from shore. I pointed the bow toward the coconut palms of a motel beach, and when I landed I found a sign proclaiming that this was the Gold Key Motel, Islamorada, Florida.

I checked my map and saw that Islamorada was about a hundred miles from Key West. I had come almost three hundred miles since leaving Tampa nineteen days ago, which was faster than I'd expected, considering all the stops and my leisurely pace. There was time for a side trip out of my way to Key West, and I thought it would be good to paddle an extra two hundred miles of easy island-hopping to prepare myself for the more widely-spaced islands of the Caribbean.

The tiny strip of beach behind the Gold Key Motel was deserted at this hour. There was a table and chairs, swimming pool, and an outside shower near the water's edge. I dug a can of ravioli and a bottle of shampoo out of my kayak, and after eating, took a cold shower to wash away the Everglades grime. There were no mosquitoes at all here, making the place seem like paradise compared to where I'd been. Those who have not experienced the torture of being attacked incessantly by at least three species of biting insects for more than a week cannot truly appreciate the ecstasy I felt at being able to sit out in the open unmolested by bugs. I was too exhausted to go any farther. There didn't seem to be anyone around the motel, so I spread my sleeping bag on the ground under some bushes behind a maintenance building and slept until daybreak.

In the morning I carried my filthy clothes to a Laundromat in town and ate breakfast at Burger King. I wandered the streets while waiting on my laundry, taking in the sights. There was an island feel here that was different than the other parts of Florida I'd seen. Lush greenery was everywhere, and a cool Atlantic breeze swept down the streets and rattled the palm fronds, taking the humidity out of the air. The tourists were thick, but there were other travelers like me as well. Near the Burger King, I watched as two middle-aged men with hair down to their waists headed down Highway A1-A under the weight of huge backpacks, most certainly bound for Key West. I had been to the Keys once before. When Ernest and I came out of the Everglades after our canoe trip, we drove to Key West for a couple of days, so I knew what it was like. People like those backpackers come from all over the country, as if on a pilgrimage to the southernmost U.S. city at the end of A1-A. I would fit right in, arriving by kayak.

Crowded Islamorada offered no prospects for camping, so I paddled along the Overseas Highway to the west, hoping to find a quiet place to catch up on my sleep. Five miles from Islamorada, I paddled under the bridge through a cut between two keys and into Atlantic waters for the first time. I wanted to check out Indian Key, shown on my chart as uninhabited. There was a small dock for boaters visiting the island, and as I approached closer, I saw a sign that said camping was prohibited because it was a state preserve.

I went ashore and found other signs with information about this historic little island. In 1840, a town was built on the island and for a short time Indian Key was been a thriving wrecker's colony. These devious pirates set up a bright light on stormy nights to lure ships seeking shelter from rough seas. The hapless sailors who fell prey to this ruse were unaware of their mistake until their vessel broke apart on the reefs they had been tricked into hitting, their cargo spilling into the waves to be claimed by the unscrupulous wreckers.

A map on one of the signs showed the layout of the town, complete with the street names and the location of stores and other buildings. Archaeologists had excavated most of the ruins, though not much remains other than several cisterns. I walked down the dirt streets and ambled through the town square, trying to imagine what it must have been like in the 1840s. According to the information on the signs, the colony did not last long. A Seminole war party paddled ashore one night in canoes and massacred the entire community. Indian Key has remained uninhabited ever since.

The cleared streets offered the only paths for walking on an island that was covered in a tangle of subtropical vegetation. Thorn bushes, agave, and other cactus formed an impenetrable understory, and in places large exotic trees I could not identify rose above this scrub, but none reached a great height on this storm-swept island that was only a few feet above sea level. Most of the shoreline consisted of jagged coral battered by ocean swells, but on the north side of the island, under a dense stand of mangrove and buttonwood, there was a narrow beach completely hidden from the view of drivers on the nearby Overseas Highway.

There was a guest register attached to the signpost on the dock where visitors could sign in, and I saw that no one had been there in two days, probably due to the overcast weather that looked like it was going to get worse. I was exhausted from my crossing of Florida Bay, and decided to take a chance on breaking the law and camp on Indian Key. I was beginning to feel like a fugitive, with all this hiding and illegal camping, but there was no reasonable alternative. I moved the kayak from the dock area to the overgrown north side of the island and pulled it under the concealing mangroves, just in case someone did show up. After pitching my tent in the densest part of the thicket, I spent the rest of the afternoon exploring the ruins of the town and examining the strange plants on the island.

That evening as I cooked dinner, I noticed the wind was steadily increasing and the seas smashing into the island were getting bigger. I turned on the VHF radio to get a NOAA report and was shocked to hear that Tropical Storm Keith was headed for Florida. I was so excited about arriving in the Keys that I didn't give the weather a second thought, until now. I thought I was safe from hurricanes, traveling so late in the year, but this late-season storm was predicted to move ashore sometime Tuesday night, the warning area extending from Cape Sable north almost to Tampa. Indian Key was just barely out of its path, but I knew that such a storm could change course with little warning. Keith was packing sustained winds of sixty-five knots at the moment. If it built to hurricane force, even if it went to the north, the Keys would get their share of heavy weather. I knew what hurricanes were all about. Though I was only five at the time, I remembered Camille, the killer hurricane that devastated the Mississippi Gulf Coast in 1969. Even one hundred miles inland, we had wind speeds over one hundred knots, and thousands of sea gulls had been carried to our town, trapped in the eye of the storm.

I knew Indian Key was no place to be in such a storm, but I felt secure for now. It was more than twenty-four hours away, so I decided to sleep there one night, and make a decision as to what to do next based on the morning forecast. I figured I could always paddle back to Islamorada and check into the Gold Key Motel if the Keys were going to be in for a real blow.

The wind was blowing a steady thirty knots by daybreak, and the sea was white with foam. My first reaction was to break camp and get to secure shelter on Islamorada, but the radio report insisted that Keith would make landfall in an area just south of Tampa. The storm would not reach hurricane status. Small craft were advised to stay in port throughout the Keys, however, and a storm surge of four feet was expected in the local area.

I walked around Indian Key to evaluate the situation. The streets in mid-island were high enough to be safe from a four-foot storm surge, and the cisterns, five to six feet deep and lined with stones would provide shelter from wind and flying debris. I decided to stay. No one would venture out to the island in such weather, and I needed more rest. I moved my tent from the mangrove thicket and pitched it on one of the streets. Someone had left an axe on the dock, and with it I cut heavy stakes and drove them into the rock ground to secure my shelter. I cleared dead branches and other potential projectiles out of the immediate area and moved my kayak near the tent, weighting it down with large stones.

These preparations made, there was nothing else to do but wait. I walked to the windward side of the island and watched forty-knot gusts blow spray off the tops of turbulent whitecaps that filled the horizon. The wind smelled clean, the way it always does before a storm. Standing there, I remembered seeing a halo around the full moon two nights before as I crossed Florida Bay. I had read somewhere that a halo around the moon was a sign of an approaching storm.

Throughout the night the wind howled and rain poured, but the resilient trees on the island didn't break under the strain and my tent held together. The radio reported seventy-knot gusts on Cape Sable, just thirty-five miles to the north. On Wednesday morning the seas were still chaotic, but I was low on drinking water so I broke camp and paddled under the Overseas Highway to the more protected waters on the Gulf side.

Paddling west under the bridge in choppy seas that kept me soaked, I reached Fiesta Key by noon. I tied up to a seawall at a KOA campground to top off my water supply. A couple of vacationers fishing from the seawall offered me a cold beer and said tent sites were thirty dollars a night in the campground. This changed the plans I'd entertained about camping there, but after a couple more beers and a brief account of my trip, I learned that these two guys were experienced campers and paddlers themselves, earning their living as counselors taking troubled juveniles on twenty-eight-day wilderness canoe trips. Hearing of my difficulties finding places to camp, they offered space for my tent in their campsite, so I avoided the fee and enjoyed my first hot shower in almost a month.

The next morning was Thanksgiving Day. I left the KOA early after procuring a couple of green coconuts from one of the palms there. I paddled on to the west, hoping to find a waterfront restaurant where I could reward myself for reaching the Keys with a proper Thanksgiving feast. I found nothing along my route that day though, and settled for a can of cold ravioli for lunch and rice and tuna for dinner. I thought of my friends and family back home in Mississippi with their turkey and dressing; sweet potato pies and cranberry sauce. But I wouldn't have traded that day with any of them. It felt good in a perverse way to eat such a simple meal on that abundant holiday, like a kid playing hooky while everyone else was in school.

Friday morning the wind was strong out of the east, so I decided to experiment with an improvised downwind sail, something I wanted to try in case I needed it on the long open-water crossings in the Caribbean. I had a parafoil kite, often used by sea kayakers for downwind sailing, but it required twenty or more knots of steady wind to stay airborne and pull the kayak. I had tried it once before the trip, but so far had not had such strong tailwinds again. This time I used my spare paddle as a mast and a plastic tarp as a makeshift spinnaker. It pulled the kayak along surprisingly well, and I sailed effortlessly for fifteen miles to Marathon Key.

Needing groceries, I stowed the sail rig and paddled into one of the residential canals that run like streets between the waterfront homes of the island. I tied up to a private dock with the permission of the owner and learned that as usual, I had landed more than two miles from a store. I set out walking until I found the supermarket, stopping on the way back to treat myself to much needed fresh vegetables and fruit at a Pizza Hut salad bar.

Just west of Marathon Key, I spotted an apparently deserted islet on the Atlantic side of the highway and headed for it, always preferring the seclusion of an island campsite to any spot reachable by road. The shore of this island was rocky, and battered by waves, much like Indian Key, but there was one strip of sand that looked like a possible landing site. A grove of weather-beaten casuarinas trees and clumps of low bushes was the extent of the island's vegetation. I could see no signs proclaiming private property or "No Camping."

A speedboat with a well-tanned young man at the helm and two bikini-clad babes stretched out on the bow blasted by me en route to the same island as I struggled against the wind, which was now against me, blowing twenty knots and kicking up a nasty chop. The driver gave me a contemptuous glance as he passed, obviously proud of his sleek vessel and sexy crew, and probably regarding my kayak as a "non-boat." I slogged steadily on, still a half mile out, while the powerboater circled the tiny island looking for a place to land or anchor. In those conditions, he didn't have a chance. I approached the jagged shore with impunity and made a perfect surf landing on a pocket of sand between the rocks. I carried my gear to a level spot under the pines and began pitching my tent, while the man with his disappointed female companions circled, tried unsuccessfully to anchor close to shore, then gave up and jammed the throttle wide open for Marathon after one last hateful look in my direction. I jumped up and down, waving and grinning.

"Sell it and get a kayak!" I yelled after him.

As the boat disappeared into the distance, I felt a great sense of peace and security on the tiny island that was as inaccessible as a fortress as long as rough seas pounded its rocks. I walked the perimeter. The entire island was maybe sixty yards long and thirty yards wide. There were signs that others had camped there, but probably only in better weather. The island was so small it was not shown on my map, so for lack of a better name, I called it simply: "The Rock." I stayed two nights, reading most of the day on Saturday while a steady rain pattered the roof of my tent.

I left The Rock on Sunday morning for the crossing to Bahia Honda, the first key on the other side of the Seven-mile Bridge that connects the Middle Keys to the Lower Keys—the group that includes Key West. The sea was rough on the exposed crossing, and I paralleled the long bridge from about a quarter mile out on the Atlantic side, drawing stares, waves, and horn blowing from the stream of traffic above. On the other side of the bridge, Bahia Honda State Park offers campgrounds, but I only stopped to take a cold freshwater shower. I had my eye on another tiny island like The Rock that I could see southwest of the park beaches. I waited until sunset and headed for it. There were no trees on this island, and wide sandy beaches encircled most of it, making landing easy. There was however, a sign planted squarely in the center. After stepping ashore, I could see that it read: "Restricted—Bird Nesting Area."

I looked around carefully. I could see no birds or law enforcement officers, so I pulled the kayak up on the beach and set up camp in spite of the sign. I knew it wasn't nesting season, and I was getting disgusted with all the signs that seemed to sprout from every beach, telling me what I could or couldn't do. It reminded me of the old '70s song by the Five Man Electrical Band about the signs, and I sang it out loud as I put up my tent in the fading light:

"Sign, sign, everywhere a sign, blockin' all the scenery, breakin' my mind . . . Do this, don't do that . . . Can't you read the sign?"

I felt more and more isolated from society. I couldn't follow all the petty little rules concocted by people who had no idea what it was like to be immersed in the elements day after day. I had no intention of breaking any *real* laws or causing harm to any person or property, but I just couldn't do this trip without breaking somebody's "No Trespassing" rules on an almost daily basis.

The soft sand near the sign felt like a bed after spending two nights on the unyielding surface of The Rock. I slept peacefully and left at dawn. Key West was only forty miles away. I paddled on, suspended by calm, transparent water three or four feet deep above an endless expanse of grass flats. Occasionally I would see a rocky hole in the grass to break the monotony, and in one such hideaway I drifted over a three-foot nurse shark and stopped to prod it with the paddle. The shark took off, but a green moray eel emerged from a crevice and snapped at the end of the paddle. Seeing the bottom and the abundant life beneath my hull added a new dimension to paddling. I stopped often to take a closer look with mask, snorkel, and fins, towing the kayak along as I swam.

Later that day, as I approached Sugarloaf Key from about five miles offshore, the wind increased and I punched through choppy seas paying little attention to the water, my gaze fixed on my destination and my thoughts wandering to where I would spend the night. Suddenly, my left hand felt as if it had been stung by dozens of wasps, and I jerked it back to see the stringy purple tentacles of a Portuguese man-of-war clinging to the skin. I had seen plenty of these creatures floating on the surface since I'd been in the Keys, but somehow I did not see this one and my paddle scooped up the trailing tentacles and swept them right onto my hand. I thrashed my arm wildly in the water, trying desperately to rid myself of the burning strings that clung tenaciously to my hand. The pain was excruciating, even after I managed to wash away all the stinging cells. I had been stung plenty of times by jellyfish, but this was not even in the same league. I could not believe the pain. My entire left arm quickly became paralyzed from the shoulder down, forcing me to grip the paddle in the center with my right hand and slowly propel the boat towards shore with a figure-eight stroke. I had Benadryl in my first aid kit, but unfortunately I had stored it in the stern compartment where it was unreachable from the cockpit. After almost three hours of one-handed paddling, I reached Sugarloaf Key, where there was another KOA, advertised as the southernmost KOA in the United States. I tied up in some mangroves and took two Benadryl capsules. Then I found my way to the showers and a bought a cold Coke. My arm was still numb, so my paddling for the day was done. This was definitely another one of those unexpected incidents that I had never dreamed of while planning the trip. I was just lucky that I had not been even farther from land when it happened. Feeling drowsy from the Benadryl, I pitched my tent in the campground and went to bed at dark.

By morning my arm had recovered, so I left the KOA at daybreak, continuing on towards Key West. I passed deserted islands all morning, most posted with large signs that read: "U.S. Government Property, Do Not Approach Within 100 Yards. Trespassers will be prosecuted." These islands were obviously part of Key West Naval Air Station. Fighter jets streaked overhead and a low-flying Navy helicopter turned around and passed back over me for a closer look.

That afternoon I reached Stock Island, but still had not found a likely campsite. I didn't want to arrive late in Key West, because my intention was to simply circle the island, spend a few hours taking in the sights of Duval Street, and then turn around and head back east to Key Largo.

The only likely place to pitch a tent that I found was a deserted strip of land behind the campus of the Florida Keys Community College. I set up camp there in the concealment of a fallen pine tree and, undetected, slept until morning. There were more military installations along my route as I approached Key West from the Gulf side, including arrays of satellite dishes, bristling antennas, warships at anchor, and huge blimps with the words "Atlantic Sentry" emblazoned on their sides. I had seen some of these blimps the day before, so high they appeared as a white speck in the sky. I assumed they were used to keep an eye on Cuba, just ninety miles to the south.

I slowly rounded the southwest end of Key West, passing more government property, military residences, private beaches, and marinas. I could find no likely landing spot, so I circled the island until I was back on the Atlantic side and headed east again. There I passed resort hotel beaches crowded with sunbathers and swimmers, including several topless women. I stopped at a beach concession that rented windsurfers to inquire about leaving my kayak on the beach while I went into town. Permission was denied, so I pushed off the beach and paddled on. I was ready to forget the whole idea of visiting Key West when I passed one more large resort hotel and noticed a woman sweeping the sidewalk in front of a small building that housed an array of rental catamarans, windsurfers, motor scooters, and bicycles. I was sure she would send me away like the others, but decided it was worth one more try. I had paddled a long way out of my way to get there.

Seeing me land, the woman, who looked about my age, came down to greet me. She was wearing a nameplate that said "Lisa." I explained my dilemma and she said she would check with the manager. She came back a few minutes later and said it would be fine to leave my boat there for a few days. I was shocked at this offer and quickly pulled the kayak up on the beach, telling her I only needed a few hours to look around and have a decent meal.

The rental office where Lisa worked was called Key West Watersports and was a concession of the Casa Marina Resort Hotel. She introduced me to Steve, another watersports instructor who was interested in kayaking, and I told them my story and let Steve take the kayak out for a spin. Steve came back with a wide grin and a dozen questions, offering to buy me a couple of beers later if I would tell him more about sea kayaking. I didn't plan to stay until nightfall, but the prospect of drinking in a bar sounded good, and I also liked the idea of hanging around and talking to Lisa.

Feeling my kayak was in good hands at Watersports, I ambled into downtown Key West with no worries, glad to be away from the water and among people for a brief time. I found my way to Duval Street and followed it to the west end, where each day tourists and citizens of Key West alike come to Sunset Celebration. It was amazing seeing hundreds of people turn out just to watch the sun go down. Mallory Square was alive with activity when I got there. There were musicians playing: an old West Indian black with steel drums, a young Rastafarian with dreadlocks pounding out a reggae pulse on a conga, and a fellow wearing a kilt and playing bagpipes. There were jugglers and circus-style tightrope acts; a lady with a nine-foot python that tourists could touch for a dollar, and vendors selling everything from popcorn to green coconuts. When the sun finally did sink into the ocean, the entire crowd clapped and cheered, as if this were the first time it had ever happened.

After dark I left the square and met Steve at Turtle Kraal's, his favorite bar. Steve had been to the Bahamas as crew on a sailboat, and he raved about the clear water and great diving to be found there. This talk and the island atmosphere at Sunset Celebration left me anxious to get going to the islands. But Key West was an interesting stopover, and the friendly people I encountered made it tempting to spend more time there. Steve told me that I could get away with sleeping on the beach near my kayak, if I scaled the fence surrounding Watersports when the security guard was on the other end of the beach. This tactic worked out fine the first night, so I decided that more than one night was in order.

The following day a reporter from the Key West Citizen got wind of my arrival by kayak, and came to the beach at Watersports where I posed for a photo beside my boat and answered his many questions. I hung around the shop talking with Lisa and some of the other employees, and ended up back on Duval Street that night. I was having fun, and before I realized it, a few hours turned into four days, and my money was disappearing in quantities that would have lasted me weeks out in the wilds, camping and paddling. In this short time I made real friends and felt at home, and the temptation to stay was strong. Many before me who visited this island for a few short days were still there years since. It was time to move on and escape this potential trap. Steve and Lisa were on the beach to shove me off when I had the kayak packed and ready to leave.

"Those TV commercials are right," Steve said as I fastened my sprayskirt and adjusted my rudder. "It really *is* better in the Bahamas."

They watched until I paddled out of sight, awkwardly getting back into the rhythm after so many days of not being in the kayak. After a mile I was back in the endless cadence of my traveling stroke, and the boat slid easily over crystalline water until Key West fell astern, turned blue with distance, and finally, faded from sight.

# THREE

# KEY WEST TO THE BAHAMAS

A man who is not afraid of the sea will soon be drowned,
For he will be going out on a day when he shouldn't
But we do be afraid of the sea,
And we do be drowned only now and again

**—FISHERMAN'S QUOTE FROM THE ARAN ISLANDS**

Leaving Key West, I retraced my route to Sugarloaf Key, stopping to camp that night in a mosquito-ridden mangrove hideaway that made me wish I were still sleeping on the beach at Watersports. I missed the food, the music, and the people of Key West. It was a lonely night, but I was determined to press on. The next day I stopped once again at the KOA on Sugarloaf but decided not to camp there. There was an uninhabited key visible about five miles out on the Atlantic side, shown on my map as Key Lewis. I decided to paddle out there, hoping to find nice beaches and fewer mosquitoes.

I reached Key Lewis by sunset, and as I approached it my hopes sank like the rapidly fading light when I saw large signs planted in the shallows well off the island warning against trespassing. The island was government property, according to the signs, which were intended to keep anyone from even thinking about landing. I saw no evidence of people or buildings, so I ignored the warnings and paddled closer. There appeared to be no solid land, only jungle-like tangles of mangroves growing directly out of the water.

Movement in the trees caught my eye, and I heard strange calls coming from the foliage. I thought it must be birds until I saw dark shapes sitting in the branches and then dozens of large animals shaking the limbs and moving towards me. They were monkeys! I drifted in amazement a few yards from the edge of the forest. The monkeys were jumping up and down and chattering at the sight of my kayak. I recognized them as Rhesus monkeys, a large species often used in scientific research. I wanted to land and dig out a fresh roll of film, but the monkeys seemed aggressive. I feared that if I tried to camp there, they might steal all my gear and haul it off into the trees. They might even gang up and attack. Perhaps the government was doing some kind of disease or biological warfare research with these animals and keeping it a secret by working on this isolated key. I was exhausted and ready to camp, but it was not worth the risk.

I paddled parallel to the shore and the monkeys followed, their strange calls reverberating in the twilight, lending an eerie feel to the island. More groups of the monkeys materialized as I paddled along the large key, and I realized there were hundreds, if not thousands, of the animals on the island. One aggressive male got so excited as he scolded me that he lost his balance and fell from a branch into the water. As interesting as they were to watch, I had to leave, as I faced a long night crossing to get back to the main keys where I could search for another place to camp.

It was a moonless night, and the sky was filled with stars that seemed as near as the city lights on Big Pine Key, five miles to the north. I set my course for the little key with the bird nesting sign where I had illegally camped the previous week. I reached it after midnight, weary and spooked from the long paddle over black water. Once I thought I saw a large fin that disappeared just a few yards from my

Twenty miles of wilderness beach on Cape Sable, Everglades National Park.

kayak. Each loud splash as some big fish jumped out of the water would cause a brief moment of panic and inspire me to paddle faster. For some reason, this was one night I did not at all feel comfortable being on the water.

I woke the next morning on the little key to the sound of a motorboat approaching the beach. Through the netting of my tent door, I could see a flashing blue light and a uniformed officer at the helm. The engine went to idle and the officer's voice boomed over a radio PA system, informing me that camping on the island was illegal. I crawled out and explained my situation. The officer said he would give me thirty minutes to pack up and go before he would return to write me a citation. I quickly broke camp and made the ten-mile crossing back to The Rock, off Marathon, fighting headwinds all the way. There was no sign that anyone had visited the island in my absence. I stayed only one night this time, enjoying a brief respite from signs and law enforcement officers.

During the next two days I made many of the same stops I'd made heading out to Key West. I resupplied on Marathon, took another hot shower at the KOA on Fiesta Key, and once again set up camp on Indian Key, where I had weathered Tropical Storm Keith. I then paddled to Islamorada, where I needed to replenish my most important supply of all—cash. I had gone through about four hundred dollars in five weeks, a large chunk of it blown in Key West. I had left the bulk of my traveling fund with my father in Mississippi. I called him and had him wire another five hundred dollars from my stash to Islamorada.

With money in my kayak, my next goal was Key Largo, where I had a prearranged mail drop. I was expecting to pick up some guidebooks to the Bahamas and Caribbean that I had sent there, and my friend Pat Milton was sending a replacement for the camp stove I had thrown into the Gulf when it died near Naples.

Getting to Key Largo on the Gulf side would mean winding through a maze of mangrove islands with their ever-present swarms of mosquitoes, so I decided to try the Atlantic side instead. I headed east of Islamorada, excited to be in unfamiliar waters once again, where every turn might lead to a new discovery. I entered the Atlantic through the pass at Windley Key, and after passing a large resort on my left, found another pocket of mangrove swamp where a makeshift houseboat was moored in a green hideaway. The owner, who introduced himself as Mike, told me that he had built his living quarters on the old pontoon boat in Tampa and, like me, had made his way down the west coast of Florida to the Keys. He had been living on the houseboat for four months. He made his living cleaning swimming pools and houses with a pressure washer that he towed behind an old single-speed bicycle.

He had no living expenses other than food and consequently spent most of his days lying in his hammock, smoking dope and looking out over the ocean.

"The land's private, but they can't say anything about my boat. They don't own the water," he said. "You can camp right over there if you don't stay more than a few days," he said, pointing to a narrow strip of land near the mouth of the inlet. "The cops don't come out here but about once a week."

I took him up on the campsite. It was a good place for me to get organized and make my plans for crossing over to the Bahamas. I studied my charts and discussed the crossing with Mike. He thought it was feasible after seeing my specialized equipment. This crossing weighed on my mind for months, long before I left Tampa, back when the trip was just a dream. I knew the Gulf Stream would be my biggest obstacle to reaching the islands. The Gulf Stream is an ocean current so wide and deep that it contains more flow than all the fresh water rivers of the world combined. Running through the Florida Straits between Cuba and the Keys, then north between the Florida peninsula and the Bahamas, it carries warm tropical water along the eastern seaboard until it meets the cold Labrador Current and changes course across the North Atlantic to warm the shores of Europe. The section I had to cross between Florida and the Bahamas averages thirty to fifty miles wide as it squeezes through the narrow straits with a speed of more than three knots at midstream. The current would set me north at a rate of three miles per hour while I paddled east across it at approximately the same speed. It would be like trying to swim across a strong river for the opposite bank without being swept downstream. The difference was that this river was fifty miles wide and the opposite bank was Bimini, a tiny island less than five miles long and so low I wouldn't be able to see it until I was a few miles away. At my paddling speed, it would take up to twenty hours to cross the current, which could set me as much as sixty miles to the north. I had no handheld Global Positioning System receiver (GPS) to give me continuous position fixes. GPS receivers were just coming on the market at the time and were way beyond my budget. My deck-mounted compass was my primary navigation tool, backed up by a handheld Radio Direction Finder (RDF), now rendered obsolete by GPS technology.

With the RDF, I could receive an audio signal from a transmitter tower on Bimini, allowing me to readjust my heading to stay on course for the island, and by triangulating with signals from mainland Florida, I could tell how far north I was being swept, but none of this knowledge would help me with the physical problem of battling the current in a human-powered boat. If I missed the Bahamas because of a navigational error or simple exhaustion that would prevent me from maintaining my speed to the east, the Gulf Stream would sweep me into the North Atlantic on its path to Europe.

Because of this problem with the current, I concluded that the most sensible point of departure was Key Largo, even though it would be a ninety-mile crossing to Bimini, while the Miami area, due west of the island, is less than fifty miles away. Starting that much farther south would give me a more favorable position in the current, allowing me to paddle across the stream on due east heading while the current angled me directly to Bimini. The crossing would take up to thirty hours this way, but I would be paddling across the current rather than fighting it by choosing this course.

The other major consideration, of course, was the weather. The Gulf Stream has a reputation for mountainous waves that occur when strong north winds blow against the current. I had been listening to the NOAA weather radio reports on Gulf Stream conditions since I'd been in the Keys. It was the time of year when winter cold fronts occasionally made it down to south Florida, seldom bringing cold weather, but always packing sustained north winds that make the Gulf Stream dangerous. It was not uncommon to hear reports of seas ten to fifteen feet offshore and eighteen to twenty-four feet and higher in the Gulf Stream during such northerly blows. Between the fronts, the Florida Straits could be as placid as a sheltered bay. But the window of opportunity for crossing in smooth conditions was often narrow this time of year. Because of all these factors, there was no doubt in my mind that attempting this crossing in a kayak was a serious undertaking requiring meticulous planning and the right conditions.

I stayed a couple of nights in the hidden campsite near Mike's boat, discussing the crossing with him and going through my equipment. It was only about seven miles to the edge of the continental shelf from my camp, so I paddled out there one day to get a look at the offshore conditions. I could see the sand bottom 60 feet below as I approached the edge, and then nothing but inky blue beyond the drop-off. The swell was running seven to ten feet. I tested my desalinator, trailing the intake tube into the sea and pumping the unit with the output tube in my mouth. The water it made was sweet and fresh. I hoped I wouldn't need it though, as it required vigorous pumping and trickled fresh water at a ponderously low slow rate. I tuned in the RDF to the Bimini beacon. The Morse code signal came in loud and clear: two dashes, two dots, one dash, three dots, one dash, three dots . . . repeating over and over. The signal was strongest when the compass read sixty degrees. Precisely where the chart indicated Bimini should be. I began to feel confident that I could find it.

The next day I invited Mike over to my camp for breakfast and showed him how to make pancakes. Then I broke camp and paddled east toward Key Largo, looking for a jumping-off point where I could camp while waiting on a weather window and making ready for the crossing.

The prospects for finding a free campsite looked grim as I paddled along the Atlantic side of Key Largo in the late afternoon. The only places not occupied by waterfront homes or other developments were the mangrove swamps and the rock jetties that protected the entrance to residential canals. Near the entrance to Marina Del Mar, I passed two large sailing yachts at anchor, a trimaran and a black-hulled schooner that had the look of a pirate vessel. I continued on past the marina, setting my sights on a tiny offshore key that appeared to have some dry land under its cloak of green mangroves.

Naturally, when I drew nearer, I was disappointed to see a sign claiming that this island, like so many others, was a bird nesting area off-limits to human intruders. The island had no beaches at all but appeared to be made up entirely of baseball-sized chunks of coral rock. There was no place to land on the side facing the sign, so I paddled around the island until I found a hidden tunnel under the mangroves where I could pull my kayak out of sight in knee-deep water. A quick inspection of the island revealed that it was fit only for birds, and even they seemed to have abandoned it. There was nothing but rocks and debris washed ashore from the sea. The only vegetation was red mangrove and twisted buttonwood trees. I was too tired to go anywhere else, so I cleared a spot under the trees and pitched my tent. I had to break branches out of the way to erect it, and I put some waterlogged pieces of broken plywood under the floor to provide a semblance of smoothness on the sharp rocks. It was the most uncomfortable place I'd ever camped, but at least the tent was well hidden. I was too tired to be concerned with comfort.

In the morning I broke camp early and paddled back to the Marina Del Mar, where huge motor yachts dwarfed my kayak. The marina was certainly not designed to accommodate small boats. The only place I could find to tie up was in a slip big enough for a fifty-footer. The dock was so high at low tide that I had to stand in the kayak and haul myself up with my arms. I walked to the post office but was disappointed to learn that there was no mail for me under general delivery. I would have to wait another day.

I bought some of the food supplies I would need for my Gulf Stream crossing and stopped at a dive shop to purchase chemical light sticks that I planned to use to illuminate my compass at night during the passage. Then I went back to the miserable little rock pile of an island and set up my tent in the same place. Motorboats passed close by on their way in and out of the marina, so I couldn't build a fire for fear of being seen and forced to leave. I had expected the new stove to be in the post office, but without it, there was no alternative to a cold supper. I crawled into the tent and studied the charts that night by candlelight, making notes and a detailed list of everything else I needed to buy before leaving. There would be no way to cook at sea, so I planned to carry at least three day's supply of ready-to-eat, high-energy foods. I planned to pack this supply all around me in the cockpit in case something went wrong and I could not reach land as soon as expected. I decided to begin the thirty-hour crossing at 3 A.M. so that I would be in the middle of the Stream during daylight hours and hopefully, during the second night, be able to see the light beacon on Bimini to confirm that my navigation was on target. If all went well, I would step out on Bahamian sand by daylight on the second morning.

On Wednesday, I paddled back to the marina, and still there was no mail waiting for me at the post office. The weather for the crossing was good, but I could not leave until I received my package. I went to the grocery store and bought the items on my crossing list. Mostly snack foods like cheese, granola bars, dried fruit, crackers, nuts, candy—but also small cans of ravioli, spaghetti, and beans with pull-tops for easy opening at sea. This done I returned for a third night to my rocky hideaway.

I was no longer tired from paddling, so it was impossible for me to fall asleep on the uneven plywood and rocks that made up my bed. I tried piling all my spare clothing under my sleeping bag, but that didn't help much. I tuned in the weather station on my VHF radio and listened to the report on Gulf Stream conditions. A cold front sweeping down across the continent was bringing north winds and creating chaos out there in the current; seas offshore running eight to twelve feet, higher in the Gulf Stream, according to the report. I switched off the weather and tuned in to the tantalizing RDF beacon on Bimini. It seemed so clear—and so close . . . I put away the RDF and put a Jimmy Buffett tape in the Walkman, listening to Caribbean tales set to island music while I read my Air Force survival manual by candlelight. This fascinating book included illustrated descriptions of techniques for catching fish and signaling for help while stranded at sea in a life raft. It was comforting to read that many people had survived weeks at sea with minimal equipment and supplies. I tried to imagine what it would be like adrift for weeks in my kayak as I tossed and turned on my rocky bed and listened to waves crashing ashore a few feet away.

Other sounds outside drew me out of the tent to investigate. I discovered that I was not alone on the island when I saw several large rats in the beam of my flashlight. I secured the sprayskirt over my kayak's cockpit opening to keep them out, and hoped they would not try to chew through it to get at the food inside. Like the raccoons I encountered on most of these mangrove islands, the rats showed little fear of humans. If they wanted it badly enough, the rats or raccoons could chew through the watertight bulkheads behind which my food was stored. This would render my boat unseaworthy, and if it happened on a more remote island, I would be marooned in any but the calmest conditions.

I spent a sleepless night worried about the crossing ahead of me and after sunrise once again broke camp and left the rat-infested island to paddle to Key Largo. My trip to the post office this time was fruitful. My new stove had arrived, as well as a letter from Ernest, the first letter I'd received since leaving Tampa. I was free to leave for the Bahamas now, but the weather was not cooperating. The cold front predicted by the NOAA forecasters had arrived, and twenty to twenty-five knot winds swept through the streets and whipped up whitecaps on the near-shore waters. There was nothing to do until this wind changed. I refilled my water jugs and bought a cheap inflatable air mattress at a dollar store. If I had to be stuck camping on the rocks for a few days, I would have to try to get some sleep.

Back at the marina, I opened the hatches of my storage compartments to cram in the new mattress and some extra food I picked up at the grocery store. I was aware of being watched from the sidewalk above the dock.

"Now *that's* camping out," a man's voice said. I looked up and at the same time the small boy holding the man's hand repeated his father's statement. "This is my son Grant," the man said, introducing the blonde-haired boy who looked to be four or five. "I'm Ben Olsen. My wife, Sylvia, and my oldest son, Sky, are around here somewhere. They're going to want to see this too."

I didn't have anywhere else to be, so I recited the often-repeated narrative of my trip up to this point and outlined my paddling plans. Ben was amazed that I had paddled all the way from Tampa, and incredulous when I announced my plan to paddle to Bimini.

"Isn't that a bit too risky?" he asked. "Why don't you just hitch a ride across on a sailboat or something like that?"

I told him that I had considered that option, but figured no one would be willing to put my long kayak on the deck of their boat, and besides, I had heard that all the sailboats cross from Miami or Ft. Lauderdale. There would be no place to camp there while trying to arrange a ride. And anyway, the kayak was seaworthy, and I was in shape from five hundred miles I had already paddled. The weather would calm down, and I knew I could make it.

Ben still seemed unconvinced. The Gulf Stream was at its roughest this time of year. He knew it well. I had assumed that this was another tourist family, but I was wrong. They were sailors, and, in fact, the black-hulled schooner anchored nearby that I had admired when I first paddled into the Key Largo area was their ship. Ben said it was a forty-two-foot Tom Colvin design, custom-built in aluminum. They were Bahamas-bound themselves.

"In fact, I was just considering offering you a ride across myself, if you decide not to paddle," Ben said with a grin. "Your boat will easily fit on *Whisper*'s foredeck."

"I'll think about it," I said. "But if this weather lets up, I really want to do the crossing on my own."

Ben said that they would sail in a few days if the weather permitted. I joined them for lunch at the salad bar in a Wendy's that was just across the street from the marina. The Olsen family lived in Iowa, of all places. As incongruous as it seemed, they were farmers who kept a cruising schooner in south Florida, escaping the Midwest winters each year after the harvest of corn and soybeans was brought in and spending several months until spring planting season sailing the Bahamas. They had done so for years. Ben asked me to stay in touch during our wait for favorable weather and update them of my plans each morning by calling on the VHF.

I paddled back to the little island to set up my camp again. Once ashore I opened the package containing the new stove and discovered that Pat had included several packages of Mountain House freeze-dried food from his store. I opened one labeled "beef stroganoff" and had water boiling within minutes. I inflated the air mattress I bought in town and stretched out in luxurious comfort in the tent, despite the rocky ground. By candlelight, I read the letter from Ernest:

Scott,

I take it you arrived safely at Key Largo. How are the Keys? I predicted they would be as bad as the Everglades as far as mosquitoes and mangroves. Right or Wrong?

It's frosty here, 5:30 P.M. on Sunday, fire in the fireplace, sun has set. I'm sipping whiskey and listening to guitar on cassette tape. Very un-rough life—but hey, I plan to watch *Nature* on TV tonight, so I'll still be in touch with the wilds. I went on a 10-mile hike in the Homochitto Forest the other day. Very nice—big hills and hollows, crisp autumn woods.

Hope you found some way to get some exercise. I know from experience how easy that kayaking is—sitting in a comfortable seat, occasionally dipping the paddle as the wind and waves carry you where you want to go.

I look forward to hearing about your experiences, that is, if you find time to write. I know how demanding all that partying is in places like Key West. Any prospects for getting over to the Bahamas?

Merry Christmas,

Ernest

That night the rats got bolder. They ran around the perimeter of my tent, scratched at the nylon walls, and climbed all over the kayak where it was moored in the mangroves. Several times I went outside to hurl rocks and vile language at them, sending them scurrying for cover briefly until I crawled back into the tent. The next morning, packed up to leave for the day, I saw that I had left a plastic fuel bottle full of gasoline for the stove sitting on the rocks near my tent during the night. I was furious to discover that the rats had chewed a hole in it, ruining the bottle and spilling my fuel.

Once at sea far enough from the island to evade the insects, I called *Whisper* on my VHF. The Olsen's weren't leaving for at least a couple of days, and I couldn't either. The north wind was still blowing steady. I paddled on to Key Largo and spent most of the day wandering around, putting off my return to the rock pile as long as possible. I couldn't get away from Florida soon enough. I was sick of the miserable campsites I had been forced to retreat to, driven into mosquito hellholes by the tourists, wealthy residents, and no trespassing laws of the Sunshine State.

At sunset I returned to my campsite and spent that evening and the next day bringing my journal up to date. It was surprisingly cold—in the upper fifties with twenty knots of north wind. It felt like freezing to me after becoming acclimated to the subtropics. This was the first day I left my tent up during the daylight hours on the little key. I camouflaged it with mangrove branches and stayed inside writing as an endless stream of motorboats sped by within two hundred yards of the island. I reread Ernest's letter and wrote back in reply:

Ernest,

I'm including 50 or so pages of my journal with this letter. Got your letter the other day. Nice of you to remind me of "crisp autumn woods, sipping whiskey on the porch while the sun goes down," etc.

Here I am, camped on a birdshit-encrusted rock pile, under siege by a pack of plundering rats, while I hide in the mangroves to avoid being seen and asked to leave this wonderful place. I wish you could be here, but I know your idea of "roughing it" is lying propped up against a log on a Black Creek sandbar, sipping rum by a glowing fire as the embers slowly bake inch-thick rib-eyes.

Try sleeping on fist-sized lumps of coral sometime. Throw in a thick tangle of mangroves, clouds of no-see-ums, a pack of rats, and hundreds of idiots in motorboats screaming past all day . . .

Soon, however, I will be lying on the soft sands of some un-named Bahamian cay, soaking up the tropical sun, occasionally getting up to dive into the crystal clear water to retrieve a fat lobster for dinner. I'll be thinking of how your "crisp autumn woods" are then—in the middle of January—under a cold gray sky, probably drenched with freezing rain and chilled by a stiff north wind! Of course, you won't have to venture outdoors then, and why should you? You can watch *Nature* and see expeditions like mine on *National Geographic Explorer.*

You are right about me needing some exercise. So far I have been quite lazy. The wind and current have been at my back for the entire 500 miles I have traveled so far, scarcely requiring me to dip my paddle blades. My muscles are rapidly becoming atrophied from disuse . . .

Well, the sun is sinking into the ocean, and I can't afford to waste a candle to keep writing. I'll send a postcard from the Bahamas. Please keep the journal pages in a safe place. I may want to read them again someday. Have a good Christmas,

Scott

The next day the wind was still blowing twenty-five knots out of the north. Seas in the Gulf Stream were running eighteen feet and higher. It was December 18, and I had been in Key Largo a week. It was clear that I wouldn't be able to paddle across the Gulf Stream anytime soon. I decided to paddle over to *Whisper* and talk to the Olsens further about the possibility of sailing with them. The Olsens were at home when I arrived alongside, and I was invited aboard to check out the accommodations. *Whisper* was well equipped for cruising. Ben said that he had chosen an aluminum-hulled vessel for its great strength and easy maintenance. He said they might sail around the world someday. The boat certainly looked capable of it, and I could imagine the junk-rigged schooner lying to the anchor in some Polynesian lagoon. Though there were two dinghies and a sailboard already on deck, Ben said there was plenty of room for my kayak. I went below and he showed me the aft cabin that would be my quarters if I chose to go. Though small, the cabin seemed luxurious compared to the rock pile I had been camping on.

I paddled back to my lonely camp to spend the night, then returned to *Whisper* the following day to help Ben weave safety netting to hang under the schooner's long bowsprit. Ben suggested that I sail with them as far as Eleuthera, well to the east of Bimini. If they dropped me off in Bimini, I would still have a seventy-mile open water crossing of the Great Bahama Bank to reach Andros or some of the other islands that are spaced closer together. From Eleuthera, I could easily cross to the Exumas, a string of islands spaced as closely as the Florida Keys and extending 150 miles to the southeast, along my intended route.

Ben advised me to buy supplies in Key Largo, as there would be nothing in the remote area where they would drop me off. I would need to make any phone calls before we left, and have any future mail forwarded to Georgetown, Exuma, the first real town along my route.

At the dock in Key Largo the next day, I met a fellow named John Gookin who said he was also a serious kayaker. He had paddled in the Sea of Cortez and among the reef islands of Belize. He was in Key Largo on his honeymoon, and he and his new wife were on their way to a restaurant when they spotted me paddling in from my campsite. He knew what it was like paddling and camping for weeks on end, so he offered me the key to their room so I could take a shower while they were out. The room was the honeymoon suite at the Holiday Inn. I stood in the hot shower for a half an hour. It was utter decadence. Drying off in front of the huge mirror, I was surprised to see how deeply I'd tanned during the past weeks of living outdoors. I left a thank-you note for John and Mary beside the key, grateful to have finally met someone who understood exactly what I was doing.

It felt sinful to slide back into the wet cockpit of the kayak as clean as I was, but I forced myself to do it and paddled back to the rock pile against a strong headwind and choppy seas that quickly rechristened me in seawater again. Ben had given me some paperback novels to help pass the time, so I spent the following two days on the island. I set up my solar panel and charged batteries for my VHF, RDF, Sony Walkman, and flashlights during the daytime, and at night I paced restlessly around the perimeter of the island, burning off pent-up energy by stretching and doing push-ups. Now that I was not paddling every day, I had trouble sleeping at night.

On December 21, it rained steadily all night, and I woke with a puddle of water surrounding my sleeping bag. The tent had leaked. I was getting fed up with all the equipment failure I had experienced so early in the trip. I lit a candle so I could make a list of all the problems:

*Eureka Aurora Tent*—$200.00 (given to me free by the manufacturer)—leaks unexplainably and zipper catches on flap at bottom of door, making it difficult to close (invariably when there is a black cloud of mosquitoes and no-see-ums trying to follow me inside).

*Coleman Multifuel Stove*—$57.00—totally defective, almost blinded me when it sprayed fuel in my eyes. Tossed it in the Gulf. (The new one Pat sent seems to be working—for now.)

*Ikelight Underwater Flashlight*—$34.00—threads locked up and it could not be opened to replace the batteries, had to buy a $35.00 replacement.

*"Water Resistant" Tasco Binoculars*—$70.00—completely corroded and useless, need new pair to aid in navigation but budget won't allow it.

*Large "Waterproof" Gear Bags* (2)—$20.00 each—leak with slightest exposure to water, reason for binoculars getting ruined, as well as a lot of food.

*Waterproof Document Bags* (2)—$15.00 each—used for wallet, journal, passport, etc.—seams cracking apart, leak.

*Waterproof Chart Case*—$15.00—designed to keep charts handy on deck—stays full of water, many charts ruined because of it.

*Teva Sports Sandals*—$52.00—supposed to be good for wear on beaches and in water—Velcro straps do not hold and pop loose with every step—extremely aggravating to walk in.

*One Case Waterproof Matches*—$5.00—What a joke! Bic lighters are the only reliable means I've found of starting a fire or lighting the stove.

*5-Gallon "Reliance" Collapsible Water Container*—$5.00—Unreliable—leaks continuously, forcing me to paddle to Key Largo almost every day for more water.

I felt better after making the list. I wondered if the engineers who designed such faulty equipment could do better if they had to live outdoors with it every day as I had to on this trip.

By December 23, the north wind had clocked around to the east, making conditions a bit calmer in the Gulf Stream but still unfavorable for paddling or sailing in that direction. I resigned myself to having to spend Christmas on the rocky islet at Key Largo with the rats, instead of in the Bahamas as I had hoped.

But everything changed the next day, on Christmas Eve, when I ran into Ben and Sylvia at the marina in Key Largo. Ben invited me to join them and their friends on the big trimaran, *Afterglow*, anchored near *Whisper*, for a Christmas Day feast. Then, he said we would make preparations to sail for the Bahamas that very night. I was elated at this. I paddled back to my camp to spend one last night on the little island. On Christmas morning, when I awoke the screens of my tent were coated in no-see-ums, as it was a windless, humid day that bore no resemblance to any holiday season I'd ever known. I broke camp under siege by the pests and scattered rocks and driftwood where my tent had been, erasing all evidence of my stay there. This rock pile had been my home for twelve nights. I left it to the bugs and the rats and hurriedly paddled over to *Whisper*.

I tied up alongside the schooner and unloaded all my gear out of the kayak so we could hoist it to the deck and lash it to the port lifeline stanchions for the crossing. We spent the afternoon making preparations for the passage, including several trips by dinghy to the marina to fill jerry cans with fuel and drinking water. This done, we finally went over to *Afterglow*, where I met another cruising couple, Kenny and Marianne, who had two little girls about the same age as Sky and Grant. I learned that they lived aboard year-round, staying in Key Largo when not cruising the Bahamas. Sylvia and Marianne produced a traditional Christmas meal complete with all the trimmings, despite the cramped working space of the galley on the boat. There was turkey, fresh grouper, homemade bread, vegetable casseroles, cranberry sauce, and apple pies. This bountiful feast shared with such good company was a blessing to a lone traveler like me, like the shower offered by the honeymooning couple. Such unexpected gifts had never crossed my mind when I was planning every detail of the trip during all those months leading up to this. I missed my family and the reunion they were sharing on that day, but here I felt accepted and as welcome as if I had known my hosts for a lifetime.

The Olsens and I left *Afterglow* around 10:30 P.M., and shortly after boarding *Whisper* and stowing the dinghy and motor, we hauled in the anchor and motored away from Key Largo in the glow of a full moon. Ben waited until we were past the reefs five miles out before setting the main and jib. We would still need the inboard diesel to make progress into the light easterly wind, but at least having the sails up made Ben feel better. I didn't know what to expect on the passage. Tonight would mark a lot of firsts for me. It was my first time on a voyaging sailboat. It was my first open sea passage on any kind of boat. And it was my first time to leave the United States. The lights of Key Largo and my home country grew dimmer and dimmer as we headed out to sea, and eventually disappeared below the horizon. I was free at last after seven long weeks in Florida, and I had no regrets about not making the passage in the kayak. What mattered most was that I was moving on again. I looked expectantly to the full moon that was hanging low over the dark seas to the east to guide *Whisper* to the islands.

Though the wind was relatively light, once we reached the Gulf Stream we encountered large residual swells left over from the previous days of strong winds. The big rollers tossed *Whisper* about as easily as five-foot waves toss my kayak. Though I was totally inexperienced, Ben gave me the helm and showed me the bare essentials of keeping the sails from luffing as the boat yawed and pitched with each passing wave. He warned that I might have to change course due to shipping traffic in the busy Florida Straits, and showed me how to take a bearing using his expensive Steiner binoculars with their built-in lighted compass to tell if a distant ship was on a converging or diverging course. Then, to my amazement, he left me alone on deck and disappeared down the companionway to join Sylvia and the boys, telling me to wake him for the next watch at 4 A.M. I was awed by his faith in leaving his yacht and the safety of his family in the hands of a complete novice and nervously scanned the horizon for the lights of approaching ships.

The sea became rougher farther out in the Stream, and *Whisper* crashed head-on into big swells that sent spray all over the deck. I was glad I was not making this passage alone in my kayak. It was lonely enough being out there on the deck of the big yacht. The oil-black seas rose and fell in every direction, easily visible in the light of the full moon and stars.

At 2 A.M., I spotted a cruise ship lit like a city and repeated checks with the binoculars confirmed a collision course. I made a correction to give the ship right of way, and we passed within a half-mile of her stern. Ben came on deck at 4:00, and said that Sylvia, Sky, and Grant had all been seasick. I was feeling queasy myself, and the nauseous feeling grew worse when I went down into stuffy cabin to try and sleep. I barely made it back up to the starboard rail before losing my Christmas dinner. Only Ben among all of us on board had the stomach for these seas.

When the sun finally rose out of waves dead ahead, I soon forgot my discomfort as I sat on deck under its warm influence and stared at the water beneath our hull. It was the deepest shade of blue imaginable.

I had never seen water like that before—so transparent that you could see perhaps a hundred feet down into it to where the light faded into the abysmal blackness of oceanic depths.

We spotted land by noon—a group of isolated rocks on the edge of the Great Bahama Bank called Riding Rocks. Deep water abruptly ends at the edge of this bank, which is a vast area of hundreds of square miles of shallows only ten to thirty feet deep. The transition was dramatic. One moment we were sailing over indigo blue ocean, and the next we crossed a clearly discernable line into turquoise and green waters beneath which a rippled sand bottom appeared close enough to reach down and touch. Just inside this line of shallows we passed a shark that was easily as long as my kayak, and by far the biggest shark I'd ever seen.

Riding Rocks was not an official port of entry for the Bahamas, and we were supposed to sail north to clear customs at Cat Cay, but we anchored there anyway and sailed to Cat Cay the following morning. *Whisper*'s engine failed just as we approached the dock, making it impossible to slow down by shifting into reverse, and we drifted into a docked vessel named the *Ben Vassey*. Her crew was on deck in time to fend us off with boat poles, so no serious damage was done to either yacht, and we managed to get *Whisper* secured to the customs dock aft of the *Ben Vassey*. Sylvia and the boys would have to stay on board, while Ben and I, each masters of our own vessels, took our paperwork and headed for the customs and immigration office.

The first Bahamians I saw were customs agents across the dock from where we tied up. One officer was standing on the dock with a submachine gun trained on two men who were sitting nearby with their hands on top of their heads. Several other officers with crowbars and axes were tearing apart the interior of a large American motor yacht that obviously belonged to the two detainees under guard. I assumed they were looking for cocaine or marijuana. These islands were rampant with drug smugglers trying to get their illicit cargo into the United States.

Resting in the shade of a grove of tall coconut palms that surrounded the building, Ben and I waited two hours to see the immigration officer. As I waited I worried that I would not be admitted to the country since I did not have a boat big enough to sleep on. I had heard conflicting reports about the legality of camping here. Ben told me to simply avoid the subject if possible when talking to immigration. When at last it was my turn to go inside, the Bahamian officer did not seem concerned about my accommodations. He did require the serial numbers of the two guns I had in my possession, so I went back to *Whisper* to write the information down and when I returned I paid a fee of twenty-eight dollars for a six-month cruising permit and a fishing license.

"I hope you got good charts, mon," the officer said as he handed me my permit and returned my passport. "De Bahamas a big country, you know. Lot de islands, dem far apart, an' de sea, she get mean sometime. You got a long way to go to dem Caicos Islands."

I thanked him and left much relieved. I couldn't believe how easy that had been. I had cleared into my first foreign country in my kayak, and had been granted six months—far more time than I needed to transit the seven-hundred-mile chain of the Bahamas. When Ben was finished we sailed *Whisper* out of the harbor to the south end of Cat Cay, where we anchored for the night. Ben tinkered with the engine and tried to decide whether to go back to Florida for repairs. Had they gone back, I would have disembarked then and there and left on the seventy-mile crossing of the banks to continue my trip, but Ben decided to keep going and said they would drop me off on Eleuthera as originally planned.

While in the Bimini area the next day, Ben and I donned masks, fins, and snorkels and went hunting with our spears in the clear waters under *Whisper*. Bahamian law prohibits the use of sophisticated spear guns, but the more primitive Hawaiian sling is allowed. All I had was a simple pole spear, which proved to be too slow to be effective in such clear water. Ben loaned me an extra sling and spear, which I quickly learned to use. The butt of the long steel shaft fits through the hollow handle of the sling, and into a fitting on the rubber bands, similar to a slingshot, which I had plenty of practice with growing up in Mississippi. Aiming is instinctive, as with a bow and arrow. The sling propels the heavy steel spear with enough force to impale a fish about five yards away, and even if it does not kill it quickly, the 6-foot shaft greatly impedes the fish's ability to swim away.

I got the first fish, one that we identified as a porgy with the aid of Ben's guide to tropical fishes. We swam over the reef in ever-widening circles around *Whisper*, towing the dinghy to put the fish in and periodically diving to shoot at likely candidates for the fish fry we were planning. Ben soon shot a large amberjack and a queen triggerfish, and with dinner in the boat we headed back to *Whisper*.

The following day and night, we made the seventy-five-mile run east across the banks to Chub Cay, a resort in the Berry Islands group. It was an easy trip, cruising over calm, transparent shallows, leaving little for us to do while the autopilot took the helm. We entered the marina at Chub Cay to take on fuel and water, both of which were sold by the gallon, the water priced at fifty cents. Prices in the small food store were equally disturbing, easily double those back in Florida for the same items. I bought a few extra supplies to cram into my kayak when I departed *Whisper*, and paid five dollars at the telephone office for the privilege of making a collect call to my parents. I found a dive shop nearby and went in to inquire about buying a Hawaiian sling and spear, as my foray with Ben convinced me that I could feed myself for free in these islands with the right equipment. A young man with a British accent running the shop was shocked at my request.

"Why no! We don't sell anything with which to *kill* things," he said with an air of practiced aloofness and self-righteous vegan superiority. "We only dive on the reef to *observe* the marine life."

"You don't eat anything that was once alive then?" I grunted and walked out in disgust. I would have to find hunting weapons elsewhere.

I went back to *Whisper* with my expensive groceries, and soon we were under way again, heading a few miles north to find a quiet anchorage in the Berry Islands before heading to Eleuthera. We passed close by several islands and I was surprised by the topography. I had pictured the Bahamas flat, like the Florida Keys, but here were rocky cliffs and rolling hills—not exceptionally high—but rugged. Surf smashed into the stony coastline, and groves of Australian pines reminded me of pine-clad islands I had seen off the coast of Maine.

We anchored near an uninhabited cay and the next day went ashore and explored. Ben and Sylvia had been sailing among these islands for years, yet had never tasted a green coconut. In Florida, I had met people who had coconuts hanging from the palms in their yards and didn't even know what they were. I showed the Olsens how to open the green nuts, and they were all impressed with the delicious sweet water inside. We completed our natural breakfast with other wild edibles, including the heart of a cabbage palm, and some prickly pear fruit. That afternoon we sailed farther north and anchored between Frozen and Alder Cays. Both were uninhabited, about a hundred yards apart, with a reef connecting them and creating a beautiful lagoon of multihued water bordered by sandy beaches. Beyond the shore were dense groves of coconut palms, completing the perfect picture of tropical tranquility—the image I had so often conjured in my South Seas dreams.

I off-loaded my kayak to do some exploring of my own. Ben and Sylvia were in no particular hurry, and now that I was away from Florida, I wasn't either. We stayed in the anchorage several days, and when I wasn't making long forays among the other islands in my kayak, I went spearfishing with Ben and helped him load all the coconuts we could gather on board *Whisper*. Sylvia set up a chair on the beach and gave haircuts to Ben, Sky, and Grant, offering me one as well. I had not had a haircut since the previous spring, when I had begun serious preparations for this journey, and I saw no reason to have one now. I would cut my hair and shave my beard when the trip was finished—maybe.

Paddling around these islands was a delight. The kayak seemed to glide on a cushion of air as I cruised over reefs thirty feet below that looked close enough to jab with the paddle. It was a world apart from Florida, with no signs warning against trespassing, no oil-covered tourists, and no hotels or condominiums. There were no buzzing speedboats or personal watercraft, and the only boat I saw was a large chartered sailing yacht loaded with guests, many of whom were trolling fishing lines as they sailed by. When one of the lines got hung up on some near-shore rocks, I freed it for them easily by paddling up to the reef and standing up in the cockpit, nearly capsizing in the process. This earned me a loud applause from the crew and guests, and the skipper tossed me an ice-cold Miller Lite for my effort. I drifted slowly, savoring every drop of the cold beer. Ben had plenty of beer on *Whisper*, but no refrigeration, and drinking hot Heineken takes some getting used to.

Much refreshed, I landed on the beach at Hoffman's Cay and followed a steep trail to the top of the island where there were ruins from an abandoned nineteenth-century farmhouse. There many such ruins in the Out Islands of the Bahamas, evidence of the hardships early settlers faced on these rocky, waterless islands. I searched for fruit trees, as I'd heard that many of the old farm sites still have orange groves and other imported plants, but I found none here. I pushed on along an overgrown path that seemed to lead nowhere and then suddenly came upon a view that took my breath away. I had almost walked off the edge of a cliff into the biggest sinkhole I had ever seen. Before me was a circular hole in the center of the island that was at least seventy-five yards in diameter. Vertical and undercut walls dropped twenty feet to the surface of the black water that filled the hole. Though the water was dark, it was clear and looked bottomless. I sat on the edge and stared down in wonder for a few minutes before heading back to tell the Olsens about my discovery.

When Ben heard this, he wanted to know if the water was right under the edge of the cliffs.

"Yeah, why?" I asked.

"Great. I can do some high dives."

"Maybe, but you better climb down and check it out first."

He was ecstatic when he saw the place, calling it a first-rate swim-hole. He stripped and walked naked to the edge of the abyss. Despite suggestions from Sylvia and I that he either jump first or climb down to check for unseen rocks, he dove headfirst into the black water, popping to the surface about a minute and a half later to report that he had found no bottom. During the days I had been on *Whisper*, this forty-nine-year-old farmer from Iowa had constantly amazed me with his swimming and diving ability. While spearfishing, he frequently would free-dive to depths of fifty to sixty feet, then effortlessly search cracks and crevices in the coral reef for lobster and grouper. Though I was an experienced scuba diver and had been down to one hundred feet plenty of times with compressed air, I could not go beyond twenty-five feet on a free-dive, because of sinus blockages that made rapid equalization impossible.

I followed Ben into the sinkhole—feet-first—and we swam around, checking it out. The water was salty, and obviously connected somehow to the ocean by means of underground passageways that were beyond our reach. Marks on the rocks around us indicated a tidal fluctuation. Ben climbed out of the hole again and again until he had satisfied himself with several more leaps and somersaults off the cliffs.

After we returned to *Whisper*, we got our snorkeling gear and went spearfishing out on the reef beyond the anchorage. We found good hunting grounds in twenty-five feet of water and Ben quickly located a huge spiny lobster in a crevice. I followed him down to get it and snapped a photo as he returned to the surface with the writhing creature impaled upon his spear. *This is going to be easy*, I thought, but two more hours of hunting produced no more lobster. We swam farther out, facedown on the surface with the snorkels until the sand bottom was one hundred feet beneath us, yet plainly visible in the clear water. Magnificent formations of coral reached up in places to within fifty feet of the surface. But though Ben swam down to peer into cracks and under rocks, he found nothing else to shoot.

We returned to *Whisper* with the one lobster, and Ben gathered some whelks, a kind of marine snail, from the rocks in the shallows of the anchorage. He wanted escargot before the lobster, so Sylvia dropped them live into a pot of boiling water. When they were "done" after a few minutes, Ben used a toothpick to pull them from their shells and dipped them in butter before swallowing them whole. I ate a few, though they looked disgusting and tasted and smelled like the rotten seaweed that filled their guts. The lobster was infinitely better but didn't go far among five hungry seafood lovers.

After dinner Ben announced that we would sail straight from the Berry Islands to Royal Island, which is just west of the large island of Eleuthera. I studied his charts and decided that I would part with them there. We loaded my kayak onto the deck and left early in the morning for the forty-five-mile passage across the deep waters of the Northwest Providence Channel. It was a rough passage, with seas equal to those we had encountered in the Gulf Stream, convincing me of the need to pick my route wisely when kayaking these waters and to travel only when weather conditions were optimal. Despite the heavy seas, we made good speed on a beam reach and arrived in the harbor by late afternoon.

The anchorage at Royal Island was the most crowded we had yet seen in the Bahamas, but the island itself is uninhabited. The attraction for boaters is the ruins of a splendid nineteenth-century mansion that was once the center of a sheep ranch that occupied the island. We took the dinghy ashore and explored the crumbling rooms of the estate and its many outbuildings. The vegetation was lush—almost jungle-like, with many species of trees I did not know. They grew out of the buildings, their huge roots cracking the concrete and stone walls, which were covered in moss and bromeliads. We found orange trees loaded with fruit, but these oranges were unlike any I had ever tasted. They were sour, but refreshing once you got past the first shocking bite.

Other trees bore strange fruit, which Ben and I knocked down to examine but were afraid to eat.

On the way back to the dinghy, I took off my shirt and used it as a sack to carry at least a dozen of the sour oranges. I was determined to make use of every free food source available to stretch my limited funds as far as possible. Back on *Whisper*, I spent the rest of the evening packing and rearranging my gear in the kayak. The following morning I returned with the Olsens to Royal Island for more exploring, and then after having lunch and one last hot Heineken with Ben, I said good-bye to the family I had lived with for twelve days and slipped back into the cockpit of my kayak to continue my solo voyage.

# FOUR

# ISLAND PARADISE

I should like to rise and go
Where the golden apples grow;
Where below another sky,
Parrot islands anchored lie.

**—ROBERT LOUIS STEVENSON**

I turned to wave one last time to Ben, Sylvia, Sky, and Grant as I paddled out of the natural harbor at Royal Island and headed east along the shore toward Eleuthera. I would miss the Olsen family, but I was ready to be alone and looking forward to the freedom of kayaking and living on the beach again. I was claustrophobic in the confines of *Whisper's* cramped aft cabin and eager to pitch my tent, having come to regard the nylon A-frame as home in the past months.

I thought I might camp for one night on the other side of Royal Island, but I didn't like the looks of the exposed shoreline there and decided against it after paddling around to check it out. On a rocky point at the end of the island, I saw several wild chickens. We had heard roosters crowing that morning from the anchorage. After two weeks of sailing with strict health-food nuts who were mostly vegetarians, I craved fresh meat. It was a temptation to break out my .22 rifle and shoot a hen for dinner, but there were several boats in the nearby anchorage and I was afraid the shot might be heard and reported, so

Climbing a coconut palm for drinking nuts in the Berry Islands (photo by Sylvia Olsen)

I refrained and paddled on. The customs official at Bimini who granted me my cruising permit and gun permit had made it clear that all the ammunition I had with me was to be accounted for. Recreational shooting and hunting were forbidden. The diminutive cartridges for the .22 were so small, however, that quite a few loose rounds were scattered throughout my gear and clothing that were not included in the official inventory. When the time and place was right, I would put the rifle to use. I had heard that many of the islands had abundant populations of feral livestock such as chickens, goats, and pigs. These living remnants and abandoned stone houses and cisterns mark countless failed attempts to homestead the waterless rocky cays that characterize the Out Islands of the Bahamas.

I made a short crossing to Russell Cay, which lies between Royal Island and the north end of Eleuthera, and on the windward side of the cay I found a deserted beach and made a rough and wet landing through heavy surf. The beach was covered with sand spurs that made walking without shoes painful. My first job was to clear out a large enough space to put my tent so their sharp spines would not puncture the floor. I cooked rice and added a can of tuna, then leaned against the trunk of the lone Australian pine on the beach and spread out my chart of the islands as I ate. I could hardly contain my enthusiasm to paddle the route I had marked off on paper, and to see what each tiny cay and island village was like in real life. With visions of adventure in my mind, I drifted off to the sound of crashing surf and was up at daybreak.

That morning I cooked my first proper breakfast in thirteen days—a stack of pancakes with maple syrup. This was the kind of fuel I needed to start a day of paddling. I had often felt starved during my time on board *Whisper*, especially in the mornings. A small bowl of fruit for breakfast may have worked for them, but after two and half months of paddling, often twenty miles or more in a day, I needed carbohydrates. I could eat as much and as often as I wanted. This lifestyle of paddling all day, making and breaking camp, snorkeling and swimming, and exploring ashore on foot took care of all the calories. I was fit when I'd begun, but now my endurance and tolerance to hardship were beyond anything I'd ever known.

Launching from the beach that morning was difficult, due to the heavy surf, and after I succeeded in getting out, I paddled back around to the protected side of the cay to avoid the high winds that were screaming across the Northwest Providence Channel. I stopped to take a saltwater bath and make myself halfway presentable before visiting the town of Spanish Wells, where I planned to get supplies. Feeling somewhat better, I paddled into the harbor, past rows of moored fishing boats, and tied up to an old wooden dock. On the waterfront street, several curious residents that saw my strange craft coming in were now watching intently as I stepped out of the boat. A rotten board in the dock planking broke with my weight and caused me to take an embarrassing fall in front of my audience, but I somehow managed to avoid landing in the water and losing my wallet, which I was holding in my hand.

I had read a bit about Spanish Wells in a cruising guidebook Ben had on board *Whisper*. The name came from the fresh water wells on the cay where Spanish ships stopped to top off their water casks. The people living there now are descendants of a group of British colonists called the "Eleutheran Adventurers" who left England three hundred years ago to settle the island of Eleuthera. Unlike most Bahamian settlements of today, the town is predominantly white and the people cling to a perfect British accent. The quaint wooden houses are well kept and the neatness of the community rivals any small village in the English countryside. Only the tropical fruit trees shading the lawns reminded me that I was still in the Bahamas. Quiet streets with mostly pedestrian traffic and a handful of vintage cars made the town seem a few decades back in time. I had only walked half a block when a man driving by stopped and offered to take me wherever I needed to go. I gladly accepted, eager to talk with a local and learn more about the place, though cars seemed unnecessary to me on an island that is only about three miles long and a mile wide. I got in and we sped down the left side of the road. I learned that most of the men of Spanish Wells are commercial fishermen, including my host. He knew a lot about the sea and seemed skeptical that I could survive all the crossings between Eleuthera and the Turks and Caicos in my kayak. He had fished those waters all his life and warned that the passages south of the Exumas were especially dangerous. But he had never seen a kayak like mine and, like most people I'd met, was completely unfamiliar with its capabilities. I thanked him for the ride and got out at the far end of town, where there was a dive shop that he said might carry Hawaiian slings.

The shop was sold out of spearfishing gear, so I walked back to the town center where there was a post office and two general stores with a limited selection of groceries. I settled for a few canned goods, rice, spaghetti, and chocolate bars, and bought two fresh baked loaves of bread from a woman who sold them from her house. The hot bread was delicious. Bahamian bread makers mix their batter with the water from green coconuts, and the result is incomparable. I devoured half a loaf while I sat on a street corner and watched the blond-haired schoolchildren that looked so out of place here file past on their way home from classes. When I returned to the dock with my groceries, I found that my kayak had created quite a sensation, and I had to answer lots of questions before I could be on my way. I hated to leave such a friendly town, but I was anxious to reach a deserted beach where I could cook a big dinner and spend some more time with my charts, working out my route to the south.

Eleuthera is an odd-shaped island, a hundred miles long, but quite narrow, with a long peninsula that juts out to the southeast towards the Exumas. From Spanish Wells, I paddled to a narrow beach on the west side of this peninsula and set up camp under a grove of Australian pines. Impenetrable thickets of palmettos, cactus, and bushes I could not identify cut my beach off from the rest of the island and blocked any further exploration on foot. I broke camp the following morning and paddled south to Current Cut, a narrow passage between the peninsula and Current Island, a long key that extends on to the southeast. The cut gets its name from the ripping 6-knot current that flows through when the tide is running in or out. I wanted to get to the other side to top off my water jugs in a little town called The Current before setting out for the Exumas. I was unlucky enough to reach the cut when the tide was running out and was dismayed to see what looked like a whitewater river in the middle. I stayed close to the rocks on the north shore and paddled furiously against the flow, making it halfway through the quarter-mile-wide cut before being flushed back out to where I had started. I landed on the beach to eat some lunch and plan a new strategy for the assault. I decided to try it from the south side, along the end of Current Island, and this time, after an exhausting half-hour battle, which I stubbornly refused to lose, I conquered Current Cut and emerged into the choppy waters on the other side. I pulled up to the wooden dock in The Current, where two black Bahamian fishermen were cleaning the day's catch of conch. They were incredulous when I told them I made it through Current Cut against the tide, and asked why I didn't simply wait for it to turn. Of course, I could have done that, but it was Saturday afternoon, and I figured the stores would soon close and wouldn't open again before Monday. I wanted some more homemade bread before I headed south to other islands where I might not find any.

"Mon, you got to be crazy! Dat current, she make 6 knot, an' all de time de big shark, dem hang out 'round de Cut," said one of the fishermen, who introduced himself as Henry. He told me I could leave my boat tied up to the dock and pointed in the direction of a house where I could buy fresh bread.

I bought two loaves and refilled my water jugs, and Henry told me that he had a Hawaiian sling and spear that he would sell me for twenty-eight dollars. I knew the price was as high as a new one would have been in a dive shop, but I figured it would soon pay for itself in all the money I would save by eating fish and lobster instead of buying the high-priced food sold in the local village stores. Henry said that he lived in Current Island Settlement, three miles to the south, and told me to camp on the beach there and wait for him to return home that night and he would bring me the spear.

I hurried to get back through Current Cut before the tide changed directions. It was a joyride blasting through the quarter-mile run at six knots without having to dip the paddle. I could see schools of big fish in the clear waters beneath me, but though I looked expectantly, I saw none of "dem big shark."

Henry had assured me that I would never have to worry about theft out in the "family islands" away from Nassau and other large towns of the Bahamas. I could see that the people of Current Island Settlement believed that by the way they left their outboard-powered Boston

Whalers pulled up on the beach with all sorts of fishing equipment strewn about inside. The homes of the one hundred residents of the settlement were on the hill above, out of sight of the beach. I set up my tent near the remains of a bonfire on the pleasantly shaded beach and cooked supper while I waited for Henry. Just as he promised, he arrived before dark with the sling and spear. The six-foot-long stainless steel spear shaft was not perfectly straight, but Henry assured me this would not affect its accuracy at the close ranges at which spearfishing is done. The sling was a beautifully carved piece of hardwood with a hole drilled for the shaft to pass through and two bands of surgical rubber tubing connected to a metal socket designed to fit the butt of the spear. It was a simple and effective design, as I had discovered while hunting underwater with Ben. I paid Henry the twenty-eight dollars, and we talked for a while around my campfire until swarms of no-see-ums drove him up the hill to his house and me into my tent.

I tried to tune in a radio station on my Sony Walkman, but was disappointed to find that I could receive only one AM station in Nassau. The broadcast consisted of nothing but gossip about who died and who was getting married, with the occasional gospel song thrown in for variety. I hadn't realized how totally cut off I would be from the rest of the world while I was among the remote outer islands of the Bahamas. I was a little concerned about not being able to get weather reports, because I had no way of knowing if a storm was approaching when I set out to make a long crossing. Paddling down the coast of Florida, and through the Keys, I could always tune in one of the ten NOAA Weather Radio frequencies available on my handheld VHF radio. Here in the far eastern Bahamas, I was too far from Florida to receive those weather stations or any FM broadcasts from the United States.

As I was packing up the following morning, an old man and a little girl came down the hill from Current Island Settlement to see my kayak and ask some questions. The subject of weather came up and the man told me he had made his living all his life from fishing these waters. He gave me some pointers on forecasting weather from natural signs and answered my questions about my intended route to the Exumas. I was facing a thirty-three-mile open water crossing from Current Island to the northernmost cay in the Exumas, and I hoped I could camp on Finley Cay, shown as a tiny speck on my chart in the middle of this passage.

"I know dat Finley Cay," he told me. "Every summer we goin' dat place to shoot pigeons. You can find good camping place on Finley Cay. De wahtah all round on de bank is shallow, an' de big boat she can't go, but you not to worry in dat canoe, mon."

At his insistence, I followed him up the hill to his house, where he topped off my largest water container and showed me around the little village. It was a quiet Sunday morning, and most of the townspeople were attending services in the church, from which familiar hymns drifted out into the streets and took me back to childhood Sundays in south Mississippi. The few residents who were at home and saw me walking down their streets seemed startled but friendly. It was obvious that few tourists visited this isolated community. I thanked the old man for his advice, and he told me that there was an excellent beach on the south end of Current Island, where I could camp while preparing to make my long crossing.

I made my way back down to the kayak and paddled the five miles on down to the end of the island before noon. The beach was as good as the old fisherman had claimed. Crystal clear water washed the soft white sands and beyond the seashore was a dense forest of cabbage palms, gumbo limbo, and sea grape trees. I climbed the lone coconut palm on the beach and pulled down the four green drinking nuts it bore. Climbing palms was easier since Ben and I had fashioned loops of nylon webbing to put around our ankles when we had climbed so much while gathering coconuts on Frozen and Alder Cays. With the ankles held loosely together, it was easy to rest while climbing by simply clamping the soles of the feet to the trunk. Once at the top, it was easier to pull the nuts down, since with the feet secured, it was safe to let go with one hand. I had also found that the tough stem that each coconut hangs from is easily severed by giving the nut a hard spin, which twists the stem until it breaks.

After unloading the kayak, I followed the example that Ben and his family had often set when we had come to an isolated beach, and stripped off all my clothes. It was the natural thing to do in such a perfect climate and in such complete solitude. Wearing only fins, mask, and snorkel, I took my new spear and headed to the reef in front of my campsite to find lunch. It was only a matter of minutes before I returned to the beach with a six- or seven-pound jackfish, and I was soon frying thick fillets that I had first rolled in cornmeal. I ate until I was stuffed and still had fish left. Living off the sea here was going to be easy, I thought, as I spent the afternoon walking the beach and exploring the woods behind my tent.

The following day I paddled down to the south tip of the island and found that the seas were rough and the skies overcast. I decided not to try the crossing that day. I returned to my camp and spent the afternoon studying charts and dreaming of islands farther south, more tropical and surely, I thought, even better than this wonderful place. This was the nature of my trip; it was all about keeping the kayak moving. I suppose if I had not thought what was over the horizon was going to be better, I could not have endured the hardships of going on. Here on Current Island, I had found perfect beauty and easy island living, but I was not content to stay.

I cooked an early dinner of brown rice, boiled in the water from two of the coconuts I had gathered. Pete Hill had told me about this trick when we were camped together in the Everglades. It was as good as he said it was, the sweet liquid giving the rice a custard-like flavor. I looked forward to experimenting with all the many uses of the coconut palm, that ubiquitous symbol of tropical islands that would be a part of my life for the duration of this journey.

My solitude was interrupted after dinner when a sailboat dropped anchor off my beach and three people came ashore in a dinghy. They were a couple from Washington, D.C., vacationing with their teenage daughter. They told me they had chartered the boat for a week and planned to stay in this anchorage just one night. In the morning, after breaking camp and packing up, I paddled out to their yacht to bum a gallon of water so my supply would be topped off before I set off for remote Finley Cay.

I headed south from Current Island, towards the empty horizon where my chart showed that Finley Cay should be. On a solo crossing like this, it is difficult to have complete faith in charts and compass. As Current Island slowly receded into the distance behind me, I wondered if Finley Cay was really out there, nineteen miles ahead. There was no evidence of it or any other land in the vast expanse of blue that stretched before me, yet the entire crossing would be over the shallow waters of the Yellow Banks, with average charted depths of less than twenty feet. Once beyond sight of Current Island, I could see no land in any direction, but the bottom was clearly visible as I glided over air-clear water. Isolated coral heads scattered here and there broke up the monotony of miles of sand bottom that looked like an underwater Sahara.

Finley Cay was so low that I could not see it until I was within about five miles of it. I did not reach its lonely beaches until almost six hours after leaving Current Island. Shallows of two feet or less extended more than a mile around the cay, making it impossible for deep draft vessels to approach. The kayak was the perfect craft for exploring such waters, and from the beaches of Finley Cay, I could see no sign of other boats or human activity in any direction. It was by far the most remote and isolated island I had ever visited, and it was a delight to walk the untouched shore and see no footprints or other sign that anyone had visited recently. In the tangled vegetation in the middle of the island, however, I found the remains of some kind of radio communications tower, obviously abandoned many years before.

The pink coral sand of Finley Cay was the softest I'd ever seen, so fine that walking through it was difficult. With each step I sank down past my ankles in it, and soon concluded that it was too exhausting to walk far in the stuff. I was tired from the crossing anyway, so I spent the afternoon near my kayak. That night I stretched out on the beach looking up into a sky jam-packed with stars—the kind of sky that can only be seen in a place far removed from the lights of mankind. The tiny speck of light from a passing jet was my only reminder that somewhere out there was a world where people have no idea pristine islands like this still exist.

I would have stayed a couple of nights on Finley Cay, but when I woke in the morning, I discovered that my largest water jug had leaked all night, leaving my supply too low to linger. I didn't want to depend on the desalinator except in an absolute emergency, so that morning I embarked on the fourteen-mile crossing to North Sail Rocks, at the extreme north end of the Exuma Island chain. Most of the crossing would be over the Yellow Banks, but near the Exumas, the nine-hundred-fathom depths of Exuma Sound would be to my east. If I missed the island chain and went too far to the west, I would cross over the even deeper Tongue of the Ocean and the next landfall would be Andros Island, sixty miles away.

Halfway into the crossing, at a point where I was out of sight of land, a Bahamian fishing vessel motoring out of the south spotted me and changed course to intercept me. Apparently the crew saw me paddling the tiny boat and thought I was on a lifeboat of some sort and in need of rescue. As they came within hailing distance, all hands were on deck to see my strange vessel. They were all local islanders, who undoubtedly had never seen a sea kayak this far from land.

"Where you goin' in dat boat, mon?"

"Exumas!" I shouted in reply.

"Where you comin' from, mon?"

"Eleuthera . . . Florida . . . Mississippi!"

The captain shook his head and informed me that I was crazy but pointed in the direction I had already been heading and said, "Exumas dat weh, mon!"

They motored slowly away and I was alone again, squinting into a morning sun that passed through my sunglasses as if they weren't there and burned my already deeply tanned face. I tied a wet bandana across my nose and pulled my wide-brimmed canvas hat down over my eyes as I continued the seemingly endless crossing. The sea was lifeless, no sign of another living creature on it, in it, or above the mirror-like surface. Not a breath of wind stirred. I was paddling in a mirage of nothingness that reflected every cloud above and blended indiscernibly with the sky on the horizon in every direction.

By mid-afternoon, I still had not sighted land and was beginning to get worried. A fourteen-mile crossing should have only taken three or four hours, since I was not fighting a headwind. I scanned the horizon in all directions, and directly to my left, to the east, I could make out what could be distant rocks, barely protruding into the otherwise empty horizon. A double check of my charts revealed that there should be no rocks to the east of my rhumb line between Finley Cay and Sail Rocks, and careful scanning of the horizon in all directions revealed no other land in sight. Those rocks to the east had to be Sail Rocks, but it seemed impossible that I could have drifted so far off course. The only explanation was that an unseen and unfelt current had been bearing me steadily to the west as I paddled south. My instincts told me to keep paddling south, that those rocks couldn't be Sail Rocks, but I forced myself to believe the charts and swung the bow of my kayak around and began paddling steadily towards the east. Two hours later, I neared the rocks and could see distant islands stretching away to the south and knew I was looking at the Exumas. It had been a close call. If I had not spotted the rocks and changed course, I would have been paddling a long time before I crossed the Tongue of the Ocean and would have undoubtedly become more confused, with no reference to know my exact position.

The dead calm of morning abruptly changed to twenty knots of headwinds as I neared Sail Rocks, and the last mile to the scant shelter they provided was a hard-won battle. I was disappointed to find that there was no beach where I could land and rest. Shipborne Cay, five miles to the south, was the first real island in the northern Exumas. It didn't matter that I was already exhausted; I would have to paddle there before I could sleep. I could see another group of large rocks about two miles to the south, and decided to hop there on my way to Shipborne, to break up the distance, even though there would likely be no place to land.

A clearly visible line of color in the water marked the division of Exuma Sound, with its oceanic depths, from the shallow banks I'd been traveling over. Ahead I could see breaking waves blocking my path, formed by huge Atlantic swells rolling in from the east and stacking up at the edge of the shoal water. I would have to paddle through the breakers, but I'd done that before and saw no reason for concern. I drifted away from Sail Rocks, eating one of the sour oranges from Royal Island, while being carried by a strong current into Exuma Sound. I continued paddling toward the next group of rocks, enjoying the waves and staring at the bottom one hundred feet down beneath the impossibly clear water. I could see where it dropped off into the abyss at the edge of the shelf I was cruising over.

The farther I got into the crossing, the bigger the waves became, and soon I was bracing constantly with the paddle to keep from capsizing. I still wasn't worried, until I was within a half mile of the rocks and found myself in a chaos of huge, unpredictable waves. Each breaker spun the kayak around and buried me up to my neck in whitewater froth until the buoyant hull popped back to the surface. A few minutes of this and I went from complacent to terrified. All around me were jagged outcrops of coral rock that jutted out of the water waiting to tear my boat apart if the monstrous waves swept me into them. I had never been in seas so big. The wave faces were as long as my seventeen-foot kayak and I paddled seemingly straight up the oncoming slopes, fighting to keep my bow into them to avoid being rolled. Each time I reached the peak of a wave the kayak would plunge off the back and nose-dive into the trough left by its passing. I alternated survival bracing techniques with furious paddling to get into the lee of the big rocks. I screamed in fear and cursed and prayed, until at last I saw an opening into a sheltered lagoon and passed between the rocks at breakneck speed, surfing almost vertically down the face of one final big wave that did its best to destroy me. I rode its fury a good fifty feet and slipped between two coral heads unscathed, finding myself suddenly in the calm of protected shallows, the sandy bottom once again clearly visible just a few feet below. It had been my closest call on the trip. If I'd smashed the boat there and somehow survived the swim to the rocks, I would have found myself clinging to nothing but a barren reef, miles off the route of all boat traffic and with little hope of rescue. Still trembling with an adrenaline rush, I mumbled my thanks to God—and to Mike Neckar, for building such an incredibly seaworthy vessel.

Thinking the excitement was over for the day, I rested the paddle across the cockpit coaming and peeled another orange as I drifted in the lee of the rocks. Suddenly, something hit the stern of the kayak with an overwhelming force, like being rear-ended in a car by a truck. The boat shot forward and spun to one side, but I managed to stay upright. I turned in time to see the shadowy outline of a large shark disappear into the depths. I froze with fear, thinking the shark would return momentarily for a serious attack, but when it did not, I assumed that it was just checking me out and rammed the rudder out of curiosity.

I reached Shipborne Cay in the last hour of daylight, and set up my tent on a deserted beach near an abandoned nineteenth-century farmhouse built of coral rocks. I was tired and looked forward to a good night's sleep after such a rough day, but it was not to be. Shortly after midnight, the wind began to howl, and an hour later it was so strong that it snapped the main support pole of my tent and pulled apart one of the door zippers. Then a brief but torrential rain drenched my flattened tent and soaked me in my sleeping bag.

Despite being wet and uncomfortable, I had just fallen asleep again before dawn when I was awakened by squealing and trampling outside.

I looked out to see a huge sow hog with half a dozen piglets rooting through the food and gear I had left beside the boat. I yelled and chased them away before they did any real damage. Apparently they were feral hogs descended from the domestic stock brought to the island by the farm owner who had built the stone house.

I gave up on sleeping, and after cooking a pancake breakfast, accessed the storm's damage to my tent, which was my only home and would have to last for many more months. I cut the splintered section out of the fiberglass ridgepole, and found that though it was shorter, it would still serve its purpose. The zipper was beyond repair, and I realized with a sinking feeling that it would be difficult to seal out the swarms of no-see-ums and mosquitoes should I find myself in another bug-ridden mangrove jungle like the Everglades.

After packing my waterlogged gear into the kayak, I paddled south and soon came to Allen's Cay, where a large number of sailing yachts were lying at anchor. Ben had told me that the iguanas are the attraction at uninhabited Allen's Cay. It is one of the few islands where large numbers of Bahamian iguanas still survive. Elsewhere throughout the country, islanders have hunted them to extinction for their meat, which is reputed to be delicious. I landed on the beach, and several of the two-foot-long lizards wandered down to greet me, since so many of the yachties feed them. I didn't linger long at Allen's Cay after meeting the iguanas, since I wanted to push on to Highborne Cay, a few miles to the south, where there was a settlement and I hoped I could get more food and water.

By noon, I was fighting a fierce headwind as I pulled into the harbor at Highborne Cay. There was a long concrete dock extending out from the beach, with an enormous motor yacht tied up to one side of it. I paddled single-mindedly against the wind, aiming for the sand on the other side of the dock. I was in a bad mood after my struggle with the wind all morning and the lack of sleep during the stormy night. The last thing I needed was to be heckled by a bunch of rich Americans in a yacht that looked more like a cruise ship than a private boat. Though I couldn't see the occupants through the dark tinted windows of the plush vessel, I could feel their eyes upon me as I struggled to pull my heavy-loaded kayak up onto the sand. The rope holding the grab handle on the bow had to pick this most inopportune moment to break, and when it did, I was pulling so hard that I went sprawling backwards into the sand. I was certain that those on the yacht were laughing and jeering at the unshaven vagabond in his tiny little kayak.

I put on sandals and began walking up the road to find a store. A man who lived on Highborne Cay stopped to give me a ride in his pickup, saying that the store was more than a mile away. I was grateful not to be walking on the hot, hilly road in my less-than-optimistic mood that day. The little store had the usual limited supply of canned goods and basic staples, so I bought all I could carry and walked back to the beach.

Back at my kayak, as I was loading food into the boat through the stern hatch, a uniformed crewmember from the palatial yacht approached and invited me aboard. He said that the owner wanted to meet me and that I was welcome to take a hot shower on board.

*A hot shower*! I couldn't believe it. I lost no time in following the crewman aboard *Destiny*, where Charlie Leech was waiting in the spacious main salon with a cold beer to greet me.

"I saw you coming in against that wind with a pissed-off look on your face, and I said to myself, that guy's going somewhere in that kayak," Charlie explained. "They'll show you to the showers. Go ahead and get cleaned up, then we'll have a drink while you tell me about your trip. I've never seen anything like it. I'd have had a brass band playing if I'd known you were coming."

The interior of *Destiny* was like a palace, and a pretty young woman who said she was one of the chefs led me down below through two staterooms. The bathroom was nicer than the one in the honeymoon suite at the Key Largo Holiday Inn, where I'd had my last hot shower almost two months ago.

After I'd changed into my last set of clean clothes, Charlie introduced me to his girlfriend, Gail, and two other couples aboard, Dennis and Dee, and Tim and Donna. They didn't own *Destiny*, Charlie explained, but had chipped in together to raise the "considerable chunk of change" it had cost to charter the yacht, complete with skipper and crew, chefs and a maid, and all the gourmet food and booze they could consume for ten days of Bahamas cruising. Charlie was about fifty, his hair cut in a short crew cut, with an ample gut hanging over the waistline of his shorts. He reminded me of the comedian Rodney Dangerfield, especially his accent and mannerisms. It was obvious that he was a natural ham who could keep a party going non-stop, booze or no booze. He told me he had gotten rich from a family business in Manhattan and was planning to have a good time from now on. He and his friends listened intently to every detail of my journey, filming the whole interview with a camcorder while I relaxed and drank another beer. Charlie insisted that I stay for dinner that night, and when I told him about the iguanas on Allen's Cay, he said that we should run up there in the dinghy to kill some time that afternoon.

*Destiny*'s "dinghy" was an 18-foot center-console Boston Whaler with a 150-horsepower outboard, and Charlie drove it like a maniac to Allen's Cay. He'd brought along handouts for the iguanas, and my mouth watered as we fed those lucky lizards fresh broccoli and apples. It had been weeks since I'd had anything like that. *Destiny*, of course, was equipped with refrigeration and freezers, so no luxury would have to be spared during the cruise. There were scores of hungry iguanas on the beach eager to accept our offerings. Charlie marveled at them, calling them "well-designed machines."

That evening we sat down with wine and candlelight at *Destiny*'s dining table to a feast the chefs had spent all afternoon preparing. I had answered Charlie's earlier query about my age by informing him that the following day, January 13, was my birthday. After dinner a Key lime pie with twenty-six candles was brought to the table and the entire crew sang happy birthday to me. It turned out to be quite a party, as we spent the rest of the evening drinking margaritas. Some of the mixed crew slipped off for some swimming and their own private party at a secluded beach nearby. Charlie called it all "lifestyles of the rich and ridiculous."

Sometime after midnight, when most of those on *Destiny* had passed out, I made my way down to my kayak, which was still where I'd left it that morning. I spread my sleeping bag out on the sand beside it, too drunk to bother erecting the tent. I woke at dawn with rain-drops splashing off my face, and leapt up to pack away all my scattered gear as the heavens broke open and dumped a pouring shower on Highborne Cay. The crew of *Destiny* was casting off the dock lines, and I waved goodbye as I stood in the rain and watched them slowly motor out of the inlet and begin their voyage back to Palm Beach. The party was over, and I was back in the real world of a sea kayaker. No more hot showers, fancy meals, cold margaritas, or conversations with beautiful women for me. It was back to rice and tuna for dinner and plain water to drink. I felt a touch of regret as I struggled to drag my heavy-loaded boat back to the water's edge.

The rain felt cold, but I quickly warmed up once I sealed myself into the cockpit and fell into my steady traveling stroke. I was paralleling the next cay south of Highborne, staying within a few yards of the shore in fifteen feet of water. I had barely gone a quarter of a mile when I heard a surge in the water behind me. I turned and was horrified to see a black fin slicing the surface, headed directly for my stern. I braced for the impact and somehow managed to avoid capsizing as the kayak was spun nearly 180 degrees by the shark's strike. With trembling hands I fumbled for my bang-stick, which I'd been keeping handy on the deck since that first shark rammed me a couple of days before. I peered into the clear water, which was poorly illuminated in the early morning light of a rainy day. Then out of nowhere I suddenly saw the shark circling beneath me for what could be a serious attack. Shaking with the fear that can only be inspired by the imminent prospect of being eaten, I unscrewed the safety on the bang-stick and waited. I was startled at the incredible speed with which the shark rushed me when it broke out of its circle pattern, and I scarcely had time to raise my weapon in preparation for a desperate defense. Instead of taking a bite however, it passed about three feet beneath me, rolling to one side as it contemplated me with one mechanical-looking eye. I could clearly see that it was about twelve feet long, its head and body wider than my kayak. I wasn't sure what species it was, as its body just looked dark in the poor light.

The shark disappeared after that final pass. I waited motionless for a few minutes to be sure it wouldn't return before I cautiously paddled to the nearest beach, being careful not to make any unnecessary splashes. I collapsed on the sand, needing a few minutes to contemplate this incident. From what I'd read of them, sharks were not supposed to be so aggressive. I'd spent more than a hundred hours scuba diving in the ocean and had never had an incident with a shark. Now I had been rammed twice in three days, both times within a fifty-mile stretch of islands. What was it about the sharks of the Bahamas that I didn't know? I inspected my kayak for damage. The heavy aluminum rudder had been folded to a U-shape by the blow. I had to take it off and use a big rock to pound it back to a semblance of straightness. Obviously, the shiny rudder and the splashing paddle had excited the shark, but on closer inspection, it decided to pass on a Kevlar sandwich for breakfast. I worried that the next one might not be so picky in its culinary preferences, but I had no choice but to go on or quit right then and there. It was like falling off a horse and then getting back on to ride. I steeled myself and relaunched, paddling with frequent over-the-shoulder glances for the next few hours. When nothing else happened I was able to push the threat to the back of my mind and resume enjoying the scenery that was slipping past me.

That afternoon I reached the northern boundary of Exuma Cays Land and Sea Park, a twenty-two-mile stretch of the Exumas where all plants, animals, and marine creatures are protected. My spearfishing would have to wait until I was south of the park. Camping was also technically illegal in the park, but a man in a small powerboat who stopped to talk told me that I could camp on Little Cistern Cay with no problems. I continually got the impression in the Bahamas that I was welcome to camp practically anywhere and stay as long as I wanted. This was hard to get used to after weeks of hiding out like a fugitive on Florida's west coast and the Keys. I had concluded that it was impossible to travel any distance in a sea kayak without trespassing or breaking somebody's "No Camping" rules. The physical nature of kayaking limited how far I could go each day, making it necessary to stop and rest when I reached my limit, whether there was a campground or not. Thankfully the very nature of the kayak; small, silent, and unobtrusive, made it possible to pass along a coast mostly unnoticed. At night the entire boat could be withdrawn into even minimal foliage, allowing me effectively to disappear. But here in the Bahamas, I had the luxury of camping in the open. I built fires on the beach at night and didn't worry about breaking camp and moving out at the crack of dawn.

That night on Little Cistern Cay, another vicious squall swept over my campsite, and my fiberglass ridgepole snapped again, sending the tent down on top of me. I thought of the engineers who designed the thing, snug in some office, never having to spend a sleepless night in a soaking wet sleeping bag. I was getting fed up with overpriced "expedition" gear that was barely adequate for a weekend outing at a park. Why couldn't something like a tent or camp stove be designed to last? After less than a month into the journey I had flung my expensive stove into the ocean in a fit of rage, and the second one Pat had sent to me in Key Largo was little better. It became obvious to me that all this stuff was built to last a season or so for the weekend recreational camper. It had to fail after that, so there would be a need for replacements. This was the business plan of the gear manufacturers. I was disgusted with it and determined to buy as little as possible from now on. I would prove to myself that most of the stuff people buy is unnecessary. Due to necessity, I had become quite expert at cooking on tiny fires that required only a few twigs. I could boil a pot of rice or produce a stack of pancakes in about the same time it would have taken to set up the stove.

I was able to repair the pole the following morning after the storm abated by once again cutting out the splintered section. Though it was now six or eight inches shorter, it still seemed to serve its purpose. I worried that it would soon break again, eventually becoming too short to function. The tent was more critical than the stove, and it would be hard to live without it due to biting insects. It would be difficult to get a replacement in these remote islands. I would have to call Pat in Pensacola, so he could order one from the manufacturer. Then I would have to paddle to some settlement with infrequent mail boat service and wait there until it arrived.

After breaking camp and leaving Little Cistern Cay, I had one hell of a time making an eight-mile crossing to the next cay—an all-out battle against a 25-to-30-knot headwind and frenzied whitecaps. It was the most difficult fight against the wind I'd had so far on the trip, and it raised new doubts as to whether I'd be able to buck the wind on the several thirty-plus-mile crossings that lay ahead, beyond the Exumas and Long Island. John Dowd's warnings about the steady southeast trade winds began to make sense to me now. Wind like this was an intangible concept when I was looking at maps and calculating crossing times at home. It was a factor I didn't consider to be a problem, since on the northern Gulf coast the wind rarely blows for very long and certainly not from a constant direction. Now I could see the wisdom of John Dowd's group when they did their Caribbean kayak expedition ten years before. By starting in Trinidad, they were able to tour the islands all the way to Florida with the prevailing winds behind them. Nevertheless, I was determined to go southeast. Part of the appeal of the trip for me was the idea of leaving home waters and heading out into the horizon to new and strange places. I was open to any possibility, including settling down and living somewhere if I found a place that was particularly captivating. Flying somewhere and paddling home would not have been the same at all.

# FIVE

# THE CRUISING COMMUNITY

... Yet I cannot tarry longer
The sea that calls all things unto her
Calls me,
And I must embark
For to stay, though the hours burn in the night,
Is to freeze and crystallize and be bound in a mold

**—KAHIL GIBRAN, *THE PROPHET***

Despite my troubles with the wind that day and the doubts it created about my ability to complete the trip, I reached Wardrick Wells Cay, where construction was under way to build a new headquarters for the land and sea park. Peggy, the park warden, was in the meantime working out of the large trawler yacht she lived on at anchor off Wardrick Wells. She offered me a cold beer when I paddled up to inquire about camping. She understood what it was to travel as I was doing and told me I could camp on the adjacent beach, regardless of park rules. There were several large tents already there, and Peggy explained that the workers building the headquarters were young people from Operation Raleigh, who were living in camp during their work assignment there.

I paddled over and introduced myself to the members of the team and learned that Operation Raleigh is a volunteer group from the United Kingdom, similar to the U.S. Peace Corps. They were just knocking off for the day, and Hendrick, a young man from the outskirts of London, was on cook duty and invited me to join them for dinner. There was a total of seven in the group, four women and three men. All were from England, except for the woman named Tessa, who said she was from Melbourne, Australia. Most of them rotated to various projects around the world; Tessa told me she had recently been working in Chile.

While I was waiting for dinner, a Canadian man and his daughter, who were cruising alone on their small sailboat, *Heron I*, came over to look at my kayak. Lawrence Pitcairn told me that he had paddled with the Canadian National Canoe Team in years past. He was intrigued by my kayak and my brief account of the journey. He and his daughter, Laura, had found some conch while skin diving, and he told me that he was about to clean them on the beach. Eager to learn how to prepare this readily available food source in case I needed it in the future, I followed Lawrence and Laura to where he had left the conch and watched the procedure attentively. The indigenous natives of these islands made good use of this giant marine snail, as evidenced by the walls of conch shells they left behind. Some of these walls were several feet high and hundreds of yards long, each shell in them exhibiting the telltale human-made hole necessary to extract the meat.

Lawrence showed me where to make the hole, using a hammer. This makes it possible to slip a knife inside and cut loose the attached muscle. Then you pull the slimy creature out by its foot and cut off the eyestalks and other inedible parts, including the tough skin. It's an unappetizing sight, to say the least, but when it's finished, you have a considerable chunk of rubbery, white meat—pure protein. Lawrence insisted that it was perfectly good raw and handed me a thin slice after eating one himself. It wasn't bad, but like Ben's whelks, I decided that I wouldn't do any damage to the conch population unless I found

Mt. Isabela de Torres forms an impressive backdrop for Puerto Plata harbor, Dominican Republic

myself in dire straits. Seventeen-year-old Laura wasn't enthusiastic about conch either and kept herself at a safe distance throughout the procedure.

Back at camp, Hendrick showed me the supply tent for Operation Raleigh, where they had boxes of freeze-dried British military rations. They were sick of this fare after living on it for so long. Today's menu called for several packets labeled "Spaghetti Bolognese," and after Hendrick added the necessary hot water, we all sat down to eat, following the meal with freeze-dried banana custard. The food was good as far as I was concerned, so the following morning before I left, Hendrick loaded me down with a two-week supply of the rations, which he said was surplus that they would never eat. I gladly accepted this windfall of free grub. I would eat compliments of the British taxpayers for a while! After stuffing all these food packets into my kayak, I left Wardrick Wells, stopping by to say good-bye to Peggy on the way out. She had a ham radio on her boat, and said she would call ahead to other ham operators on boats to tell them I was coming through.

South of the park, where I camped on a small, uninhabited cay, I received more unexpected hospitality. A young man from Florida was angling for bonefish in a small skiff with a Bahamian guide, and upon spotting my camp; they came over to give me three cold sodas. I was content to be in the Bahamas as I cooked dinner that night. Never had I been in a place where all the people went out of their way to be friendly. Even the animals were friendly, except for the sharks. As I ate, several fat curly-tail lizards crawled about my feet with no sign of fear, waiting for their share. I gave them bits of cheese, which they nibbled at while they watched with apparent curiosity as I set up my tent on their island.

My next civilized stopover was at Sampson's Cay the following day, where I found outrageous prices in the only food store. I paddled on to Staniel Cay, only five miles farther south. As I approached the crowded anchorage at Staniel, a dinghy intercepted me and a couple in it told me they had heard from Peggy by radio that I was coming. They knew I was from Mississippi and had come to tell me that there was a couple on a sailboat called the *Miss Reb* who were also from Mississippi. I was excited to meet some folks from back home, as I had not seen any since my trip began. The dinghy was gone when I paddled over to *Miss Reb*, so I set up camp on a nearby island and caught up on my neglected journal while I awaited their return.

In the morning I was invited aboard *Miss Reb* for coffee and learned that the couple from Jackson had built the boat themselves and had been living aboard for five years. They had been as far as the Virgin Islands and planned to eventually sail around the world. They provided much useful information about the route ahead and gave me an empty Clorox jug, saying that they had found the one-gallon containers to be much more reliable for carrying water than the leaky "Reliance" container I was using.

Later that morning, when I pulled my kayak up on the beach at Staniel Cay, a Bahamian on a moped stopped and began questioning me about my trip. His questions turned to preaching when he found out I was traveling alone, had no family of my own, and was not in church on Sundays. His advice also covered the physical dangers after he learned of my run-ins with sharks. In his opinion, the large barracudas that were always hanging around the reefs were equally aggressive.

"Dat Barry, he cut you up, mon. I git out de wahtah when Barry, he come 'round."

After the part-time preacher putted away on the little moped, I walked up to the store he'd directed me to and purchased some canned goods, chocolate bars, rice, and bread and butter. I returned to the shaded beach near my kayak, where I sat down to eat. The bread was the same as that I had enjoyed so much on Eleuthera. What made it even better was the excellent canned butter imported from New Zealand. I was told by several yachties that this product would keep a long time without refrigeration.

Dinghies from the many yachts in the harbor came and went, landing on the beach beside my kayak. I watched as a man with two female companions approached in a wooden rowing dinghy. Most of the cruisers were much older than I was, but this trio had to be in their early twenties. They landed and the man went straight to my kayak, walking around it with obvious awe and appreciation.

"Somebody's *traveling* in this thing," he said to the women. "Look at that compass on the deck!"

I emerged from the shadows where I had been eating unnoticed and introduced myself. Mark, from Norfolk, Virginia, and his Danish girl-friend, Lis, had sailed there from the Chesapeake. The other woman was a friend of Lis's who had flown out from Copenhagen to Nassau to join them for a few days. Mark invited me out to their vintage wooden sailboat, *Elske*, for dinner, and there I met the other crewmember, Chelsie, a big Chesapeake Bay retriever who leapt over the side and swam out to greet us as we approached the yacht. Lis and her friend cooked dinner, and afterwards Mark invited me to stay aboard for the night, since there were likely no isolated beaches on Staniel Cay where

I could camp. Grateful for the company and the chance to hang out with some people close to my own age, I spread my sleeping bag in the cockpit beside Chelsie. I regretted not being in my tent when rain in the middle of the night forced me to retreat to the crowded cabin, where I found just enough room to crash on the narrow sole.

The next morning over coffee, Mark told me we were anchored near Thunderball Cave, the famous attraction of Staniel Cay. The cave is in a tiny cay not far from Staniel and was the location for an underwater James Bond thriller film called *Thunderball*. The entire rocky islet, which rises abruptly out of the water to a height of about thirty feet, is hollow, with an opening in the roof that illuminates the pool of water inside its base. The cavern below the surface of this pool is teeming with fish. Rock walls around the perimeter of the cay extend down to the pool on all sides, but open up just below the surface. The only way to enter the cavern is to swim underwater from the outside, beneath the walls until you reach the spacious inner chamber. Mark was not an experienced snorkeler and could not be persuaded to swim into the cave, so Lis and I left him in the dinghy and went in to check it out. It was fantastic. We surfaced inside an eerie grotto with a ceiling more than twenty feet above, from which hung stalactites dripping with water that plopped to the pool with an amplified echo. The light coming through the ceiling was just enough to illuminate the transparent water in the cavern, and we could see schools of big yellowtail and red snapper, the best food fish on the reef. They swam past with no fear, as if aware of the law protecting them from spearfishing in their exotic haven.

The sight of the fish whetted my appetite, so after leaving Thunderball Cave, we motored in the dinghy out to a reef on the edge of the open sea, and Mark and I tried unsuccessfully to spear the elusive yellowtails and groupers we found there. The fish near this popular anchorage area were skittish from being overhunted and would disappear into rock crevices at the first sight of an approaching swimmer.

I went ashore on Staniel Cay again later that day and saw Laura and Lawrence from *Heron I* and spent some time talking with them about my kayak. Mark and his crew were leaving that afternoon for George-town, so I paddled south myself, planning to make a few miles before dark. I got no farther than the next cay south of Staniel though, because I was so attracted by the beautiful beach on Bitter Guana Cay that I had to pull in and set up my tent even though the sun was still high. This pristine beach was bounded on all sides by high, cactus-covered hills, and on the south end, rocky cliffs rose abruptly to fifty feet and hung out over the clear, aquamarine waters. The desolate cay seemed like an alien world with its pockmarked limestone and huge craters. It was the kind of island I would have expected to find along the Baja coast rather than here in the Bahamas. The moon was full that night, and I hiked about the island for hours, sometimes stopping on a rocky crag overlooking the windward side to watch and listen to the breakers that slammed the foot of the cliffs. I stayed up late when I returned to camp, sitting by a beach fire and attempting to blow some blues on my harmonica.

I stopped in the town on Little Farmer's Cay the next day, since Ben had told me it was their favorite hangout in the Exumas. As I pulled my kayak up on the beach, three men who had been watching through the windows of a waterfront bar came down to greet me. One of them was Terry Bain, the mayor.

"Welcome to our island. Our home is your home, my friend," he said as he shook my hand and took in my answers to his questions about how I had come to land there in a kayak. He told me that *Whisper* had already been there but had sailed for Georgetown a couple of days before. I was overwhelmed by this exceptionally warm hospitality at Little Farmer's Cay, but for some inexplicable reason, I didn't want to stay there. Perhaps I just wanted another night of solitude like I'd had on Bitter Guana Cay. After buying a loaf of bread and filling my water jugs, I said good-bye to Mr. Bain and paddled on until I found a quiet beach a short distance to the south.

The next day I found an even better campsite on Darby Island. There were a few coconut palms on the beach there—something I'd been missing for days. I was disappointed to find that not all the islands in the Bahamas have dense groves of palms like those the Olsens and I found in the Berry Islands. In fact, most of the uninhabited cays I'd seen had no trees or palms of any kind—only desert-like scrub brush and cactus. The few coconut palms I did see were usually on private islands and were planted by the owners. To me the coconut palm was the icon of the tropics, and I always felt like the trip I was doing was worthwhile when I saw one.

I set up my tent near these palms on Darby Island and, after climbing one to get a couple of green drinking nuts, gathered up my spearfishing gear and headed for the water to hunt the main course. There was a submerged rock wall near the beach, and I swam along this taking futile shots at yellowtails and red snapper that were always quicker than my spear. In deep water beyond the wall, I encountered a granddaddy barracuda that was about six feet long, and remembered the words of the preacher from Staniel Cay: "Dat Barry, he cut you up, mon." I turned around and swam to shallower water. I couldn't believe my luck when I saw a huge lobster crawling backwards across the sandy bottom, far from the safety of the rock crevices. I approached to within easy range and speared it through the carapace. I was excited as I rushed back to camp with my first lobster writhing grotesquely on the end of the steel spear. Lobsters are tenacious of life, and even after I did as Ben had taught me and stuck the point of my dive knife into its head and twisted it back and forth, the six legs and two long antennae flailed about with snapping noises, giving the giant crustacean a mechanical appearance. I twisted off the fat tail, where all the delicious white meat is found, and even after I dropped it into a pot of boiling water, it continued to contract involuntarily. The difficulty of killing this creature and its stubborn struggle to live made me wonder if it was worth the trouble and if I could stomach spearing another one.

Fifteen minutes later, however, when the tail had turned to bright red and the meat within was snow white, I decided that it *was* worth it. I spiced it up with Tony Chachere's Cajun seasoning and some

Louisiana hot sauce, and washed it down with water from a green coconut. This was living off the land and sea at its finest.

The following day was dreary and overcast, unusual for the Bahamas. During the past two weeks, the sun had been my biggest enemy, even more incessant than the wind. It blazed in the cloudless blue skies and burned my already browned skin. Often I could find no relief from it in the barren Exumas, and when I stopped for lunch I would crouch in the shade of a rock and try to eat bread with the melted canned butter. I was relieved today to have a brief respite from the burning rays, but the skies seemed to grow stormier as the afternoon advanced and the strong southeast wind reduced my progress to a pitiful one mile per hour. I had set for my goal that day the small settlement of Barreterre, just north of Great Exuma Island, but it was still miles away when night was approaching, and the islands nearby offered no possibilities for landing or camping on their rugged shores. I could see the low profile of a sandy cay about four miles to the east, so I headed for it, splashing through choppy seas and fighting wind that threatened to tear the paddle from my hands.

Dark clouds swept over the open expanse of water south of me and I watched with fascination as a towering waterspout danced slowly across the horizon. I kept my bow stubbornly pointed at the little island, anxious to complete the crossing before the weather got worse. I also did not want to paddle these waters after nightfall, when sharks are more active. When I reached the other side, it was fully dark, and what had looked from a distance like a beach was actually smooth rock. I couldn't land there through the surge without damaging my boat, so I followed the shoreline to the south, where I came upon a sailboat anchored in a protected cove. The couple on board filled my water jugs and told me they had been watching my crossing through binoculars. They couldn't believe I was out paddling in such rough conditions and informed me that another waterspout had passed close behind me as I paddled. I was glad I had not looked over my shoulder, as I might have panicked at the sight of a seagoing tornado so close at hand.

I paddled another half-mile past the sailboat, finding an ideal sandy beach for camping. The bad weather didn't last, and soon the moon illuminated the white sand so that it almost seemed like daytime. I could see the few lights of Barreterre to the west as I cooked some of the freeze-dried rations from Operation Raleigh. I decided that since it was Saturday night, I would take a full day off. I needed the rest, and I figured I probably wouldn't be able to buy the supplies I needed from Barreterre on a Sunday anyway. I spent my time on the tranquil beach recharging my Ni-Cad batteries with the solar panel, writing in my journal, and planning my budget for the remainder of the trip. My cash was getting dismally low. I hadn't counted on these strong winds that would slow my daily progress so much, nor had I allowed for the high food prices in the Bahamas. Most of the basics were double or triple the prices I was used to the States. I wondered if I could stretch what I had far enough to get me the remaining several hundred miles or so to Puerto Rico, the first island where I could legally work.

On Monday, I paddled into Barraterre and bought a few items at the tiny general store there, thinking it would take two days to make the thirty miles to Georgetown. I had been hearing a lot about this town on the southern end of Great Exuma Island. Ben and his family considered it almost paradise, and he told me it was a mecca for cruising sailors who congregate there to wait for the right weather to make the difficult windward trip to the Caribbean. I looked forward to seeing it for myself, and to seeing the Olsens again, as I expected them to be there when I arrived.

I left Barraterre with the wind at my back for a change. A cold front sweeping across North America brought the unusual change in wind direction. North winds are a rarity in the trade wind belt, and it takes an unusually strong front to reach this far south. I was eager to take advantage of such an opportunity to make easy miles, so I unpacked the parafoil kite that had been stowed on the rear deck all these months and began untangling the lines. I had experimented only a little with the parafoil, finding it frustrating in the variable winds of the Gulf of Mexico, but I knew that sea kayakers had used them as sails to make rapid downwind progress in the right conditions. So far on the trip, I had not had even a single day of steady tailwinds of sufficient strength, so the parafoil was almost forgotten.

Launching the kite from a kayak is the most frustrating part of parafoil sailing, and my previous attempts had resulted in tangled lines and attendant profanities when the kite plummeted into the sea each time the wind speed dropped. This time, however, it was different. I held the ten-square-foot plastic kite at arm's length in front of me, and the wind filled it with a snap, carrying it up and away from me. The three-hundred-foot nylon line sang as it spun off the hand reel, and the kite rapidly climbed to a height of one hundred feet above the waves, far out in front of my bow. I rested the paddle across the coaming and hung on to the reel as the kayak surged forward to an unheard-of cruising speed of six knots.

Barretterre dropped below the horizon in my wake, and soon I was in deep water about a mile off the coast of Great Exuma, enjoying the ride as I sat back and effortlessly moved at twice my paddling speed. The settlements of Rolleville and Steventon slipped past to starboard as I paralleled the rugged coast of the island. As I was only able to run before the wind, I was being carried farther from shore on my southeast heading as the beaches curved away to the south, but I didn't care. I wanted to ride this wind as long as I could. Five miles out, beyond the reefs in oceanic depths, schools of flying fish skimmed over the waves in front of my bow, gliding easily a hundred yards at a time before disappearing again into the waves.

I reached Georgetown in just over five hours, covering thirty miles without dipping the paddle. The anchorage off Stocking Island was easily recognizable by the number of cruising sailboats present. There were at least a hundred. It was the only place in the Exumas where so many boaters gather. Not wanting to deal with a crowd and the many questions the cruisers would have when they saw me, I reeled in the parafoil just north of the anchorage and set up camp on the deserted beach there. After cooking and eating a simple dinner of rice and tuna, I turned on my VHF and tried to call *Whisper*. There was no answer from the Olsens, but the radio channels were alive with chatter from all the boaters in the area.

In the morning I paddled across the harbor from Stocking Island to the other anchorage at the edge of Georgetown. As I worked my way through the cluster of sailboats there, Mark, from *Elske,* called my name and I paddled over to go aboard for coffee with him and Lis. They said they had been there for two days, after an easy sail from Staniel Cay. Mark said that this anchorage near the town was called Kidd Cove (said to be a favorite anchorage of Captain Kidd) and there were almost as many boats anchored here as the one hundred or so out at Stocking Island. Mark pointed to a small pocket of beach where I could land my kayak to go into town, so I said goodbye until later and paddled ashore. My first priority in this outpost of civilization was to find a laundry. My clothes had not been properly washed since Key Largo.

I left a garbage bag full of dirty T-shirts, shorts, and underwear at the full-service laundry, and set out to explore Georgetown. There was something familiar about this place, and then it struck me that the town was not at all unlike many rural Mississippi communities such as Prentiss, where I grew up. If not for the ocean and a few coconut palms here and there, I could almost imagine myself back in my hometown.

Near the center of Georgetown, a bridge passed over an inlet to a small bay where most of the dinghies from visiting yachts were tied up to a dock provided for this purpose. There were two grocery stores that were larger and better stocked than any I'd seen in the Bahamas, and other small stores were randomly spaced along the single main street north and south of the bridge. On one end of town there were government buildings and a post office, along with two small hotels, the Peace and Plenty and the Two Turtles Inn. The telephone office was on the opposite end of town, and away from the business areas, colorful tin-roofed houses, neat and well maintained, lined the streets.

Both the boaters and the locals walked at the same unhurried pace. A T-shirt stand sold shirts that encouraged this behavior: "Georgetown Bahamas—Nobody Move, Nobody Get Hurt." It seemed that people here took this philosophy seriously. Nothing seemed important enough to justify expending extra energy.

Georgetown lies only a few miles north of the Tropic of Cancer. I was excited about being so close to the official tropics and looked forward to crossing that demarcation line soon. But though there were coconut palms and other exotic plants, Georgetown didn't seem any more tropical than the other islands I had seen miles to the north. I couldn't quite see it as the paradise Ben Olsen had raved about, but it was a pleasant enough place to hang out for a while, and there was certainly no lack of fellow boaters to swap sea stories with. I recognized many faces that I'd seen in the past two weeks as I worked my way south, but far more people recognized me. Many were total strangers who said things like: "Aren't you the guy paddling the kayak?" or "We saw you a couple of weeks ago at Allen's Cay . . . you *paddled* all the way to Georgetown from there?"

Unbeknownst to me, word of my solo journey had spread like wild-fire throughout the Exumas yachting community, propagated by ham radio operators and word of mouth exaggerations. Most of these sailors were unfamiliar with sea kayaks and were amazed at my ability to paddle through the same islands they were sailing among in much larger and infinitely more expensive and complicated vessels. I didn't know it that first day in Georgetown, but I would soon be repeating my story so many times that I would grow tired of hearing it.

Finding a place to camp in Georgetown did not seem likely, so I paddled back across the harbor to Stocking Island and landed on the "Volleyball Beach" that Ben had mentioned in his descriptions of Georgetown. Someone had erected two volleyball nets one year, and it had been a tradition ever since among the yachties to gather at 3 P.M. for a couple of hours of informal games. I arrived at the time of this competition and was surprised to see how many people had turned out. Each of the four teams consisted of ten to twelve players, and another two dozen spectators watched from the sidelines.

Not wanting to pitch my tent too close to this activity, I found a spot just around a long sandy point out of sight of the volleyball nets. A grove of tall casaurina trees provided shade. Someone had hung a tire swing from a branch for the kids, and a crude tree house was nailed between the branches of another tree. I quickly took possession of the area, stringing my hammock between two trees, setting up my tent, and digging a fire pit in the sand for cooking.

Behind my campsite, the beach gave way to island scrub forest. Just inside the tree line I found an unusual signpost set up by one of the cruisers who had too much time on his hands. A chunk of island limestone hung by a string from the sign, which proclaimed the stone to be a "weather rock." Handwritten instructions were posted for skippers needing meteorological information:

> Weather Rock:
> If it's wet—it's raining. If it's dry—it's not . . .
> If it's hot—the sun is shining.
> If it's hanging straight down—there is no wind . . .
> If it's out at angle—there's good wind for sailing.
> If it's straight out—it's a hurricane!
> If there's ice on it—this ain't the Bahamas and it's time to sail south!

The heavy rock wasn't out at the slightest angle, despite the strong breeze that threatened to blow my tent away. I couldn't stake it down in the deep powered coral that made up the sand of the beach, so I gathered piles of rocks and empty conch shells to weight down the corners. People from the volleyball game began wandering over as I gathered materials for a cooking fire. Everyone wanted to examine my kayak and gear, and they all seemed to ask the same questions. There would be no privacy here, as in addition to the visitors on the beach, there were several sailboats anchored close by in the twenty-foot depths just beyond the shallows in front of my tent. I didn't mind the company for now though. I craved conversation after so much time spent alone.

I planned to stay in Georgetown no longer than two or three days, but after this time had passed, I was not anxious to leave. I learned that Georgetown's anchorage was also known as "Chicken Harbor" by serious voyagers because of the large number of Canadian and American yachtsmen who sail there on their way to the Caribbean from Florida and then "chicken out" and go no farther. This is because south of the Exumas, the islands are more widely spaced, and stronger trade winds straight out of the southeast make progress down island a head-on bash into rough seas. The route from the Bahamas to the Virgin Islands and points beyond in the eastern Caribbean has long been known as the "Thorny Path" because of its difficulty. The sailors who "chicken out" at Georgetown to go no farther south are not in want of like-minded company. In winter, when the trades are blowing their strongest, three hundred or more yachts often congregate in these waters, their crews making excuses to stay longer, passing the time with volleyball and partying.

Deprived of social interaction during much of my solitary journey, I was more interested in the latter pursuit. I learned that on Friday nights, the Two Turtles Inn in Georgetown is the place to be. That was the time of the weekly Friday night barbecue, when all the boaters congregated to swap dreams and sea stories amid a free-flowing torrent of rum and beer. I went to the barbecue my first Friday night in Georgetown with Mark and Lis, who had been joined that day by Mark's sister, Lisa. Lisa had just flown in from Norfolk to spend a couple of weeks sailing on *Elske*, and was easily recognized as a newcomer to the islands by her snow-white, untanned skin. Mark was beginning to be infected by the "chicken" fever that was going around in Georgetown and was having doubts about continuing on to the Virgin Islands after listening to too many tales of disaster spread around by some of the older salts in the harbor. *Elske*, Mark explained, was built in 1933, and her old wooden hull might not stand the pounding of motoring head-on into wind and waves for several hundred miles. He suggested that he might consider going on if he had another man on board to help but didn't know if Lis and Lisa could pull their share of all-night watches. It was an invitation, and I told him I would consider it, but I had been aboard *Elske* enough to note the dilapidated condition of the once-beautiful old vessel. I wouldn't say so, but I felt safer in my kayak.

Though I wasn't eager to join Mark on *Elske*, despite the arrival of his good-looking sister, I was already thinking of the possibility of hitching a ride on some other sailboat. Everyone warned me that I would not be able to make the eighty-mile crossing from the Caicos to Hispaniola against the wind, and even if I could, there were only a few ports on the north coast of the Dominican Republic where foreign vessels were permitted to land. I was told that I would never be able to get permission to paddle the coastline of that country, so my best bet would be to go as crew on a sailboat and then resume my paddling in Puerto Rico, a U.S. territory. Even John Dowd had warned me before I left home about potential problems on the tightly restricted coast of the Dominican Republic. His group of four paddlers had been arrested there, despite the letter of permission they had obtained in advance from the Dominican navy.

My dwindling cash supply was another reason to consider crewing on yacht to Puerto Rico. It would take another two to three months to paddle there, by which time I would be broke, or I could hop a ride on a faster boat able to take a more direct route and possibly get there in two to three weeks. Once there, I could find a way to earn some more money and then continue on by kayak. There were quite a few boats in the harbor going down island, but I was to learn that cruiser-types don't stick to a tight schedule, and most only had vague plans at best. I mingled with the crowd at the Friday night barbecue and put the word out that I was seeking a passage. Then I returned to my campsite, zigzagging across the dark waters of the harbor at 2 A.M., more than a little tipsy from the rum drinks that were somehow hard to keep track of.

My days in Georgetown were filled with exploring the immediate area on foot and by kayak, and meeting so many people I could no longer keep their names straight. I went to the afternoon volleyball games and sometimes joined in. Everyone wanted to know more about my trip and my reasons for traveling this way instead of in a more conventional boat, so I had numerous invitations for dinner and drinks aboard the yachts in the harbor, and could probably have stayed as long as I wanted without ever having to cook another campfire meal. I usually made my own breakfast, however, and spent the mornings hanging around camp, reading in my hammock or snorkeling in the clear waters just off the beach.

One afternoon while napping in my hammock I was awakened by a piercing Tarzan yell and looked up to see a big French-speaking guy about my age climbing down from the nearby tree house to where his attractive blonde girlfriend awaited. Switching to English, he introduced himself as Jean-Louis, saying they were both from Switzerland and that his girlfriend spoke no English. Jean-Louis was ecstatic about my kayak and my journey, saying that he hunted ducks from a similar craft as a boy. I answered his questions, and he rapidly translated my answers to the girl, who stared at me with wide blue eyes and a shy smile that suggested she might prefer my company to the loud-mouthed maniac by her side. Jean-Louis bragged that he had sailed around the world three times already and embellished his voyages with tales of a shipwreck in his first boat off the coast of New Guinea. He claimed that he and a different girlfriend reached shore in a life raft and walked fifty miles of uninhabited coast to reach a native village.

Jean-Louis dressed in a flamboyant style to match his yarns of adventure, with a multi-hued Hawaiian-print shirt, equally loud flower-print trousers, sandals, and bougainvillea flowers woven into his foot-long ponytail. The girlfriend, still standing there in silence, was much more conservatively dressed in jeans and a T-shirt. As we talked, the one other member of their crew walked into my camp from where he had been wandering on the beach. His name was Scully, and he was a Rastafarian from the island of Dominica, out in the far eastern chain of Caribbean islands known as the Windward Islands.

Scully wore nothing but a pair of cut-off shorts, and evidently had never owned a pair of shoes, judging by his broad, calloused feet that enabled him to walk over the sharp coral rocks at the water's edge in front of my camp. Dominica had been high on my list of desirable islands to visit when I planned this trip. I listened eagerly to Scully's descriptions of his homeland. It was an island of jungle paradise, according to him, with abundant fruit, good drinking water cascading in streams from the mountains, and plenty of places where I could camp out of my kayak indefinitely.

Scully didn't have the long dreadlocks typical of a Rasta, and he explained that this was because the authorities in Dominica had caught him with ganja and cut his hair. It was the worst possible punishment for him, as he had been growing his dreadlocks all his life. But Jean-Louis had plenty of ganja on board the *Spirit of Sinbad*, and Scully had joined him and his quiet girlfriend in Martinique, in hopes of seeing Florida. Georgetown, just five miles north of the Tropic of Cancer, was as far north as Scully had ever been.

The *Spirit of Sinbad* was an unlikely-looking vessel for this young and obviously unemployed crew. Jean-Louis explained that the fifty-two-foot aluminum-hulled racing yacht had been sunk and that he salvaged and repaired it at a bargain price. They were on their way to Miami, where they planned to work for a while, then buy cheap jewelry to trade later on as they made their way around the world. Jean-Louis claimed to be a modern-day version of the sailing merchants of old, buying cheap items in one country and selling them for a profit at the next landfall where they were not available. He offered to take me with them, saying my kayak would easily fit *inside* the huge yacht, and that they could use an extra crewmember. The prospect of seeing the South

Pacific was tempting. But I had little money, they obviously had none, and I did not want to return to Florida, even for a day.

In addition to these new friends, other cruisers I'd met farther north in the Exumas chain were showing up again in Georgetown. One morning while paddling across to Georgetown, I saw *Whisper* sailing into the anchorage and later caught up with the Olsens in town and walked with them to the post office. While there, I ran into Lawrence Pitcairn and his daughter Laura, from *Heron I*. It was good to see people I knew again, but there was no mail held for me under general delivery, and I was disappointed to have no news from my friends back in the other world I had left behind.

Later that same day, Mark, Lis, and Lisa moved *Elske* from Kidd Cove and dropped anchor just off the beach in front of my camp. Mark told me about the recent arrival of a sailboat called *Foxglove*, skippered by a fellow from Maine with his nineteen-year-old blonde daughter, Becky, and her brunette friend of the same age, Christine. After making sure we were out of earshot of Lis and Lisa, Mark told me the rumor he had heard about *Foxglove*. Becky's father, divorced from her mother, had recently met a woman who wanted to move on board *Foxglove* and cruise the islands with him. Expecting her to arrive in Georgetown soon, he had recently given Becky and Christine notice that their vacation was over and that they needed to start thinking about a trip back to Maine. Mark said that he had seen the soon-to-be-castaway crew and assured me that these two single young women were the hottest in the anchorage, if not all the Bahamas, and not wanting to go back to New England in February, they were looking for berths on another boat. Mark's dilemma was how to get rid of Lis and Lisa, so he could offer these poor girls a ride. I would be welcome to join him if he succeeded.

Not having seen Becky and Christine yet, I wondered why he would be so anxious to part with his Danish girlfriend anyway. When they came to visit my camp on the beach later that afternoon, Lis with typical

European disdain for modesty, removed her bikini top and proudly revealed her ample and well-tanned upper half. Emboldened by her example, Mark's sister Lisa went topless as well, wisely applying plenty of sunscreen. Mark and I sat in the shade with Chelsie, the retriever, aware of the many sets of binoculars trained on the beach from several boats in the nearby anchorage.

Utterly foreign to me before this journey to the islands, I was becoming aware of and immersed in the cruising subculture. I began to realize that these yachties had a loosely organized yet vibrant community they carried with them from island to island in their ceaseless quest to leave behind whatever it was that had inspired them to trade shore life for a life afloat. Perhaps the biggest difference between this life and the life they had left behind was the amount of free time they had, which inevitably led to boredom. Like any other small town, the community of sailors at Georgetown's anchorage was rife with rumors and gossip, and everyone seemed to know something about everyone else's business.

*Foxglove* was not the only boat that was much talked about in the anchorage during those days. There was also *Winning Edge,* a twenty-seven-foot Hunter single-handed by a crazy Frenchman named George. Everyone who had a VHF radio had heard George Bouillon's arrival into Georgetown. In barely comprehensible English, he called for help when he sailed into the harbor:

"Can somebody tell me what eez dis place? I sail out of Nassau . . . put on ze auto-matic pee-lot, drink a bottle of ze cognac, and wake up here."

I met George one afternoon as I paddled back to camp after a visit on *Heron I.* He was rowing to his boat from the beach in a dinghy, his tanned bald head shining in the sun.

"Come for ze beer!" he shouted, pointing at *Winning Edge.*

Amazingly, George recognized the make of my kayak and told me that he was a personal friend of Mike Neckar, the builder. Over hot Beck's beer he told me that he had lived in British Colombia for years.

He was greatly impressed with the quality of my boat after a closer inspection. I told him of my travels and of my plans for hopping a sailboat to Puerto Rico. George said he would be glad to offer me a ride himself, but "only ze short one," as he hoped to pick up female crew anywhere the opportunity presented itself along his intended route to Martinique. When I mentioned the desperate young ladies on *Foxglove*, George got on the radio within seconds:

"*Foxglove, Foxglove* . . . it is *Winning Edge* who call you—over."

He repeated this plea three times but still did not raise *Foxglove*. However, we both met Becky and Christine in Georgetown the following morning, and George invited them to *Winning Edge* for dinner that night.

George drank no water. He started his day off with two hot Heinekens or Becks ("I don't to eat in ze morning") and so he kept no fresh water in *Winning Edge*'s storage tanks. When the girls came to dinner on schedule, George discovered that he had no fresh water on board for cooking. I had none in my camp to give him, so he simply cooked the rice and vegetables in seawater. Now, I had often cooked rice in a 50/50 solution of seawater and fresh to conserve my limited freshwater supply while camped on isolated islands, and it was okay so long as no extra salt was added. But straight seawater, of course, rendered the food practically inedible, and Becky and Christine later confessed to me that this had been a deciding factor in their decision not to sail with George. I was to find out later though, that George had been a professional chef in France and could cook quite well when sober.

Becky and Christine also visited my camp and were quite intrigued with my method of travel. Christine, especially, expressed a desire to try kayaking and hinted that she would probably be adventurous enough to go with me, but alas, my kayak was a single-seater. Such a shame that I still had the two plastic Chinooks Ernest and I had started out on Black Creek in, utterly unattainable here from where they were stored back in Mississippi. There was nothing to be done short of borrowing Ben's hacksaw to cut out two more cockpits in the Necky.

Oh well, they probably wouldn't like it anyway after a week of rice and tuna. I had chosen the path of solitude for now, and I would have to stick with it.

A week after I met him, Jean-Louis moved the *Spirit of Sinbad* to the anchorage near Volleyball Beach and I went aboard to visit one afternoon when a rare cold front sweeping down from North America brought the usual wind shift to the north and a daytime temperature of only sixty degrees. Jean-Louis was repairing a spare sail and Scully was shivering on deck, wearing two pairs of long pants and two shirts. Jean-Louis laughed at the Rastaman, who had never been this far "north." I told Scully that this was not *real* cold. *Real* cold was what he would find *way* up north, where they were headed, in Miami.

"I come from de sun, mon." Scully said as he shivered with his arms crossed over his chest and his back turned to the north wind.

Jean-Louis dashed below and returned with a photo of snow-covered peaks near his home in Switzerland. "I told him this is what it's like in the United States, but he doesn't believe me."

"It's true, Scully," I said, taking the picture and holding it in his face. "This is what you'll find in Miami this time of year. Why do you think I'm going south? You won't be going barefoot *there*. No mon! You'll be wearing *five* or *six* pairs of pants."

Jean-Louis rolled with laughter, delighted that I backed up his tales of the rigors of winter in Florida.

"I an' I goin' bok to Dominica," Scully said. "A mon not supposed to lib dat weh, you know."

We went below into the spacious cabin of the *Spirit of Sinbad* so Scully could get out of the wind. Jean-Louis had said before that they had not refurbished the interior since salvaging the yacht. Looking around down there at the wide-open interior, with no floors, bunks, or even bulkheads that were not structural, I began to think his story of how he obtained the yacht might be true. The essentials were there, however, including a well-equipped navigation station with sophisticated electronics, and a serviceable galley where there was a huge bowl of cooked white rice on the countertop. Near the stern, on a mattress laid across a sheet of plywood, the beautiful Swiss girlfriend slept, unaware of our presence.

"See, we have plenty of room for your kayak." Jean-Louis reminded me as he looked about the cavernous interior of the *Spirit of Sinbad.*

I was briefly tempted to throw in my lot with this strangely assorted crew, but the thought of nothing but white rice three times a day for weeks on a Pacific crossing frightened me. And besides, I was determined to get to the islands I had set out to reach, whether I could paddle there or not.

Jean-Louis said that the *Spirit of Sinbad* was designed for racing and was very fast. "Maybe we'll win the America's Cup," he laughed, "and sell it to buy drugs!"

Scully grinned. It seemed like a good idea to him.

Someone outside yelling my name cut our conversation short. I went topside to see Lawrence, standing on the deck of *Heron I,* anchored nearby. He said that a lady from the yacht *Celebration* was calling for me on the radio, inviting me to dinner.

I used Jean-Louis's radio to find out what this was all about. I had met the owners of *Celebration* a couple of days before, when I had learned that they were looking for a crew member, but after talking to them, I gathered that they were not interested in sailing any time soon. But when I reached them on VHF channel 16, they asked me to please come on over for dinner, because they wanted to talk.

When I found *Celebration* in the anchorage, I was impressed with her appearance. She was a large and well-equipped vessel that appeared almost new by the looks of her glossy Gelcoat and stainless steel fittings. I tied my kayak alongside the inflatable dinghy and climbed aboard to meet the owners: Frank Holzmacher and Josephine Adams, both from New York City. They were both retired architects and had bought the Tayana 42 with plans to live aboard and cruise for at least the next ten years.

The interior of *Celebration* was as plush as the overall appearance of the yacht suggested. There was a refrigerator and freezer, TV, built-in stereo, and a computer interfaced into the navigation instruments. Josephine had baked a homemade pizza in the well-equipped galley's oven, and while she set the table, Frank poured me a stiff rum drink. Over dinner, they explained that they had cruised down the East Coast Intracoastal Waterway from New York, sailed to Georgetown over a year ago, and had been hanging around ever since. Twice they had left with intentions of going down island, but each time had encountered rough conditions and turned back. They needed extra help standing watches, pulling heavy anchors, and making sail changes on the longer passages ahead. Frank was sixty-seven, though still in good shape. Josephine was in her forties but quite overweight. Neither of them had experience of open ocean voyaging.

I answered their questions and showed them my passport, feeling as if I were on a job interview, and Frank said they would let me know in a few days if they could take me along. He said they planned to sail direct from Georgetown to the Caicos Islands, then go to the Dominican Republic and spend some time there. After that stopover, they would sail to Puerto Rico, where they would drop me off to resume my kayak journey. If they took me along, he said they would provide all my meals while I was on board in exchange for my help. This seemed fine with me, and I paddled back to camp full of hope about this prospect for going south.

In the meantime, while waiting for an answer from *Celebration*, I continued an island lifestyle that revolved around my camp on Volleyball Beach. Ben moved *Whisper* over to the anchorage nearby, and one evening they brought food to cook out on the beach with me. We grilled hot dogs over the fire, and I watched with amusement as these "vegetarians" stuffed themselves with this "junk food." Ben ate four, and Sylvia, Sky and Grant three each.

The next morning Ben and I left in his outboard-powered dinghy to go out to deep water on the other side of Stocking Island for some serious spearfishing. It was a long ride south from Stocking Island to get to the cut where there was access to open water. As we motored past miles of deserted beach, we passed another dinghy pulled up on the sand far from the crowded anchorage. Our fast approach caught the lovemaking couple on the beach beside it by surprise, and not having time for any other course of action, the man, who was on top, merely grinned over his shoulder and waved at us as we went past.

Beyond the cut we snorkeled in about thirty feet of water, taking turns towing the dinghy and diving down to hunt. Ben soon had a nice Nassau grouper, and I got a black grouper. After he got the third fish, our activity attracted the attention of a six-foot barracuda, which followed us persistently, watching our every move and just waiting for the opportunity to steal our next kill. When a ten-foot bull shark arrived on the scene, cruising below us near the bottom, we decided to call it quits. Sharks were all too common here. Someone had caught a twelve-foot hammerhead in the anchorage right off Stocking Island the week before.

Back at my camp, we cleaned our catch and Sylvia fried the fish on board *Whisper*. The Olsens were leaving that day; a couple of their friends from Iowa had flown down to join them, and they were going to begin a leisurely cruise back to Florida. I waved good-bye to them again, this time for good, as they pulled their anchor and sailed out of the harbor. *Whisper* was a sight to see under full sail, with her junk-rigged sails and the classic schooner lines of her black hull. By comparison, the uniformly white hulls of the many fiberglass production boats in the harbor had little character.

The day the Olsens left, I got word from Frank and Josephine that I could accompany them south on *Celebration*. There were a lot of preparations to be made before we could sail. First, I had to get the remainder of my travel funds wired to me at the bank in Georgetown and, after picking up a few letters awaiting me at the post office, have any other arriving mail forwarded to a friend in Puerto Rico, where I naively believed I would be in less than a month.

To familiarize myself with *Celebration*, I helped them bring her from Stocking Island to the fuel dock at Kidd Cove, where we took on diesel and filled the water tanks. Then we made countless trips on foot to the grocery store, returning each time with the folding dock cart that was part of *Celebration*'s essential equipment, loaded with groceries and cases of soft drinks. We had our laundry done and then moved the yacht back to Stocking Island, where I broke my camp and ferried my gear out to *Celebration* in the dinghy. Like most people I had met along the way, Jo and Frank were amazed at the incredible amount of stuff I had been carrying in my kayak. We packed it into various lockers on board the yacht, and then hoisted the kayak onto the deck, where it was made fast to the starboard stanchions.

My last night in Georgetown was on a Wednesday, so I went to the dance at the Peace and Plenty and said good-bye to all my new friends. Becky and Christine, from *Foxglove*, were there, still trying to line up a ride on someone's yacht so they wouldn't have to go home. I was surprised that two single women with their looks were having more trouble than I did in securing a crewing position, but I was sure they would eventually find an agreeable captain. Christine surprised me that night by presenting me with a woven friendship bracelet that she had made for me, and she tied it around my right wrist as we shared a piña colada and told me it was for good luck.

I would miss Georgetown and all its friendly people. It was easy to see the allure of this place that kept some people anchored for a year or more. I was convinced, though, that there had to be something even better farther south. This wasn't the tropical paradise I had dreamed of. I wanted to see islands with jungle-covered mountains and cascading waterfalls. There were no streams of any kind in the Bahamas, and only limited vegetation. I was looking for a place like the Dominica that Scully described, where I could set up camp indefinitely and live off the land and sea like a beachcomber.

One thing was for certain—after what I'd seen so far, I had no desire to go back to the mainland anytime soon. All I wanted was to keep moving and to keep seeing new places. I wanted to continue living close to nature, to wake up each day and watch the sun rising out of the sea, and to sleep and eat whenever I was tired or hungry. I couldn't imagine going back to the 9-to-5 existence I had known before. My watch had long been packed away somewhere deep inside the kayak. Time didn't mean much here. I was living on island time now, and it was the happiest time I had ever known.

# SIX

# CELEBRATION

The north wind stepped readily into the harness which we had provided, and pulled us along with good will. Sometimes we sailed as gently and steadily as the clouds overhead.

**—HENRY DAVID THOREAU**

We hauled *Celebration*'s anchor on a Thursday morning and motored out of the anchorage at Stocking Island in company of three other boats that were also headed south. Though I had only been in Georgetown a little over two weeks, it seemed like much longer, and leaving these familiar surroundings and friends was almost like leaving home again at the start of my journey. *Heron I* was one of the other three boats accompanying us, but Lawrence and Laura only planned to explore some other islands in the southeastern Bahamas, since they had to be back in Winnipeg by June. I didn't expect to see them again, as their smaller boat could not keep up with *Celebration* for long. We sailed east from Great Exuma to get around the north end of Long Island, the next large island in the Bahamian archipelago, and then I had what I thought would be my last conversation with my Canadian friends as they set a diverging course for the southeast end of that island.

The other two sailboats that left with us were headed to the Virgin Islands and planned to make most of the same stops we would be making en route. *Texas Tumbleweed* was a forty-four-foot ketch crewed by a

Frank Holzmacher boarding his yacht *Celebration*, in Puerto Plata harbor, Dominican Republic. This was shortly after we weathered the storm on the passage from the Caicos Islands.

family from Houston, and *Cat Ballou* was an unusual thirty-three-foot cat-rigged cruising boat built by a Florida company called NonSuch. The couple sailing her were residents of St. Croix and had flown to Florida to purchase the vessel brand new and were now delivering it back to their home island.

Once under way, I found that *Celebration*'s modern rigging and controls were much easier to understand than those of the arcane but character-laden *Whisper*. When we had cleared the north end of Long Island and reached the safety of deep water, we set a course to the southeast, taking advantage of another cold front and its favorable winds. This was my first sailing experience under truly ideal conditions, and it was sheer joy once we cut off the engine and the powerful cutter-rigged vessel shouldered her way through the swell at an effortless seven knots. The nearly new white Dacron of the sails stood out in sharp contrast to the impossibly blue sky that accompanied the norther. The autopilot, nicknamed "Charlie" by Jo and Frank, proved its worth as a virtual crewmember by taking the helm while we lounged on the cushioned seats of *Celebration*'s cockpit and watched the rugged windward coast of Long Island slide past our starboard beam.

Jo was the self-appointed navigator on *Celebration*, and she calculated that we would reach Providenciales, in the Caicos, on the third day after two nights of nonstop sailing. It would be my longest passage at sea so far. Frank said we would need to go onto a four-hour rotating watch system, so that everyone could get adequate rest and someone was always in the cockpit to stay alert for shipping traffic.

The first night at sea on *Celebration* was a night of magic I will never forget, and that memory has kept me going back to sea ever since. Unlike the night I crossed the Gulf Stream on *Whisper*, it was a moonless night with nothing to detract from the brilliance of a perfectly clear, star-filled sky. The Milky Way formed a great curving arc of sparkling fire, seemingly close enough to be raked by our tall mast. And just off our stern, the North Star, Polaris, hung at the lowest angle to the horizon that I had ever seen it—twenty-three degrees and twenty-seven minutes—indicating that we had crossed the Tropic of Cancer and had officially left the Temperate Zone.

Perfect weather and perfect wind continued for the duration of our passage. We passed within sight of Mayaguana Island and the Plana Cays—the last we would see of the Bahamas—early the third morning. Later that day, in the Caicos Passage, I sat staring out at an empty horizon when out of nowhere a U.S. Navy warship loomed into view off our port beam and passed within a mile of our position, steaming east at about twenty knots.

Jo and Frank had a library of charts and cruising guidebooks to the islands they planned to visit, with explicit instructions for safely entering practically every navigable harbor in the West Indies. The entrance to Providenciales was a tricky one, according to the book. Shallow banks of twenty-foot depths surrounded the island, and these banks were studded with scattered coral reefs that reached almost to the surface. *Celebration*'s designed draft was six feet, but she probably sat several more inches below her waterline, loaded as she was with all of Josephine and Frank's worldly possessions, several month's supply of food, plus water and fuel.

The ketch *Texas Tumbleweed* was a vessel of equally deep draft, though apparently faster, as we had lost sight of her early in the passage only to see her once more as we approached the harbor at Provo just before sunset. The guidebook for the Caicos Islands said that safe entrance to this harbor required visual navigation, only possible when the sun was high enough in the sky to make it easy to discern water depth by the various hues of blue and green in the crystalline water. Deep blues indicated ample depths and the correct channel. Light turquoise green was to be seen over the sand banks, turning to pale yellow in extreme shallows; patches of dark brown indicated coral—to be avoided at all costs. Our approach time was wrong. The sun was already too low to illuminate the channel. We caught up to *Texas Tumbleweed* and cautiously followed from a quarter mile astern as Stan, the man of the family, steered the yacht confidently despite the low light conditions. His teenaged daughter Rachael stood on the bow pulpit bagging the headsail as they approached. It was obvious that they were anxious to make port after the three-day passage, and I was too. I looked forward to going ashore again and to seeing what, if anything, was different about the Caicos Islands, which looked on the chart to be merely an extension of the archipelago that makes up the Bahamas.

Frank grabbed the binoculars from their holder on the bulkhead near the companionway as we slowly followed Stan's lead.

"That fool's headed straight for the reef!" Frank screamed as he backed off on *Celebration*'s throttle.

Stan seemed to realize his mistake at the last minute when he suddenly brought *Texas Tumbleweed* about hard to port. The peaceful bliss of our open sea passage ended for good when Jo and Frank began a fierce argument about the correct location of the entrance. They tore the guidebook out of each other's hands and fought for possession of the helm. Meanwhile, Stan was tacking back and forth just outside the reef, at a loss as to what to do next. His calls on the radio for advice briefly interrupted Josephine and Frank's dispute, but no one could decide what to do.

"We've got to go to the left of those rocks there, then turn in!" Josephine said, as she grabbed the helm and pushed Frank forcefully aside.

"What-a-ya, outta ya mind or something, Josephine?" Frank threw his hands up in disgust, his face flushed with anger. "Just go ahead and put us on the reef!"

"SHUT UP! I can see where I'm going. It's just like the book says."

"I'm tellin' ya, Josephine. We've got to go to the *right* of those rocks! Can't ya see tha freakin' channel? What-a-ya, blind or something?"

I began to sense that neither of them knew what they were talking about. I grabbed the guidebook and looked at the situation myself. My interpretation of the instructions was completely different, but when I tried to express this, I was quickly cut off. I decided to let them have it out. It was actually quite amusing to listen to their verbal battle, carried out at a New York pace that I could barely follow. Frank threw a fit and ranted and raved, but he didn't have a chance in hell of convincing the stubborn Josephine that he knew anything about navigation. He stormed below to return to the novel he had been reading before being interrupted by our arrival at the island, telling Josephine to go ahead and run it aground, but not to ask his help in getting off the reef.

The sea was calm so there was no real danger to life if we wrecked the $150,000 yacht there. My kayak was safely on deck, and I could just put it over the side and be on my way. I was only crew, and the navigational decisions were not my concern. All of this channel and reef business was new to me anyway. My kayak could go anywhere there was at least four inches of water, and had I been approaching this island in it,

I would have simply paddled up near the reef and looked for a slot to pass through into the sheltered lagoon beyond.

Stan stumbled upon the right entrance by chance, and managed to steer *Texas Tumbleweed* safely through. Josephine followed. The channel was right where I had tried to say it would be, but I just watched and kept my mouth shut. After witnessing Frank's defeat, I wasn't about to get into a verbal sparring match with Josephine. Once in the channel, Stan opened up the throttle again, thinking he was free to cruise the remaining three miles or so to the Provo anchorage. But he strayed too far to the left side of the channel and slammed right into a small, isolated coral head. He was hard aground when we caught up.

We could not put *Celebration* at risk by maneuvering in near the coral to get close enough to put a towline on *Texas Tumbleweed*. Frank came on deck and held us in position in deep water while Rachael rowed out from the stranded yacht in their inflatable dinghy with an anchor so they could attempt to kedge off the reef. Rachael was barely making progress in the dinghy, so I dove over the side and swam over to help her. We managed to get the anchor set, but the windlass would not budge the heavy-displacement ketch. The crew of *Texas Tumbleweed* would spend the night hard aground, until morning high tide came to float them off. I swam back to *Celebration,* and we motored slowly into the anchorage. We were anchored by nightfall, and Josephine hoisted the orange quarantine flag. No customs officials would come out tonight, as it was a Sunday, so we retired early after a quick dinner. I slept for twelve hours in the peaceful anchorage, where for the first time since leaving Georgetown I could stretch out in my bunk without having to brace my feet against the bulkheads to keep from being slammed into the side of the hull.

*Texas Tumbleweed* arrived in the anchorage the next morning, and Stan reported that yesterday's accident did no damage to her hull. After they settled into the anchorage, the dinghies were launched, and we all went ashore together to report to a bar and grill called the Aquatic Center, where customs officers would meet us. The formalities were simple, and we were given clearance into the Turks and Caicos for a period of two weeks, which was far more than I hoped we would need. I didn't plan to bother unloading my kayak, as Josephine and Frank assured me that we would proceed south to the Dominican Republic as soon as a window of favorable weather presented itself.

Prices at the Aquatic Center were outrageous, but it was the hub of social activity for boaters in the anchorage. This harbor was certainly no Georgetown, and the surrounding countryside of the island was much more arid and desolate-looking than anything I had seen in the Bahamas. The Aquatic Center was isolated on a long barren point several miles from the main town of Providenciales. We were told that it was easy to hitchhike on the island, so I walked with Jo and Frank to the main road, which was unpaved, and soon we flagged down a local islander driving a dump truck. The driver wanted us to know about every new construction project on the island, and talked nonstop about the recent development that had resulted from the island's popularity among divers from all over the world. Exceptionally clear waters, unspoiled reefs, and a tax-free environment for businesses had led to almost overnight transformation on this dusty speck of rock between the Bahamas and the Caribbean proper.

All I could see from the windows of the truck was a barren desert of rolling hills with dense thickets of scrub brush and cactus. It seemed more fit for lizards and birds than anything else. But when we arrived in the town of Providenciales, I was surprised to see brand-new storefronts of glass and steel, with parking lots filled with late-model European and American sedans and sports cars. It was certainly the most modern community I had seen since leaving Key Largo. We got off the truck at a pizza restaurant owned by Californians and ordered an astronomically priced pepperoni pizza and a round of beers. I wouldn't last long on my budget in this place, that was for sure, but Frank and Josephine were paying the bill as long as I was crewing on *Celebration*.

I thought we would leave Provo after a couple of nights in the anchorage, but the weather dashed my hopes. The cold front that had given us a free ride south from Georgetown had blown itself out, and now firmly in the trade wind belt of the tropics, we faced a headlong bash against 20-to-25-knot winds for the one-hundred-mile passage to the Dominican Republic. Josephine and Frank wanted to sit it out and hope for another cold front.

Things livened up a bit in Provo when George Bouillon came sailing in one day on *Winning Edge*. I had become good friends with this free-spirited Frenchman while hanging out with him in Georgetown. I hadn't expected to ever see him again, since he wasn't ready to go when we left. He was still single-handing when he arrived in Provo, having failed in his attempts to find an eager female first mate to accompany him. He said he was disgusted with the Canadian and American yachting women in the Bahamas and was ready to continue his quest among the reputedly beautiful and willing women of the Dominican Republic.

George was undaunted by the expensive beer prices at the Aquatic Center, insisting that I join him for round after round as he talked of his plans. He said that he had left France at the age of twenty and moved to British Colombia. He had worked as chef on an oil rig off Alaska and had made enough money to retire at forty, at least for a little while. As soon as he quit his job, he made his way to Miami and paid twelve thousand dollars for *Winning Edge*, an old but solid fiberglass Hunter 27. He took off for the Bahamas immediately in his new boat and planned to sail to Martinique, where he had a friend, and where he could live indefinitely as a French citizen. Like me, George wasn't worried too much about the distant future. His primary concern was to find adventure and a good time, and a female friend to share it with.

Our stay in Provo stretched into a week; then finally the trade winds slacked off enough for us to motor-sail across the Caicos Banks to the southern end of the island group, which would be our jumping-off point for the passage to Hispaniola. The crossing of the shallow banks took an entire day of motoring at five or six knots and demanded constant vigilance because of the many coral heads scattered at random everywhere near our route. I spent most of the day leaning out from the bow pulpit of *Celebration*, looking for subtle changes in water color that indicated shoals and reefs and giving hand signals to Frank to indicate which direction to dodge. At the end of the day, we anchored near a small island named Ambergris Cay and were soon joined by *Winning Edge* and *Texas Tumbleweed*, who had followed us across the banks.

Foul winds again thwarted our plans to sail the following day, so we motored the twenty miles or so to South Caicos Island in a drizzling rain. Cockburn Town, the settlement on South Caicos, was quite the opposite of Provo. There were no modern buildings or shiny cars here. The waterfront was lined with derelict and run-down fishing boats, and everywhere was rusting automobiles and farm machinery. In contrast to Provo's population of outsiders, Cockburn Town consisted exclusively of black islanders, as far as I could tell, and the dwellings were similar to those in the rural settlements of the Bahamas, only less well kept and less colorful. The place had a depressing atmosphere and the residents appeared listless, as if aware the rest of the world was far away and no one was coming here except others like us who were only passing through on the way to somewhere else. There were few trees along the dusty streets of Cockburn Town, so most of the people sat in the shade of their modest houses to avoid the harsh rays of the tropical sun that blazed down when the clouds passed and the drizzle stopped.

George and I headed for town in his dinghy as soon as the anchors hit the bottom, not to be stopped by outer appearances from checking out this new place and having a few beers with the locals. We found a general store that sold everything from tractor parts to clothes, and there we purchased cold Heinekens and sat on the wooden benches out front with a few old men and boys, answering their questions about our respective hometowns. I told them that Cockburn Town reminded me a lot of some of the rural Mississippi towns I knew. We spent the whole afternoon there, drinking beer after beer to survive the sweltering heat, and attracting quite a bit of attention from these islanders who get so few visitors, and hardly any who cared to spend any time talking to them.

It was nearly dark when we returned to the harbor. George rowed me back to *Celebration,* where Josephine invited him to join us for dinner. She had prepared lobster that she bought fresh off a fisherman that afternoon. She had painstakingly put together an exquisite meal, with multiple side dishes to go with the steamed lobster tails, but I don't quite recall the details of the trimmings and certainly not the taste. George and I sat down at the table in a state of hysterical laughter, joking about the ridiculous extravagance of *Celebration*'s plush interior. We were so drunk we devoured the lobster as if we were eating tuna-fish sandwiches or pizza, hardly noticing what it was. If Josephine was offended at the time, I don't remember. After we ate and had another round of Frank's stiff rum drinks, George and I both passed out in the cockpit and slept until pouring rain woke us sometime after midnight. The next morning Josephine told us that she wouldn't make the mistake of wasting lobster on us again, saying that we wouldn't have known the difference between fresh lobster and frozen fish sticks.

After a couple of days of waiting in the anchorage off South Caicos, whiling the time away with diving for conch, which littered the sand bottom, we finally heard an encouraging weather report. A cold front was headed our way, promising a day or two of northerly winds. Preparations were made for the passage, and we said our good-byes to Stan and the rest of the crew of *Texas Tumbleweed.* They planned to attempt a direct passage to Puerto Rico, bypassing the Dominican Republic altogether. George, however, would sail with us, or at least attempt to keep up with us, on the slower *Winning Edge.* Before we left, he talked me into loaning him a hundred dollars, in case we arrived in Puerto Plata at separate times. He said he was short of cash for clearing customs but that he could get some wired to a bank in Puerto Plata and pay me back immediately. I agreed, even though one hundred dollars was a lot of money to me when weighed against the total I had remaining in my stash.

My spirits were high as we sailed out of the anchorage early in the morning. The cold front had arrived as predicted, bringing a shift in the wind, heavy cloud cover, and light rain, but the air was still warm and tropical. I was elated to be leaving the flat and arid islands of the Bahamas and the Turks and Caicos. In the Dominican Republic, I looked forward to seeing mountains that reach as high as ten thousand feet in the island's interior and forests that I had heard were lush and jungle-like. I also looked forward to immersion in a different culture, where I could practice my high-school Spanish. In addition, the exchange rate was reputed to be good, so, unlike the Bahamas, it was a cheap place to travel, and I could stretch my limited funds further. I was glad that George was going there, and looked forward to spending more time hanging out with him.

As we dropped the Caicos Islands astern, the rain steadily increased with a building north wind, requiring us to wear foul weather gear on deck and to put a reef in the mainsail to maintain control. Josephine estimated the crossing to take about twenty hours. At a steady six and a half knots, we were on schedule. Although George left the harbor a half hour ahead of us, by early afternoon we had passed him and left him far astern.

Josephine had cooked a big pot of what she called "schooner stew" before we left, anticipating rough conditions that would make working in the galley at sea difficult. The hot stew of cabbage, potatoes, and kielbasa sausage was a blessing as we huddled in the cockpit of *Celebration*, ruthlessly tossed by a following sea and drenched by rain. I felt sorry for George as I ate. He never thought of things like cooking in advance, and on the radio he told us he was eating crackers and cheese and steering by hand because his "auto-matic pee-lot" was no longer working.

The romance of sailing to Hispaniola was beginning to wear off by late afternoon, and all I wanted was to get to dry land. The rain was relentless and *Celebration* rolled sickeningly in seas that were rising ten to fifteen feet beneath our stern and breaking in a hissing roar of white froth. But my misery was temporarily forgotten when Frank yelled and pointed at something on the surface of the gray waves off our port beam.

Whales! They were the first I had ever seen, and they were up close and personal . . . and *huge*! There were several of them, diving and rolling to the surface, and waving their giant tail flukes in the air. We weren't sure if we should be worried or not. They were less than a hundred yards away, all of them bigger than *Celebration*. Whether out of playfulness or malice, whales have been known to ram yachts. I had just read Steven Callahan's book *Adrift*, in which he recounted his experience of having his yacht stove-in in the middle of the night in the Atlantic Ocean, most likely by a whale. His boat had sunk immediately, leaving him mid-ocean in a life raft and beginning an ordeal of survival that lasted seventy-six days.

The whales came no closer to *Celebration* and soon disappeared into the gray seascape that surrounded us, obscured by sheets of torrential rain. We had another visitor before nightfall, a frigate bird that landed boldly on the dodger right over the cockpit, apparently so exhausted that it no longer had any fear of humans. It stayed with us several hours before flying away into the stormy night.

George called us after midnight, talking so fast in his broken English that we could barely understand him. He had been motor sailing to maintain speed as he did not have a complete sail inventory on board and did not have a properly sized jib for these conditions. His engine had quit, and he was working frantically to get it started again so he could keep up with us. He had lost sight of our stern light and wanted us to signal him with Frank's bright searchlight. He had planned to maintain visual contact with us throughout the passage, as he had no means of navigation other than a compass and relied on Josephine's satellite navigation fixes for his approximate position. I was beginning to realize that George was poorly prepared for the voyage he was attempting, and that he relied heavily on others to get him out of trouble. I went on deck and waved the light back and forth in the direction we thought he would be, and after a few minutes we saw his answering signal light and pinpointed him about five miles east of us.

The wind was still increasing, forcing us to put a double reef in the main and take down the jib. Frank started the engine to help maintain control, saying the reefed mainsail would help stabilize the rolling if we left it up. I was feeling the first symptoms of seasickness and was shivering from the cold. It was not supposed to be cold in the tropics, but here in the pouring rain and wind in the middle of the night, I felt as cold as I had ever been. I couldn't imagine what George was going through, trying to get his engine running, working in the lurching cabin of *Winning Edge* amid diesel fumes, all the while trying to stay on course under sail and maintain contact with us. It was all I could do just to hang onto the rail and stay in *Celebration*'s cockpit without puking over the side.

By 3 A.M., Josephine's latest fix put us about twenty miles off the coast of the Dominican Republic. The rain had slacked off enough to permit us to see a faint glow of land lights to the south. The seas had not diminished but instead had grown frightfully bigger, building to steep hills of black water that crested and broke in resounding crashes like surf hitting a reef.

George was evidently experiencing the same conditions when he called on the radio, screaming: "I am in ze big trouble! I can't start my engine. I am going on ze rocks!"

But we knew he could not be any closer to land than we were. I tried to reassure him. "Look, George! Can't you see the lights? With the binoculars, I can almost see ze beautiful girls of Puerto Plata!" I said, mocking his accent.

This only made him mad. He screamed back that he was in deep trouble and this was "no time to make ze joke." He wanted to know if we could come and get him—somehow get close enough to throw him a rope and tow him to the harbor.

"What-a-ya, outta ya mind?' Frank asked when he heard this. "We can't get anywhere near him in seas like this. Both boats would be smashed to bits."

Josephine and I argued that we had to do something to try and help him, but Frank said we were crazy. "There's nothing we *can* do. Look around you."

He was right. The seas had grown from frightening to terrifying proportions. I had heard of such waves but never really believed the sea could get like this. Near-vertical walls of water surrounded us on all sides, until we were lifted to the peak of one and looked down into the yawning black troughs between them. We had to forget about getting to Puerto Plata and focus on survival. Somebody had to climb forward on the wave-washed deck and furl the mainsail to the boom after Frank hauled it down from the cockpit. Wearing a safety harness and tether, I crawled forward as tons of solid water swept the deck and tried to tear me loose from my death-grip on the boom. I wrestled the heavy sail into place and lashed it with a few turns of rope before heading back to the relative safety of the cockpit.

Frank kept the bow on a quartering angle to the breaking waves, using the engine to power up each cresting peak so we wouldn't be broached and capsized. It was the same sensation I had often felt when quartering my kayak up the face of a roller in the surf zone, only this was a forty-two-foot, fifteen-ton yacht that was going almost straight up each time we climbed a wave face. If we encountered a wave much bigger, I feared the yacht would be pitch-poled backwards, end over end. It had happened to others, even on bigger vessels. I felt helpless in this type of boat. In my kayak I could maintain balance with my paddle, sticking a blade into the face of a breaker to prevent a capsize as the wave carried me with it. But on *Celebration* we had no recourse but to rely on the stabilizing effect of the heavy ballast keel beneath us.

Occasionally a breaker would crash over the foredeck in such a way as to send a wall of water into the cockpit. Frank and I would momentarily be up to our waist until *Celebration*'s buoyancy brought us out of the wave and the water was shed overboard through the scuppers. Frank said he had seen such waves while serving on board a Navy ship, and he estimated their average height at thirty feet.

The well-designed Tayana 42 rode out the fury of the waves though, and I was grateful to be weathering this storm in such a seaworthy vessel and not an old wooden boat like *Elske* or a smaller one like *Winning Edge*. What could George do in this with no engine? We had not heard any more calls from him and were too busy to try and call him. Frank was certain that the cheaply built Hunter 27 would not survive this storm but said that maybe George would be lucky enough to get washed up on the coast somewhere. I couldn't help thinking the worst, that I would never see my friend again. I tried to imagine being out there in the kayak and began to think that if I lived to walk on dry land again, I would never board a boat again. I would kiss the dock the minute I landed, and go as high into the mountains and as far from the sea as I could get.

It seemed that dawn would never come as we motored into the breakers, each time expecting to encounter the wave that would do us in. When daylight did come, the seascape was even more frightening than it had been at night, as we were able to see the true proportions and fury of the waves. There was still no sign of George, and Josephine's calls to *Winning Edge* on the VHF went unanswered. It was hard to imagine that we would not see the jovial, happy-go-lucky Frenchman again, but the reality of these conditions could not be denied.

Despite our motoring into the direction of the wind and sea, we had been carried to the south along our rhumb line to Puerto Plata by the storm, and a couple hours after daylight the waves diminished markedly and the skies began to clear. The mountain that looms over Puerto Plata harbor was clearly visible, and we found the marked channel leading into sheltered waters. As we motored into the safety of the harbor and left the open sea behind, we were shocked to see *Winning Edge* already anchored, her mast swinging like an inverted pendulum as the hull rocked violently in the surge of the partially exposed anchorage.

The dominating feature of Puerto Plata harbor is the towering green mountain that rises abruptly just inland from the city. The peak was shrouded in mist and clouds, even though the rest of the sky had cleared and the rain had stopped. I knew from reading Jo's guidebook that this lush, forest-cloaked mountain was Mt. Isabela de Torres, and that it reached a height of 2,900 feet, which made it seem massive for a coastal peak. Lesser mountains and hills stretched away into the distance on each side of the main summit, all covered in carpets of green vegetation. After being at sea and among the desert islands of the Bahamas for weeks, the scent of all this greenery was overwhelming. I took deep breaths and stared at the mountain. Never had I seen such a beautiful sight, and never had I thought land could look so good. The horrors of the predawn hours were now only a memory, and I was close enough to shore that if I wanted to, I could swim to the beach.

The harbor itself was crowded and bustling with noisy activity. To the right of the anchorage was a long commercial dock where an ancient-looking gray warship and a tired old freighter were moored. Cranes unloaded dozens of containers with the Tropicana fruit company logo from the freighter, and stacked them like toys on the concrete wharf. The warship, which appeared to be of War World II vintage, was obviously a hand-me-down from the U.S. Navy, and was now flying the red, white, and blue flag of the Dominican Republic.

The opposite side of the harbor was flanked by another long dock, lower to the water and lined with all sorts of rusty towboats, barges, commercial fishing vessels, and dilapidated wooden sailing vessels. The sounds of men working drifted across the harbor from this busy dock: hammers and chisels ringing against steel hulls, electric drills and grinders, diesel engines running, and instructions and orders barked in Spanish.

Another shorter concrete dock that adjoined this work area was reserved for foreign yachts, and a dozen or so were moored there Mediterranean-style, with their sterns facing the dock and anchors off the bow. In the no-man's-land in the middle of the harbor, about fifteen more yachts were anchored in the surge with *Winning Edge*. Everywhere, the smell of diesel was overpowering, and behind the harbor, in the direction of the city, could be heard the sounds of cars, trucks, and motorcycles, all seemingly blowing their horns at once. These sights, sounds, and smells were a sensory overload to all three of us after spending so much time in the tranquil Bahamas.

We circled among the anchored yachts looking for a sizable open space to drop *Celebration*'s anchor. A larger ketch-rigged vessel flying the Union Jack had apparently dragged anchor during the previous night's storm and was now aground on the muddy, garbage-littered beach at the rear of the harbor. A motor-launch loaded with yelling Dominicans strained to pull the stranded yacht free while two Englishmen on the bow cursed and screamed in an attempt to coordinate the effort. We selected a spot near *Winning Edge* and put down two anchors off the bow to keep from ending up like the British yacht. I called George as soon as we were secure, and he stumbled up on deck, looking quite exhausted and suffering from sleep deprivation.

"My engine . . . it start again." He explained when Frank asked how he had survived those monstrous waves and reached the harbor.

"I'm glad you made it, George. I thought I'd never see my one hundred dollars again," I joked.

"You make ze very bad joke last night," he reminded me. "'George! I can see ze beautiful girls of Puerto Plata!' And all this time I am in ze big sheeet with no engine. This was no time to make ze joke."

After hearing George's story, we all went below, exhausted and ready to sack out after our all-night ordeal. I fell into my bunk in the aft cabin, oblivious to the surge that made my bunk rise and fall two feet and tilt to each side at a sharp enough angle to roll me over. I wedged myself in between the bulkheads and conked out within two minutes.

A mere half hour later, I was awakened by a rapid-fire conversation in Spanish and looked out into the main cabin to see that our boat had been invaded by five customs and immigrations officers. Josephine conversed easily with them in their language while Frank watched with a blank stare, not comprehending a word. The high-school Spanish I had taken ten years before seemed useless now, as the officers slurred their speech and spoke so fast I could hardly tell where one word ended and the next began.

I pulled on a T-shirt and joined them in the main cabin, thinking how strange it seemed to hear these black men, who could have passed for Bahamian islanders or even Mississippians, speaking this language. The officers made a perfunctory search of the yacht's storage lockers, then wrote out receipts for our firearms, which we were required to surrender into their keeping until we cleared customs to leave. They left my bang stick, but took the Beretta pistol, my .22 rifle, and Frank's stainless-steel 12-gauge pump. Josephine paid them thirty dollars for our thirty-day visas, and the officer in charge looked in Frank's liquor cabinet and helped himself to a bottle of Scotch for his tip. With this taken care of, they left in their wooden skiff, and we all went back to our bunks to sleep the day away.

George woke us up banging on the hull from his dinghy and shouting for me to come quickly: "The fellow on *Morning Star* is in ze big sheeet!" I climbed out of my bunk, feeling like I could sleep twelve more hours. I looked at my watch. It was after 7 P.M., and the sky was dark. I didn't know any yacht named *Morning Star*.

"Hurry! He's dragging ze anchor and going to ze beach!" George screamed to prod me on.

I dressed and climbed into George's dinghy. It was blowing at least thirty knots, and the bay was churning with whitecaps. What a way to wake up after crawling out of a dry bunk. We got soaked as George rowed vigorously toward a green-hulled sloop about the size of his own *Winning Edge*. There was no time for introduction as the single-handing skipper greeted us at the stern of his boat and we ran forward to the bow to pull up the dragging anchor while he gunned the engine from the cockpit to give us some slack in the chain. When the anchor was brought on deck from the oil-polluted harbor, it was coated with oozing black sludge, which George and I could not avoid getting all over our hands and clothes, as well as the pristine white decks and foresail of the pretty little sloop. But we saved the boat, and after a half-hour of frantic, back-straining work, we managed to get two anchors securely set and left the grateful skipper of *Morning Star* to sleep the remainder of the night in peaceful security.

George and I cleaned the mud and oil sludge off of us back on *Winning Edge*, and at his insistence, I agreed to go ashore with him for a beer. We rowed to the yacht dock and tied up to a derelict wooden hulk, where we found a greasy ladder to climb up. I forgot all about my promise to kiss the ground the minute I set foot on land, the horrors of the previous night already fading in my memory. There was a tall chain-link fence around the entire port area, and to enter the city we had to go through a gate guarded by three armed soldiers. I wasn't confident that I could remember enough Spanish to buy anything, or even find my way to a store, but George assured me that he had been to Mexico and that he spoke the language like a native.

George led the way like he knew where he was going as we followed the street leading from the port past the office of the Commandante of the Navy and a public park. We passed the Brugal Rum factory at the corner of the first intersection we came to and turned down a narrow side street where businesses with hand-painted signs and locked wooden doors stood deserted. It was well past closing time, but quite a few people mingled about the streets, most turning to stare at us as we passed. In not-so-fluent broken Spanish mixed with French, George inquired as to where we might buy a cold *cerveza*. I quickly realized that his command of the language was scarcely better than mine when we found our way to a store that was little more than a sidewalk vending stand, where beer was sold out an open window. George didn't understand numbers, and I had to negotiate the purchase of the two Cerveza Presidentes we ordered. We were to find out later that this was the most popular beer on the island, a product of the Dominican Republic that, like Brugal Rum, was exported to many countries, including the United States.

The store was a hangout of sorts, and I was surprised to see boys that couldn't have been more than twelve or thirteen buying and drinking beer alongside several men in their twenties. Though we couldn't understand what they were saying, it was clear that we were the subjects of their jokes, as they laughed and talked while we stood there drinking our beers. From somewhere beyond the store came the sound of loud music—a fast-paced merengue beat that reflected the happy and upbeat attitude of Latin culture. There was a sense of excitement in the air here that I had not experienced in the Bahamas, and I looked forward to returning the next day to spend more time exploring this intriguing city. But tonight, unable to carry on a conversation with our drinking buddies and still exhausted from the stormy passage from the Caicos, George and I headed back to the harbor.

When I awoke on *Celebration*, it was a bright and sunny morning and Josephine and Frank were sitting in the cockpit having coffee. I joined them, taken aback as I stepped on deck by the sight of Mt. Isabela de Torres, which seemed much closer and larger on this clear day. The peak was still shrouded in puffy white clouds, but on the lower slopes I could make out the crowns of palm trees thrusting out above a solid carpet of green forest canopy. The waterfront of the harbor was lined with palms as well, growing between run-down shanties and derelict automobiles and small boats. The noise was oppressive—the same sounds of men at work, cars and motorcycles, blasting horns, and yelling people that we had heard upon our arrival. When I commented on this, Frank and Jo said this was why they like Puerto Plata. It made them feel like they were back in New York.

"There's work going on here," Frank said. "I like that."

Not me. Work was the kind of thing I was on this trip to get away from. I much preferred the sound of surf and gulls on the quiet cays of the Bahamas, but I was excited about the mountainous interior of the island, and the possibility that I might be able to do some jungle hiking.

One thing was for sure. I didn't want to unload my kayak in this polluted harbor. There had been a recent oil spill, which explained the black sludge that coated *Morning Star*'s anchor and made such a mess of her decks when George and I brought it aboard. Already *Celebration*'s pristine white hull had an ugly film of black gunk at the waterline. It was just as well that I couldn't launch here. When Josephine and Frank announced that they would probably stay in Puerto Plata for a couple of weeks, I began making plans to tour the interior.

But first, I wanted to explore the city of Puerto Plata. With Josephine's knowledge of Spanish, getting around was no problem. We made our way to the central park and changed dollars for pesos. I was pleasantly surprised that my dwindling dollars here had about six times the buying power they would have back home. I would be able to enjoy my stay and make the best of the time spent waiting on Jo and Frank to decide to sail on.

We found out that the following day was the beginning of Carnival, and Puerto Plata would be transformed into one giant party like New Orleans during Mardi Gras. I decided to see what it was all about and made my way to the park again the next day to a massive parade of lavishly decorated floats portraying island themes. Presidente beer trucks were part of the procession, and cold beer was handed out through the open rear doors to anyone who was thirsty. I caught a ride on a flatbed truck with a crowd of *Dominicanos* and Canadian tourists and did my best to help them finish the Presidentes they carried in a fifty-five gallon drum of ice. We went around in circles for what seemed like hours, finally ending up on the *malecon*, the waterfront drive, where we passed a podium of government officials in military uniforms who watched the parade under guard by a contingent of soldiers. One of them was probably the president of the Dominican Republic, for all I knew. My new Canadian friends and I saluted these officials with upraised beer bottles. We agreed that it was a wonderful country. Was it always like this here?

When the Carnival was over, I was ready to get away from the city. I bought a map of the island in a gift shop near the park, and began studying it to plan my explorations. I had been cooped up on the sailboat for three weeks now, and I was anxious to feel open spaces and to get some privacy and maybe even a bit of solitude.

The map of the huge island baffled me, however. I didn't know where to begin. Hispaniola is the second largest island in the West Indies after Cuba, with a total land area of 29,500 square miles. The Dominican Republic occupies two-thirds of the island, with the western third belonging to Haiti. The map showed hundreds of miles of winding roads connecting scattered cities and towns along the coasts and bisecting the island to connect the north with the Caribbean side. The Cordillera Central, the central range of highest mountains, appeared to the most sparsely populated area, so that's where I intended to go. I didn't have a backpack or any way to carry all my camping gear on an overland trip, so I left with only a daypack containing clothes, raingear, and other bare essentials, planning to figure out where I would stay when I got there.

On my preliminary excursions into Puerto Plata, I learned that getting around on the island was not difficult, since there were a variety of public transportation options. At the gate outside the harbor, I climbed onto the back of a *moto*—one of the 50cc motorcycles whose drivers would carry tourists anywhere in town for two or three pesos—and asked to be taken to the *terminal de gua-guas*. The *gua-guas* are a way of life in the Dominican Republic. Mini-buses that go all over the island, they provide the locals with cheap transportation and conveniently stop to pick up and drop off passengers anywhere along the road. At the terminal in Puerto Plata, there were dozens of *gua-guas* lined up, some already packed to full capacity and pulling out. The drivers zeroed in on me—the gringo tourist with the backpack—and swarmed over me instantly, each offering his services to any place my pocketbook would carry me. I struggled with a word or two of Spanish and pointed to the rugged mountain range in the middle of my map.

"*Si! No problema*," one driver said as he took my bag and whisked me to the door of his little bus, which was already crammed with at least twenty passengers. I had no choice but to squeeze onto the edge of a seat already occupied by a couple with a small boy, and to my amazement, the driver continued to load more passengers. When he was finished, I had a smiling young woman sitting in my lap, and we tore off down the road on our merry way, the passengers singing along with the deafening merengue music that blasted from several overhead box speakers.

Some of the people pressed in around me tried to ask me questions, wondering where I was going, and amused at my wild beard and long hair, which by this time gave me the appearance of a castaway. They told me I looked like *Jesu Cristo*—Jesus Christ—because of the hair and beard. That much I understood, but with my limited vocabulary it was difficult to explain that I had arrived by sailboat, that I was on a kayak trip, and that I was now hoping to see some of the wilder regions of their country by traveling to the mountains. It was hard enough to breathe, much less talk in the stifling heat of the crowded bus. Using his horn more frequently than his brakes, the driver sped like a maniac, passing cars on whichever side seemed most convenient and dodging the chickens, dogs, cows, and children that we encountered in every mile of the roadway.

I made my way into the central mountains after a series of bus and motorcycle rides, and staying in an assortment of cheap hotels in small towns for a week. The interior of the island was much cooler and more temperate than the coast. Pine forests grew on the high slopes of mountains that looked more like they belonged in New Mexico or Arizona than on a tropical island. I spent one whole day horseback riding on a rocky trail into the backcountry, led by a small boy of about ten who took me to the base of an impressive waterfall. There was a lot to explore in the interior of this island, but not being equipped for serious backpacking and not wanting to spend too much of my limited cash on hotels and public transportation, I headed back to the coast where I hoped I could talk Josephine and Frank into moving on.

When I got there, though, I found that they had instead bought tickets to fly back to the States, and they wanted me to guard the boat in their absence. That was fine with me. I would enjoy the privacy. George and I hung out on *Celebration*, taking advantage of the well-equipped galley to cook some impressive feasts. George had finally gotten his money wired to the bank and paid me back, despite the doubts that Josephine and Frank had about his good intentions. In the meantime, while I was away in the mountains, he had asked them to loan him some more money so he could eat.

"Five dollar! Zey wouldn't even loan me ze five dollar!" he laughed as we sat in the lavish cabin of *Celebration*, which to George represented untold wealth.

We joked about untying the dock lines and sailing away on the fine yacht to Fiji or somewhere no one would ever find it.

"We could be past ze canal en Panama before zey are back from New York . . ." George laughed.

While Josephine and Frank were away, I also had other unexpected visitors on *Celebration*. Lawrence and Laura Pitcairn, of *Heron I* showed up on foot at the harbor one day and told me they had decided to sail to the Dominican Republic after all. Their boat was anchored in Manzanillo Bay, near the Haitian border. When Josephine and Frank returned, I took a bus over there and visited with them a few more days, patiently biding my time until the day we would set sail again and I could get on with my kayak trip.

# SEVEN

# A JUNGLE COAST

And o' nights there's fire-flies and the yellow moon,
And in the ghostly palm-trees the sleepy tune
Of the quiet voice calling me, the long low croon
Of the steady Trade Winds blowing.

**—JOHN MASEFIELD, "TRADE WINDS"**

Once we were in deep water beyond the entrance to Puerto Plata harbor, Frank set *Celebration* on an easterly course, paralleling the north coast of the island. Our plan was to motor-sail all night and reach Escondido sometime the following day to break up the long trip to Samana. This leg of the trip has the reputation of being one of the most difficult parts of the Thorny Path route down-island, because of the strong trade winds that sweep the coast directly from the east in the direction cruisers have to go to follow the island chain. The accepted method for dealing with this problem is to travel the coast at night, staying close inshore near the mountains, where a nighttime cooling effect counteracts the trade winds from about midnight until 10 A.M. Cruising this coast under sail in an easterly direction is almost always out of the question, so only those with strong auxiliary engines attempt this route.

We encountered rough seas as soon as we entered the open water, our progress impeded by each breaking wave that crashed into our bow. But nightfall was coming soon, and we could hope for some relief

Escondido Bay, one of the most beautiful hidden coves in the West Indies, north coast of Dominican Republic

if the wind died down as it was supposed to. Frank set the autopilot so we could sit back and relax, but when he let go of the helm the boat only stayed on course for a few seconds before veering off toward the south, in the direction of the rocky coast. He reset it and the same thing happened again and again, until I suddenly recalled what I had done to cause the problem.

The autopilot is controlled by its own below-decks compass. I went down the companionway and opened the storage locker nearest the compass. I had stored two cases of grapefruit juice, packaged in steel cans, just beneath the compass, and this was causing the autopilot to go haywire. I moved the cans, and the pilot began functioning correctly.

The trip below, on my hands and knees with my head in the locker, did not do my stomach any good in these rough conditions, and I returned to the deck nauseous and on the verge of seasickness. This feeling did not go away as we pounded on against the wind and sea. Well past midnight, the wind had scarcely abated, but with *Celebration*'s strong diesel, we were able to make steady progress despite this. The island coastline we passed was sparsely populated, and flickers of man-made light we saw on the black silhouettes of the looming mountains were few and far between. More numerous were the lights of passing freighters and cruise ships farther out to sea on our port side, requiring us to keep a diligent watch to avoid being run down.

When dawn broke we sailed closer inshore within a mile of the cliffs. I could see no beaches where a kayaker seeking refuge from wind and sea could land. The coastline looked like an impregnable fortress, with rows of folded mountains fading away in paler shades of greens and blues to the hazy purple of even higher ranges farther inland. We couldn't see the entrance to Escondido Bay until we were adjacent to it, as it was concealed from all other angles by the mountains. Josephine said that's why it's called *escondido*—the Spanish word for "hidden."

The entrance was a narrow channel of deep indigo blue water extending right up to the edge of the mountains. We passed close beneath jungle-covered hills and sheer cliffs draped with cascades of green vines. I could see wisps of smoke rising from the tops of the surrounding ridges, indicating scattered dwellings, and on the more gentle slopes, people had planted hundreds of coconut palms that lifted their feathery crowns above the surrounding mat of green undergrowth. At the back of the small, horseshoe-shaped bay was a crescent beach of dark brown sand, backed by a thick grove of more coconut palms. Smoke rose from the grove, and I could make out small thatched huts nestled in among the shadows of the palm trunks. It was a South Seas scene that I would have expected in Tahiti or Bora Bora, but not less than a thousand miles away from the mainland coast of Florida.

There were no other cruising boats in the bay, so following the advice in Josephine's guidebook, we dropped anchor far from the beach. Foreign yachts are allowed to anchor here, but since it is not an official port of entry, shore visits are not allowed. The guidebook said that locals have been known to swim out during the night to steal what they could off of yachts, hence the warning about anchoring well out. We had not been settled in long before we saw a dugout canoe put in from the beach and head straight for us. In it were three men, two paddling and the other, who wore a tattered olive-drab military uniform, sitting in the middle with an ancient-looking rifle cradled in his arm. When they pulled alongside, the uniformed man informed Josephine that he was the *commandante* for the Port of Escondido, and requested permission to come aboard. In the cabin, he looked over *Celebration*'s documentation, which he obviously couldn't read, and after asking a few questions and demanding a bottle of rum, gave us permission to stay.

We had no other visitors from the village and slept through the day as best we could in the rolling surge of the poorly protected anchorage. We woke well after dark, and Josephine cooked a hearty meal of her schooner stew to give us energy for another night of sailing. The sky was clear, and the stars seemed much closer than they had from the harbor at Puerto Plata, with its surrounding city lights. Only flickering firelight came from the dwellings on the beach here, and the silence was wonderful after a month of nerve-wracking noise in Puerto Plata harbor.

We waited until 3 A.M. to leave Escondido, and this time the downdraft effect from the mountains did seem to make a difference in the winds. The charts indicated several hundred fathoms of water right up close to shore in this area, so we stayed in close and had a spectacular view of the mountains when dawn broke. The coastline here was still fortress-like, with towering cliffs spilling into the sea. At one point we passed the gaping entrance to a sea cave, its roof at least fifty feet above the breakers.

To reach Samana Bay, we had to round a rugged cape known as Cabo Cabron. Off this point, we were overtaken by a small but fierce squall, with gusts strong enough to knock *Celebration* flat on her starboard beam before Frank and I could ease the mainsheet and spill the wind from the sail. Drenching rain fell from one small cloud in an otherwise sunny blue sky for about fifteen minutes, and then it was gone, leaving us with smooth sailing as we cleared the cape and entered Samana Bay.

Samana Bay is unusually symmetrical in shape, a nearly perfect rectangle, ten miles wide and thirty miles long, with its mouth facing directly to the east and exposed to the full force of the trade winds coming across the Mona Passage. We sailed downwind into the wide bay, passing close to a small whale that surfaced off our port bow. The town of Samana was another seven or eight miles ahead, on the north side of the bay, where a narrow peninsula divides the bay from the Atlantic coast we had just sailed past before rounding the cape. Along this north shore of the bay, we passed gorgeous beaches set at the foot of steep hills covered in thousands of coconut palms. I longed to be in my kayak in such a place and couldn't wait until we were cleared and settled in so I could off-load it for some exploring.

The anchorage at Samana is in a wide harbor separated from the vast open bay by a tiny cay that's connected to the mainland by a footbridge. This cay is the quintessential South Seas deserted island. A rounded green hump rising fifty feet or so above sea level, it is ringed with sandy beaches and bristling with coconut palms that hang out over the water in places. Most of the sailboats present were concentrated in the lee of this cay, and we found an empty space with enough room to anchor and joined them. Frank and I then offloaded the dinghy and mounted the outboard, so we could make the one-mile run across the harbor to report to customs and immigration at the concrete dock in front of the town, where a small Dominican Navy vessel was moored.

The *commandante*, a man of about forty, dressed in green jungle fatigues and polished black boots, had no launch to get out to our boat for the inspection, so we carried him in our dinghy. By this time the trade winds had resumed full force, and the harbor was choppy. The officer's displeasure was evident as the inflatable boat smashed through the chop and quickly soaked us all from the waist down. I hated riding in the dinghy anytime there were even the smallest waves, because its blunt bow just buried itself in them, shipping buckets of water into the boat and throwing spray everywhere.

Despite the soaking, the *commandante* was pleasant enough when he came aboard *Celebration* to take a quick look around. Once again, we were required to surrender our firearms for the duration of our stay in the harbor. The *commandante* took a keen interest in my take-apart AR-7 rifle, and asked me to assemble it for him. It was obvious that he greatly coveted this unique little weapon as he pulled back the slide and looked at the mechanism. Totally out of place on his professional military uniform was the large sheath knife that hung at his side. It was one of those cheap survival knives with the hollow handle and huge, saw-toothed blade that enjoyed such popularity after the release of the Rambo movies. There was a compass in a glass bubble at the end of the hollow hilt, which undoubtedly contained fishhooks, matches, and other survival gear. The blade was housed in a camouflaged plastic sheath. My folding survival rifle would have nicely complemented his armament, preparing him for adventures in the wildest jungles of Hispaniola.

Frank took him back to town with our guns, and later, after catching up on lost sleep, we went ashore to check out our new surroundings. The small town of Samana was mostly concentrated along the *malecon* (the waterfront drive) and was a lot cleaner and more modern than most of Puerto Plata. It was obviously a tourist spot, and we saw plenty of German and French vacationers in the boutiques and restaurants. The only other Americans were yachties like us. The taxis were *motos*—the same tiny motorcycles used in Puerto Plata—but here they had covered carts attached, so they could carry as many as four tourists at a time. There were street vendors pushing handcarts of cold sodas and fresh fruit, and popular among the yachters was an ice cream shop where we treated ourselves to papaya milkshakes.

It quickly became obvious that Jo and Frank were infatuated with Samana and would be in no hurry to leave. The presence of some old friends of theirs from Georgetown—Jack and Veronica—on the motor yacht *English Jack*, made it even more likely that we would be in Samana for quite a while. I was determined not to spend another month cooped up on *Celebration*, and with beckoning beaches and the vast bay around us begging to be explored; I off-loaded and prepared my kayak. There was no oil spill here, and though the water was certainly not Bahamas clear, it was clean.

At first I limited my paddling to the big harbor, using my kayak as a dinghy to go into town and checking out the nearby beaches on the little cay with the footbridge leading to it. Then I studied the charts and began making plans for a tour of the entire bay. I knew that it was restricted and that foreign boats were not supposed to be anywhere but in designated ports of entry, but after seeing the *commandante* and the one navy patrol boat at the dock that never went on patrol, I figured no one would ever know.

The selection of canned goods and other supplies was quite limited in the little grocery stores of Samana, but I bought enough rice, vegetables, and fruit for a week and packed only my most essential camping gear into the kayak, leaving the rest of my belongings on *Celebration*. It was disheartening to see how much corrosion and rust had set in during the long weeks my expensive equipment had been stored on the yacht. I could clearly see that much of my gear was not going to last the duration of my planned trip.

It was hard not to worry about the future as I paddled my loaded kayak west of the anchorage, and out of sight of the town of Samana. It was now April, and I knew that after I got to Puerto Rico, I would barely have enough money left even to start paddling, let alone replace damaged gear and travel another thousand miles over a period of several months. I had less than three hundred dollars left, and I could use it to keep moving until I ran out completely, or I could try to find work somewhere in Puerto Rico. The other option was to fly back to Mississippi where I could work and save enough money to return.

As I left the Samana area and fell into the rhythm of paddling again, I slowly began to leave my worries behind as well. The north shore of the bay was so fascinating that it required my undivided attention. Just a short distance from the anchorage I was passing the thatched huts of fishermen who mended their nets on the brown sand beaches and carved dugout canoes in the shade of palms. I stopped to admire a clear running stream that spilled off a steep jungle slope into the murky waters of the bay. As I sat near this cascade having a simple lunch, frigate birds with long, forked tails wheeled overhead along the edge of the steep cliffs that overlooked the bay.

A barren peninsula jutted south into the bay at a point east of the waterfall, forcing me to make a wide detour where I encountered breaking surf and had to brace with the paddle to keep from capsizing. The heat had been so intense during my first hour of paddling that I had removed my PFD (personal flotation device) and put it across the stern deck of the kayak, where I quickly forgot about it. Now, as I emerged drenched from the surf zone, I discovered that it had been swept away unnoticed. I was angry at myself for being so negligent of such an important piece of equipment, but though I spent an hour paddling back and forth through the waves where I'd lost it, I never saw the life jacket again. It might have been prudent to abort the tour of the bay because of it, but I decided I could go on since I planned to hug the shore during most of the eighty-mile loop anyway.

I found a passable excuse for a campsite in an area of dense mangrove swamp near the mouth of a small stream the first night and, with difficulty, pitched my tent as the mosquitoes descended. The nylon of the tent had begun to rot, and in addition to the pole that had been twice broken in the Bahamas by wind, the shock cords holding the other poles together had parted, leaving me with a jigsaw puzzle of aluminum and fiberglass pieces that would only fit together in one order.

There were fresh footprints of barefoot adults and children in the mud where I had landed, so before turning in for the night I pulled the kayak up close beside my tent and tied it to one of the poles with a string, so I would at least have a chance of hearing a nocturnal thief. No unwelcome visitors came, but before daylight, a heavy rain did, drenching me through the sagging roof of the worn-out tent. It didn't stop until well after sunrise, when I finally crawled out to greet a damp, soggy morning. It was easy to see why this eastern end of Hispaniola is so much lusher than the regions of the island west of Puerto Plata. It had rained every day since we'd arrived in Samana, and I had read that it's because the trade winds bring clouds from the sea that are stopped by these first mountains they encounter on this loftiest of Caribbean islands.

When I left my camp, the bay was dead calm, as the trade winds were completely slack after the nighttime downdrafts. The heat was suffocating due to the lack of a breeze. I passed more thatched huts on the beach and several fishermen in the bay throwing cast nets from their narrow dugouts. Naked children of all ages ran up and down the shore and splashed in the shallows, stopping to stare and wave when they saw my strange version of a canoe. On one otherwise deserted beach, I saw a man building a sizable wooden sailing vessel that was slowly taking shape around its frames in a grove of palms that nearly hid it from the bay. I pulled in to take a look and to talk to him as best I could in my limited Spanish. I gathered that he had been working on the boat for a year and a half, and that he was building it with dreams of sailing to a better life in Puerto Rico. The fellow expressed concern that my kayak was much too small for *el mar*—the sea—and warned me about the dangerous winds in Samana Bay. I tried to explain that my boat, though tiny compared to his, was made for *el mar* and impressed him with its seaworthiness by demonstrating an Eskimo roll.

The campsite I found on my second night out on the bay was a vast improvement over the swampy place I had spent the first night. Palms sixty to eighty feet tall overhung the water from the narrow strip of beach where I landed, and behind this beach a freshwater spring filled a rock basin at the foot of the bluffs above before spilling into the bay. I climbed the thirty feet to the top of the bluffs and found a flat mesa, lush with palms, ferns, banana plants, and wildflowers that formed a tropical garden. A massive tree with weird aerial roots hanging from its branches to the ground shaded an idyllic tent site, so I hauled all my gear up there where I could have a view of the bay. When my camp was set up, I spent the rest of the afternoon gathering coconuts and sampling the breadfruit and soursops I found in the trees nearby.

For dinner that night, I cooked my last packet of Spaghetti Bolognese from Operation Raleigh, and watched as thousands of fireflies twinkled against the background of the jungle beyond my camp. The sound of crickets chirping filled the air, and the presence of both these familiar nighttime insects filled me with thoughts of Mississippi. I could not recall ever hearing crickets or seeing fireflies in the Bahamas during all the time I spent camping there.

There was another town called Sanchez on the north shore of Samana Bay, and halfway between it and my campsite on the bluff, I passed a narrow harbor I had not seen on the map and was startled to see a large warship moored there. I veered to the south to give the ship a wide berth, hoping no one on board would notice my tiny kayak from three miles away. I knew that it was invisible to most radar systems because I had asked the skippers of several yachts in the Bahamas if they could detect me on their radar and they said they couldn't. This could be a decided advantage in a place like this, where I was not supposed to be at all. I stayed well offshore the rest of the morning and set a direct course for the western end of the box-shaped bay.

This end of the bay is the only shore not bounded by steep rocky bluffs and small pocket beaches. The uppermost reach of the estuary is instead low and swampy, with mangrove forests like those of the Everglades reaching far out into the water and forming a maze of channels around the mouth of the Rio Yuna, a large river that empties into the bay. This mangrove forest was even taller and more forbidding than those of the Everglades, but near the mouth of the river I found a small bayou winding beneath a tunnel of interlocking branches and decided to take a side trip to look around. Just inside the entrance, the mangroves closed overhead, completely blocking out the sun and creating a mysterious sanctuary of perpetual twilight. Though I expected at any moment to attract a vicious attack of mangrove insects, I did not get bitten by a single mosquito, deer fly, or no-see-um. I followed this enchanting waterway for more than a mile before turning back to retrace my route to the bay.

By the time I had eaten lunch while drifting in the silence of the flooded forest, the trade winds had kicked in for the day, and upon returning to open water I was greeted by muddy brown breakers that pounded the sandbars at the mouth of the river. It was a dangerous place to be caught in high wind because of the effect of the river current flowing against the wind, creating steep, unpredictable wave shapes. I ran aground on several mudflats before reaching deeper water. Once clear of the shallows, it took three hours of hard paddling in the wind to reach the southwest corner of the bay.

My map showed no settlements in this area, and I knew that it was, on paper at least, a Dominican version of a national park, called Los Haites. Cliffs towered above the bay here, and I followed the shoreline close in until I found a narrow fjord-like channel between a break in the limestone walls and paddled in to seek refuge from the wind and waves. It was like entering another world once I left the chaos of the open bay behind me. The channel was as smooth as a pond, the silence broken only by my splashing paddle. I passed a network of bamboo structures floating in the water that looked like a primitive but elaborate fish trap and indicated that someone frequented this hidden canyon. At the far end of the waterway was a tiny strip of beach piled high with discarded oyster shells. The beach was only about fifty feet wide, framed on both sides by cliffs, but the area directly behind it appeared to be a valley, overflowing with green jungle that pushed out toward the beach and climbed the steep slopes on both sides. I landed and discovered a footpath that led into this forest. The immensity of the trees and the variety of greenery surrounding me was stunning. I lost no time digging my shoes out of the kayak, applying insect repellant, and starting off up the trail with my machete in hand.

The valley turned out to be a sort of box canyon, and at the rear the trail climbed rapidly in a series of switchbacks, winding between moss-covered boulders the size of trucks and beneath a closed canopy of greenery. From an outcrop a couple hundred feet up, I had a splendid view of the lush valley I had just walked through. Beyond that point, the trail disappeared into the forest again and followed a dry streambed farther inland.

The exotic vegetation surrounding this pathway included tree ferns twenty feet tall, lianas as thick as my legs, and countless varieties of flowers, growing both from the ground and from epiphytic plants that clung in clusters to the sides of the trees. I hiked until I reached a level plateau at the top of the valley, soaked with sweat from the difficult climb in the greenhouse-like humidity of the forest. I wanted to go on, but decided it might not be wise to leave my boat and gear unattended any longer. This trail was obviously well used and had to connect the bay with a village or small community somewhere beyond this forest. It would only be a matter of time before someone would come along and discover my strange vessel on the little beach.

Back at my boat, I set up the tent near the water's edge and slung my hammock just inside the forest. This was the sort of tropical paradise I had dreamed about all those months I spent planning my trip, and I was not about to get in a hurry to leave it. I spent the rest of the afternoon exploring the immediate area near my camp, looking for water and food. Two tall coconut palms stood nearby, loaded with drinking nuts that were nearly impossible to reach, hanging as they were at least 50 feet above the ground and accessible only by a difficult climb up near-vertical trunks. Wild banana plants were everywhere, but they yielded no fruit that I could find. I knew I could get water from the stems if I needed it badly enough, but I could find no surface water anywhere in the valley. I would have been content to stay in this tropical garden indefinitely if I had been able to locate a reliable water supply.

I spent the second day in a more diligent search for wild fruits, and turned up bananas, oranges, breadfruit, and soursops. In my hammock

I spent hours lying on my back looking up at the strange birds that flitted about in the foliage, and listening to the raucous calls of others hidden in the deeper recesses of the forest. Like most of my gear, the net hammock was rotten from constant exposure to moisture in the past months, and by late afternoon it finally parted and dumped me heavily on the ground, ending my perfect idyll.

My solitude also ended the following morning, when just after breakfast I heard voices and then footsteps coming along the trail from the jungle. A moment later, three young black men walked into view. They were much more surprised to see a long-haired gringo sitting there beside a nylon tent and a weird-looking turquoise canoe than I was at their sudden appearance out of the bush. All three were barefoot and dressed in dirty trousers and shirts that were near rags. Each man carried a string bag bulging with fruit and vegetables, and like all the rural *Dominicanos* I had seen, they each carried a machete—the tropical tool of a thousand uses.

They didn't speak a word of English, but with my improving Spanish I was able to learn that they lived a few kilometers inland, along the trail I had followed out of the valley. They had walked here on this Saturday morning to meet a boat that would take them across the bay to Sanchez, where they would find a *gua-gua* to take them to the *mercado* in Samana. They were going there to sell the produce they carried in the bags. They could scarcely believe that I had paddled all the way from Samana in my kayak, so with my totally inadequate Spanish, I didn't bother trying to explain the larger scope of my trip.

They had a long wait for their boat, so one of them took some large roots out of his bag, and borrowing my largest cooking pot, soaked them in water while he prepared a fire for boiling them. Most experienced outdoorsmen have seen a variety of ways to support a pot over a cooking fire, including propping the edges of the pot up on rocks and the classic cowboy method depicted in old Westerns of suspending the pot from its bail on a stick set up to hang low over the coals. But if I learned nothing else of value on my entire trip, the ingenious method this backwoods Dominican showed me for boiling water on an open fire has since proven useful in so many camps and in so many different places that I don't know how I ever got along without it. He had water boiling in as little time as it would take most modern campers to unpack and set up a high-tech stove. All that is required is three green sticks, each about an inch and a half in diameter and cut from a nearby sapling in about half a minute with a razor sharp machete. The sticks are then pounded into the ground with a handy rock, each set at an inward-leaning angle and driven until the tops are level and just the right distance apart to support the bottom of the pot. Beneath this sturdy tripod of flame-resistant green wood, dry twigs the diameter of a pencil are stacked until they reach just to the bottom of the pot. When set afire, these twigs burn rapidly with a hot flame, even though the size of the fire is ridiculously small by most standards. By keeping this twig fire fed with fresh fuel, it is possible to boil water in as little time as practically any stove and to keep it boiling as long as needed. Even though these root vegetables required almost an hour of cooking, the green support sticks of the tripod held, though they were dried out and almost to the point of combustion by the time the cooking was complete.

When the taro-like vegetables were done, a banana leaf was spread on the ground to serve as a platter, and we squatted around this in a semi-circle. I had a trick of my own that got their attention as surely as their fire-building method riveted mine. I broke out my can of Tony Chachere's Creole Seasoning, sprinkled some on my portion of the vegetables, and invited them to do the same. They sampled the red powdery condiment gingerly at first, by sprinkling a bit on their fingers and licking it off. This resulted in wide grins all around, and then the can was passed around and liberal doses of the spicy Cajun concoction applied to everyone's food. They were so excited about it that I decided to present them the remainder of the can as a gift. I had another half-full can still tucked away in the kayak that would see me through for at least several more weeks until I could get Ernest or someone to mail me some more.

As we ate, I answered their questions about the United States to the best of my ability with my limited command of the language. After our simple jungle meal was finished, I took out the few photos from home that I carried and passed them around. The picture that intrigued them the most was one of me standing beside my car on a busy Manhattan street, and this led to many more questions about New York, a city I scarcely knew and had only visited once. I then asked them to pose for new photos as I got out my camera—a request which they were happy to oblige as they clowned around and pretended to be true savages, taking off their shirts and brandishing their machetes in an attempt to look like bushmen. But when their boat arrived, it was obvious they were excited about going to town.

The next morning I decided that it was time to leave this tranquil campsite and push on in my exploration of the bay. It was a hard place to leave, but I reasoned that there might be more such valleys, equally beautiful and waiting to be discovered. Just as I broke camp, heavy rainsqualls began to sweep across the bay, but I was not going to let that keep me from traveling. Not far from my campsite, I met local fishermen working from dugouts, and soon passed a small settlement of thatched huts on the shore.

Beyond this community, there was more wild coastline, bordered by rocky bluffs, pocket beaches, and jungle. I reached a small indentation that was sort of a cove and landed on a strip of crescent beach overhung by giant trees. I didn't intend to camp there, but after landing for a brief rest and a look around, I noticed something strange about the limestone cliff a couple hundred feet up a steep hill to my right. Most of the cliff was covered in vines that obscured its face like an overgrown beard, but there was a strange darkness behind one part of the vine cloak. I grabbed my machete and worked my way up the hill. Just as I had suspected, the vines concealed the entrance to a yawning cave, its roof suspended at least fifty feet over a flat rock shelf. Except for the tropical vegetation, the cave was almost identical to one I had found while hiking in the Ozark Mountains of Arkansas. Remembering the many arrowheads I'd found in that other cave, and knowing Hispaniola had once been home to Taino, Arawak, and Caribe Indians, I searched the leaf-littered floor for artifacts. I found no stone implements, but old middens of shells were a sure sign that ancient peoples had used the place. It would have been a perfect place to live, with excellent shelter from the frequent rains that swept the bay, and a good observation point from which to watch for any enemies that might approach by canoe.

Near the back of the rock shelf that formed the floor of the shelter, there was a deep crevice with a sandy floor, and I could see a black passageway leading off under the mountain. With visions of piles of undiscovered artifacts or even pirate's treasure (after all, this area was long a center of Caribbean pirate activity), I scrambled back to my kayak to get my large diving light. When I returned, I climbed down to the bottom of the crevice and cautiously walked into the dark chamber a few yards, finding no artifacts or Spanish gold, only piles of bones from some type of small animal. The cave was obviously part of a vast underground network, with tunnels leading to who knows where, but I didn't relish the idea of getting lost in there and disappearing without a trace on this lonely south shore of Samana Bay. If there were treasures hidden in those deep tunnels beneath the mountain, they would have to wait until I could return someday with someone to help me find them. Still, fantasizing about it gave me something to do that afternoon as I returned to the open rock shelf and sat overlooking the bay. I imagined myself paddling back across the bay to the anchorage, the kayak so heavy laden with gold that I would have to leave all my gear behind. In my mind I worked out the complex problems of smuggling the gold out of the country, and the difficult decisions that would have to be made about how to spend all that money. Perhaps I would buy a sailing yacht of my own that would be big enough to carry my kayak on the deck and whisk me off to South Pacific islands.

But the fact remained that I was sitting there in the lair of some long-forgotten people with barely three hundred dollars to my name.

I could almost feel the presence of the naked savages that had once inhabited this rock shelter, and it was easy to envision them squatting around smoky campfires, grilling fish from the bay, a fleet of long dugouts beached on the sand below next to my kayak. They had lived here for centuries without the need for gold or anything that it could buy, and, like them, I would have to learn to be even more resourceful if I were to continue traveling the islands on my limited budget.

I camped on the beach below the cave that night, and when daybreak came, I was once again visited by my old friends from hell—swarms of no-see-ums. Black clouds of the tiny insects descended upon me and attacked so viciously that I ran cursing into the bay as fast as I could, holding my breath and staying submerged until my lungs ached. I had to endure their attack long enough to break down my camp and cram my stuff in the kayak; then I pushed off and paddled far out into the bay to escape them. I then paddled on to the east until I was at a point on the south coast of the bay that was adjacent to the anchorage in Samana.

Though I had lost my life jacket, the thought of the ten-mile crossing of the bay didn't bother me, since my destination was in sight on the other side due to the mountains that rise inland from Samana. In the Bahamas or the Florida Keys, a crossing of that distance would have taken me out of sight of land. But despite the benign appearance of the bay, halfway across I was caught in a blinding squall with rain so heavy I couldn't see a hundred yards in any direction. It beat down on me with a fury, driven by wind that caused it to sting my face and threatened to tear the paddle out of my hand. The storm was intense but short-lived, and a half hour later I was once again paddling under sunny skies. I reached the north shore a few miles east of the anchorage, stopping to check out an uninhabited island called Cayo Levantado that we had passed when entering the bay on *Celebration*. Between this island and the town of Samana, I paddled through an anchorage called *Bahia de las Flechas* (The Bay of Arrows). This bay was named by Christopher Columbus, who had anchored there during his second voyage of discovery and was greeted by a rain of Arawak arrows that flew from the shore in such numbers that they darkened the sky.

Back at the Samana anchorage, Frank and Josephine were passing their days on *Celebration* doing little or nothing—Frank going through a thick novel every day. They talked of leaving for Puerto Rico, but made no commitment to a departure date. I was frustrated with waiting, especially after having just experienced a week of freedom in my kayak, camping and traveling at my own pace. But I knew I could not buck the head-on trade winds for the one-hundred-mile Mona Passage to Puerto Rico. I would have to wait for this one last passage on *Celebration* before I could once again travel independently. I spent the next few days paddling around the local area, visiting Cayo Levantado several more times and generally hanging out in Samana.

One hot afternoon I was sitting in the ice cream shop when three German tourists, a man and two women, all in their early twenties, came in and began asking me questions about the attractions of the area. The young man introduced himself as Stephan. One of the women was his girlfriend, and the other woman, Viola, was single. I was instantly charmed by this beautiful blonde and wanted to do everything I could to spend more time in her company. Josephine and Frank had told me about a nearby waterfall they had visited while I was away kayaking, so this offered a perfect opportunity to invite my new friends along as I was anxious to see it for myself anyway.

We hired one of the *motos* with the carts attached and rode this conveyance several miles west of town to a place where a small stream called the Rio de los Cocos crosses the road. The waterfall was a few hundred yards upstream, the driver said, so we arranged to have him pick us up a couple of hours later and set off up the dirt path he pointed to. Along the way we passed a couple of primitive huts with thatch roofs, similar to those I had seen on the south shore of the bay. The forest here was equally jungle-like as well, if less remote. We emerged at the edge of a deep pool of clear water, and on the opposite side of the pool was a smooth rock face where the water cascaded twenty feet in a thin sheet from the stream above. It was a magical setting—completely deserted and apparently pristine—a tropical garden of lush ferns and myriad broadleaf herbs. But when I lined up my new friends along the edge of the pool to snap a photo, my waterproof Minolta camera chose that moment to cease functioning, leaving me with no means to record the scenery here or anywhere else for the rest of the trip. I was outraged at the malfunctioning camera, but the others were ready for a swim, so I put it away and tried to forget it.

My German friends traveled much lighter than I did, carrying only small daypacks as their entire complement of luggage for a six-week vacation. This of course left no room for such trivialities as swimsuits, so in typical uninhibited European fashion, they thought nothing of removing all their clothing and diving in. Not wanting to be different just because I was an unsophisticated American not conversant in three or four languages like them, I stripped and followed them in. Swimming in cold, fresh water was a welcome change after months of swimming in the sea, and the cliff at the top of the waterfall made a perfect diving platform. We stayed there a good hour until the chill of the water became too much, then dressed and headed back to Samana.

That evening we ate at a cheap Chinese restaurant on the hill overlooking the anchorage, and Viola told me they were going back to Boca Chica, a little resort town on the south coast of the island, in the morning. She said they would be staying there three more weeks, and that there was room for me if I wanted to come visit.

Two more boring days on *Celebration* with no decision about leaving from Frank and Josephine, as well as visions of Viola that I could not erase from my mind, convinced me to make the overland trip to Boca Chica. To get there I had to take a bus first to Santo Domingo, the capital of the Dominican Republic and a city I had wanted to see anyway. The city is the oldest European settlement in the Americas, founded by Columbus in 1496. Reaching it from Samana took most of the day, the bus making innumerable stops along the way across the island to let off and pick up passengers along the road. There was another long delay to change a flat tire. When I reached Santo Domingo, I took another bus to Boca Chica, thirty miles to the east, anxious to see Viola. I could explore Santo Domingo on the way back.

I found her on the beach outside the bungalow where she was staying, and here I set foot in the actual Caribbean Sea for the first time, if it is defined as the basin bounded to the north by Cuba, Hispaniola, Puerto Rico, and the Virgin Islands. I was anxious to paddle it in my kayak, but I knew that would have to wait until I reached Puerto Rico, which I intended to round by paddling the south coast of that island.

The beach at Boca Chica was crowded with tourists, mostly European. Viola had staked out a claim under a beach umbrella, and I spent the rest of the day enjoying the view with her from the comfort of beach chairs. We ate out at a new restaurant that first night, paying too much money for what turned out to be bad food. I could not afford to do much more of that, as this trip across the island had the potential to quickly wipe out the remainder of my travel funds. But at least I had a place to stay, and I enjoyed my brief interlude in Viola's company. It seemed unlikely that I would ever see her again, as she was quite settled in Germany and happily employed at the Mercedes Benz plant in Stuttgart.

When I left Boca Chica, I arrived back in Santo Domingo on a Saturday night and rented a cheap room for just a few dollars near the historic square in the center of downtown. At dawn on Sunday morning, I walked the quiet streets past a statue of Christopher Columbus and peered into the fortress-like windows of a fifteenth-century cathedral where he is reputedly buried. In the dim light I could see hooded monks lighting candles in preparation for morning mass. I would have liked to spend more time in the old city if I had more money to spend, but I really needed to get to Puerto Rico at this point. I left for Samana, determined to nag Josephine and Frank about leaving until I could get them to overcome their inertia.

I was pleasantly surprised to find that they were ready too and were waiting on me to return and help with the preparations for the crossing. I spent an entire day making trips back and forth across the choppy harbor in the dinghy, ferrying jerry cans to replace *Celebration*'s 150-gallon water supply and then diesel to top off the fuel we had burned motoring all the way from Puerto Plata. I spent another day snorkeling under the hull with a brush to scrub off the marine growth that was starting to accumulate on the bottom from a month of being anchored in one place. It would only get worse if we stayed longer . . . Nearby, a dilapidated sailboat had so much growth on the hull it looked like a natural reef. The fifty-something year-old fellow that owned it said he had sailed into Samana seventeen years ago and just couldn't bring himself to leave. He seemed content, sharing his floating home with a beautiful local girl he had married who couldn't have been more than eighteen.

When our preparations were completed and we were ready, the weather wasn't, so we had a few more days to kill before we could leave. We spent much of this time on board *English Jack*, the fifty-four-foot motor yacht owned by Jack and Veronica, whom Frank and Josephine had befriended in the Bahamas. *English Jack* was a million-dollar vessel, equipped with a luxurious air-conditioned main salon for entertaining, so we watched movies with them on the VCR while waiting for favorable weather. Such luxury was not necessarily an advantage, however, and Jack told us of his difficulties, from the prodigious quantities of fuel he had burned to bring the yacht so far from Florida, to the theft such apparent wealth had invited from the locals wherever they went. Here in the Samana anchorage, thieves had swum out to the yacht one night and stolen the 25-horsepower Yamaha engine off their dinghy, then slashed the three-thousand-dollar inflatable with their knives. It was inevitable that flaunting such wealth in front of such impoverished people would lead to such incidents.

Jack had recently been back to Puerto Plata by car and said that George Bouillon was still there. To my surprise, Jack said that George was making arrangements for a wedding. The impulsive Frenchman was going to marry Millie, the eighteen-year-old Dominican girl he had met at a T-shirt shop the first week he was on the island. He was delayed in Puerto Plata wading through the red tape required to get permission for Millie to leave with him on *Winning Edge*.

On April 19, we got a needed break in the trade winds and decided to leave for a night passage to Puerto Rico late that afternoon. The *commandante* of the harbor, still wearing his Rambo survival knife, came out in a borrowed dinghy to clear us out and return our firearms, which were in a much rustier condition than when we'd surrendered them a month before. As soon as he was gone, I pulled up the two anchors and we motored out of the harbor.

The Mona Passage, like the Gulf Stream, has a reputation for being a particularly dangerous body of water to cross. Currents converging from the Atlantic and the Caribbean between Hispaniola and Puerto Rico, combined with strong trade winds and frequent storms, make the passage almost always rough and unpredictable. Sailboats and other large vessels are advised to steer a course well north of Mona Island and Isla Desecheo, the only land breaking up the crossing. When I had originally planned to try and paddle across, I saw Mona Island as a convenient rest stop. From the extreme easternmost cape of the Dominican Republic, it is a mere thirty miles to Mona, a weird island riddled with caves that are supposed to be haunted and that are rumored to contain a fortune in hidden pirate's gold. From Mona Island, it is another thirty-nine windward miles to the western shores of Puerto Rico. Now more knowledgeable about the strength of the trade winds, I knew I could not do such a crossing under paddle power alone. The deep water passage that sailboats were advised to take from Samana to Puerto Rico was more than a hundred miles and passed far north of Mona Island and the treacherous capes on the eastern tip of Hispaniola.

The prospect of this daunting windward bash had for many of the cruisers in Samana created an apathy and unwillingness to leave similar to that of Georgetown's "Chicken Harbor." This reluctance had begun to work on Frank and Josephine as well, and once we left the protection of Samana Bay, motoring steadily into rough breaking seas, they began discussing the wisdom of turning back to wait for better conditions. I voted to push on, and Frank concurred, saying we would likely never get any better conditions, so the decision was made. Josephine went below and returned with *Celebration's* American ensign, which Frank restored to its place of honor flying from the backstay after taking down the Dominican courtesy flag we had been flying for two months.

Once again we were troubled by a malfunctioning autopilot as soon as we set our course and turned it on, but this time the problem was not caused by canned goods stored too close to the compass; I had made sure of that before we left. The complex electronic mechanism had apparently died, as no amount of coaxing and fiddling with the controls could persuade it to steer a straight course. I took the helm and continued to steer all through the night, managing to stay awake by listening to blaring music on the headphones of my Sony Walkman and drinking several cold Cokes.

We crashed into 8-to-10-foot seas for the next thirty hours, until we at last reached the lee of mountainous Puerto Rico. I succumbed to seasickness from all the rolling and pitching shortly before dawn, and felt much better after getting the puking over with. It seemed to take forever to get close to the island after we sighted it, and by the time we made our approach to Mayaguez Harbor, night had fallen and millions of man-made lights twinkled like stars on the slopes of black mountains. It was easy to see we were back in U.S. territory. No city in the Bahamas, Turks and Caicos, or the Dominican Republic had lights such as these.

The harbor at Mayaguez is only a slight indentation in the curving coastline that offers little protection in any wind other than the prevailing easterlies of the trade winds. We dropped anchor about a half mile off the beach, and fell asleep to the sounds of traffic and music drifting out from the city on a warm breeze. In the morning we took the dinghy to the dock at a place called Club Pescado and walked into town to clear U.S. Customs and Immigration. To my surprise, this was no more complicated than making a quick phone call to a bored official who took down our passport numbers.

Josephine and Frank were interested in buying some hardware they needed for the boat, so we set off walking through the business district, checking each *ferretería* until they found what they needed. Street corner stands sold American beer, so out of patriotic duty, Frank and I bought a couple of ice-cold Bud Lights and enjoyed a change from the Heineken, Becks, and Presidente we had been drinking for months.

That afternoon we found our way to the Mayaguez shopping mall, and walking through the spacious, air-conditioned corridors between ultra-modern chain stores that were identical to those back home, I knew for sure that I was back in the U.S.A., even if I was still on a Caribbean island. When I passed the door to a travel agent's office in the mall, I decided at the spur of the moment to step inside and inquire about a flight to the mainland. Given my financial situation, it seemed to make sense to go back to Mississippi, where I had family, friends, and connections, to earn enough money to return in a few weeks and resume my trip from Mayaguez. After talking to the travel agent, I was disappointed to learn that a one-way flight to New Orleans would cost more than all the money I had. I would have to think of an alternative, or else try to find work in the Mayaguez area.

Before I made that decision, however, I wanted to go to San Juan, the capital city, where I expected to pick up mail for the first time since Georgetown. I had an acquaintance in that city, a young woman named Elaine Solis, whom I'd met in a botany class at the University of Southern Mississippi during my final semester there when I was planning my trip. I had told her of my intentions of visiting her native island along my intended route, and she had given me her address, saying that she would be there when I arrived and that I could have mail forwarded to her at her mother's house. She was incredulous that I had actually arrived in Puerto Rico when I called her that day from the Mayaguez Mall, and told me that I had lots of mail waiting for me at her house.

Leaving my kayak on *Celebration*, I took a small bus the following day from Mayaguez to San Juan. This Linea Sultana mini-bus turned out to be a much more civilized way to travel than the *gua-guas* of the Dominican Republic. The mini-bus was air-conditioned, the driver stayed on his proper side of the road, the passengers did not bring their chickens with them, and I did not have to accommodate extra women and children on my lap. The highway twisted along the rocky cliffs north of Mayaguez, providing views of the Mona Passage before turning east to follow the Atlantic coast toward San Juan. Much of the rural scenery in between was similar to that of the Dominican Republic, and, surprisingly, there were areas where some people lived almost as primitively.

When I reached San Juan in the afternoon, I spent two hours wandering around the wrong part of the city until I found a cab driver who spoke good English and quickly drove me to the right address. When we stopped on the street in front of her parent's house, Elaine was just getting out of her car.

"Now I know why you tried to paddle a kayak all the way to Puerto Rico," the driver said, as he stared at the gorgeous twenty-year-old Latina walking toward me with a big smile.

It is true that I would have paddled a kayak all the way to Puerto Rico for a woman like Elaine, but I knew that she had been engaged for a long time and would soon be married.

"You look different!" was the first thing Elaine said to me as the cab pulled away. I suddenly became self-conscious and realized that at this point I must have looked like a completely different person than the clean-cut student she had known from a year before. Though I had shaved my wild beard off while still in the Dominican Republic, my hair was still long and unruly, curled to the point of becoming dreadlocks, and bleached surfer-blonde by constant exposure to the sun. But if Elaine had changed any, it was only for the better, and I suddenly found myself wishing she were not engaged.

Elaine introduced me to her mother, and we went into the house to sit down while she got my mail. Zeida Solis spoke better English than her daughter, and translated for Elaine as I told some of the highlights of my trip at the same time I eagerly tore into my pile of letters. Some of the friends I had most expected to hear from had not written, but there were other letters from people I never thought I would hear from again. Even more surprising was the fact that some of these letters contained cash and checks, sent with wishes that they would help me continue with my journey. Pete Hill and Marty Zinn, who only knew me from the two nights we shared campsites in the Everglades, sent fifteen dollars. Lisa Roell sent twenty dollars from Key West. There was another twenty dollars from Dr. Steve Ross, a friend from the University of Southern Mississippi who was keeping up with my trip, and fifty dollars from John Herman, a coworker at the last real job I held. Ernest sent me ten dollars and a couple of other letters as well. There were letters from other friends and from a cousin.

This unexpected money would certainly help, but the total was not enough to enable me to continue the trip as the senders had intended. I asked Elaine's mother about the prospects for finding work on the island, and she couldn't offer any encouragement, saying that unemployment was high, as well as the cost of living. I could not live in my tent and go to a job every day. She suggested that it would be easier to go back to Mississippi for a while to earn money. She offered to let me store my kayak in their yard, but it would be expensive to get it to San Juan. They had a second home in Rincon, a beach house only fifteen miles from Mayaguez where *Celebration* was anchored. I could leave it there, but they were not there often. She did however, have an elderly neighbor, a widow by the name of Mrs. Charlotte Sirutis, who lived in Rincon year round and might let me store it at her house.

Zeida made some phone calls and found me a deal on a one-way flight to Miami for less than one hundred dollars. She and Elaine then took me out to dinner in a mall similar to the one in Mayaguez and then dropped me off at a reasonably priced hotel near the historic part of old San Juan. I took the Linea Sultana bus back to Mayaguez the following day, then off-loaded my kayak and gear from *Celebration* for the last time. I stayed on board a couple more nights, helping them restock the yacht's dwindling food supply at the low-priced supermarket in Mayaguez. They bought $1,500 worth of canned goods and other non-perishables. It was such a big order the store manager himself made several trips in his personal Jeep to deliver cases of food. I spent most of a day helping them ferry it out to the boat by dinghy and carry it down the companionway to where we stacked it on the cabin sole until they could sort it all out and stow it in the yacht's lockers.

With all this stuff in the way, it was time for me to leave, so the next day I said my good-byes to Josephine and Frank at dawn and paddled north toward Rincon. The sea was flat calm, and I could faintly hear distant city sounds as Mayaguez awoke and came to life. Jagged mountains that were a pale shade of purple rose in the distance behind the city and were framed in a soft yellow glow as the sun rose behind them. I watched spellbound as I paddled, feeling a lump in my throat as I realized this would be the last sunrise I would see from my kayak for an undetermined amount of time. But on the other hand, this beautiful dawning of a new day seemed to be a promise as well, and it was one that was to be fulfilled with some of the best kayaking of the entire trip.

After a few hours of leisurely paddling and contemplative drifting, I reached the beaches of Rincon and moved closer to shore, gliding past rolling brown dunes and groves of coconut palms. I saw the Solises' bright pink beach house, looking just as Zeida had described it, and just north of it, the American and Puerto Rican flags that flew in Mrs. Sirutis's yard.

Charlotte Sirutis was a lady who had done lots of canoeing in her time, much to my surprise, and she understood exactly what my trip was about. Her husband had circumnavigated Long Island in a canoe

when they lived in New York. Of course it would be fine to leave my
boat with her as long as I wanted. It would be safe, and I could call her
from Mississippi to check on it. She had a secure garage, enclosed by
the iron bars so typical of Puerto Rican houses, and the boat would be
protected from the weather and safe from theft while it awaited my
return to this excellent jumping-off place to resume my journey.

I unloaded my much-degraded gear, hosing down what was left of it
with fresh water to prevent further damage in my absence. I put the
clothes and other things I would need for my trip in a new duffel bag I
had purchased at the Mayaguez Mall, and left my camping gear, paddling equipment, and guns and ammunition in the kayak, sealed inside
the watertight storage compartments. Then I left Rincon on the Linea
Sultana bus and returned to San Juan. Zeida had another letter for me
from Ernest, but unfortunately there were no one hundred dollar bills
enclosed, so my plans for leaving the island remained unchanged. The
cheap flight I found to Miami required no advance reservations, so
Zeida phoned the airport and found out there was a flight out that very
evening at 7:30 P.M. All I had to do was be there thirty minutes in
advance with seventy-eight dollars in cash. It didn't matter to me that
the plane would land in Miami, almost a thousand miles from
Mississippi. At least I would be on the continent, and I could make my
way to my home state one way or another.

It was fully dark when the 727 climbed out over the Atlantic and set
a course for south Florida. As I was borne along at five hundred knots
through the night I could see nothing below that indicated the presence of the hundreds of tiny islands and cays that had taken me six
months to traverse by kayak and sailboat. There was hardly time to
reminisce about all the people and places I had visited before the jet
began its descent into the sea of lights that is Florida's densely populated east coast.

# EIGHT

# PUERTO RICO

... for a man is rich in proportion to the number of
things he can afford to let alone.

—HENRY DAVID THOREAU, *WALDEN*

At the Miami airport, I took a taxi to the Greyhound station to see how
much it would cost to ride a bus back to Mississippi. I didn't have
enough to get to Hattiesburg, but I could afford the fare to Mobile,
Alabama, and that was close enough. My brother, Jeff, who lived in
Hattiesburg, could make the two-hour drive down to get me if I could
get that far.

Jeff walked right past me at the terminal in Mobile when I arrived the
following evening after almost twenty-four hours of frustrating stops in
more towns than I could count. I grinned as I watched him search the
crowd for the clean-cut, pale-skinned brother he had said good-bye to
on Black Creek. When I tapped him on the shoulder, he turned around
to see a wild-haired stranger with an island tan so dark he would have
mistaken me for a foreigner. I gave him a two-minute synopsis of the
trip as we carried my duffel bag to his truck, explaining why I had to
break up the journey and come back to Mississippi to find some work.

"How much money have you got left?" he asked as we drove out of
the city.

The beach at Rincon Puerto Rico, where I stored my kayak for a time while I returned to the States to earn money to continue the trip

I checked my wallet. "Four dollars," I said.

We both laughed. I had achieved my goal of separating myself from the quest for material things and status. Jeff thought I was better off than he was. He worked everyday of his life, but still wealth eluded him and it took every dime he made just to stay afloat with a wife, three kids, and all the bills that living in society demanded to be paid.

At least it was almost summer in Mississippi. The warm weather of May was practically the same as that of the tropics I had left behind, so I didn't have to make any major acclimation changes. I spent some time with my parents and took an old tent I still had from my earliest days of camping and set up a semi-permanent camp in the woods of my father's family farm. My dad had a big field of watermelons he had planted on a whim on part of the property, so we agreed to go in on halves with the profits. I would do all the work of hoeing and keeping the coyotes and deer out of them, and then the selling when harvest time came.

In the meantime, I prepared a slide presentation of my journey and made a trip to Pensacola to speak to the Gulf Coast Outdoor Club. Pat Milton, my friend who helped me before by getting gear for the trip was an enthusiastic sea kayaker. He owned a camping equipment store and was the president of this club. He advertised and organized the event so that the resultant audience was an enthusiastic group of canoeists and kayakers who were fascinated by my tales of sharks and desert islands. Although I extended an invitation to any of the members who wanted to accompany me on the next leg of my journey, I was not really surprised that there were no takers.

Though I was certainly no farmer, my dad and I got lucky with the watermelon crop that year and just in time for July 4 had acres of huge, perfectly formed and deliciously sweet melons. After talking to some other people in the business, I decided that the way to make the most profit off the watermelons was to sell them myself out of a truck somewhere on the side of the road. Since I had no vehicle of my own, I borrowed my dad's Nissan pickup. Each morning before sunrise, I loaded it until the suspension could take no more and made the hour-and-a-half drive to Jackson, where I found an ideal location to peddle the melons along busy Highway 80. The watermelons brought four dollars each, and most days I sold out by mid-afternoon. It was an ideal way to make money, really, as I passed the time waiting for customers by reading adventure travel books and studying my maps of the Caribbean. Sitting there in the sultry heat of a Mississippi summer, I felt like the *Dominicano* fruit vendors I had seen everywhere on the island, peddling their wares from pushcarts and bicycles.

During most of this time until the watermelons were sold, I lived much as I had while on my kayak trip, sleeping in my tent and cooking simple meals over a fire. My camp was not far from Bowie Creek, which runs through the property, so I had good source of water for washing and bathing. But despite the fact that I was still living apart from society, I was not content there and longed to get back to the islands as soon as possible. I saved most of the money I made off the watermelons by simply not spending any money, but when the harvest was done I still did not have enough to return to Puerto Rico.

Since it was already late summer and the Atlantic hurricane season was at hand, I decided to wait it out and work some more so that I could replace all my essential gear. As it turned out, this was a wise decision. Hurricane Hugo devastated St. Croix and parts of Puerto Rico that year, but luckily for me, Rincon and the rest of the west coast of the island were spared from the destruction.

By the time cold weather began creeping down into central Mississippi, I was determined not to wait any longer. I bought a plane ticket from New Orleans to San Juan, and after purchasing this and all the gear I had to replace, I had just seven hundred dollars in my pockets when Jeff drove me to the airport.

I wasn't worried, though, as the jet descended that night toward the most brightly lit island in the West Indies. Seen from the final approach, San Juan was a sparkling carpet of lights that filled the plain between the mountains and the Atlantic coast. I had resigned myself to a long night of hanging around the airport, since the flight arrived at 10 P.M. and the Linea Sultana bus did not run until after 8 A.M. I didn't dare start spending my limited travel funds on such luxuries as a room for the night. All I wanted was to get back to my kayak where I could start living out of my tent again. I passed the rest of that first night on a bench outside the airport, alternating short naps with periods of writing in my journal.

Getting to Rincon took most of the next day, but when I arrived at Mrs. Sirutis's garage, I found my kayak just as I had left it. I had come prepared to make some repairs and planned to spend a few days getting ready to travel again. Mrs. Sirutis said I could camp on the beach in front of her yard, so I set to work immediately.

The gear inside was a mess; there was mildew or rust on almost everything. I cleaned the interior of the boat and resealed the bulkheads to the hull with some silicon marine caulk I brought for the purpose. I set the kayak aside to let this dry for twenty-four hours and sorted through the other stuff. I had brought a brand new tent; identical to the first one I had started the trip with. It was another Eureka Aurora, a modified A-frame that Pat Milton had arranged to get for me through his store's contact with the manufacturer. The company had graciously sent me another new one for this next leg of the trip. The only thing they wanted in return was for me to send the old one back so they could analyze how it had held up to the rough conditions I had put it through, since it was advertised as an "expedition" model. I packaged what was left of it in the box the new one came in and mailed it back to Pat. He later told me that when the people at the factory received it, they asked if it had been repeatedly run over by a truck. I guess most weekend campers don't break poles and destroy zippers.

That first night back in Puerto Rico, I pitched the new tent on the narrow strip of beach between Mrs. Sirutis's fenced-in backyard and the angry surf caused by swells rolling in from the Mona Passage. Rincon is known for its surfing, and this time of year the breakers were much larger than they had been in the summer when I had first landed here. Before dawn a larger than normal breaker hit the beach especially hard, sending a flood surge of seawater two inches deep into my tent. When that happened, I knew I was back. All the time in between spent in limbo in Mississippi seemed to vanish. I would have to quickly get used to discomfort again.

The next morning I walked to the grocery store in Rincon several times, each time returning with a bag or two of groceries and other supplies to stock up for my departure. My water bottles and cookware were no longer serviceable, so I bought a new pot and skillet and got four gallon-sized Clorox containers from Mrs. Sirutis to carry my water supply.

The bottom of the kayak was also damaged from repeatedly dragging it across the sand to escape the surf zone on countless landings.

Although Kevlar is extremely impact-resistant, I was to learn that it does not stand up to abrasion very well, and the sort of abuse I was putting it through had eventually taken its toll. Much of the hull along the keel was badly worn, in some places to the point of leaking. I asked Mike Neckar, the builder, about this in a phone conversation before I left Mississippi. He didn't think it was anything to be concerned about. "Just put a few layers of duct tape on it and you're good to go another thousand miles," he had assured me. Not being familiar with epoxy and fiberglass lay-ups at the time, I did not have the tools or know-how to do otherwise, so I followed his advice and used duct tape.

There was never a question about which route I would take to continue east from Rincon to get around Puerto Rico. Although it would have been much shorter to follow the north coast of the hundred-mile long island, this route is exposed to the open Atlantic Ocean, and much of the shoreline is rugged and rocky, offering few places to land. It is also more populated, especially in the San Juan area. The south coast, on the other hand, would offer numerous bays, outlying islands, and mangrove swamps. Being less populous, it would be much more suited to my mode of travel.

In Rincon, I asked some of the locals about the conditions I could expect along this route. I was told that camping could be dangerous on some of the beaches near the cities—and though I would avoid San Juan, there would be two major cities—Mayaguez and Ponce, along this route. It was not the first time I had heard warnings about crime in Puerto Rico, but I didn't plan on camping near populated areas anyway. I would take my chances with the insect hordes of the mangroves rather than put myself in a vulnerable position on a popular beach.

The first day back in the kayak would, out of necessity, be a long one. Most of the shore between Rincon and Mayaguez is developed, so I would have to paddle at least twenty miles to get well south of that city. I worried that I would not be in shape to paddle hard those first few days. Leaving 30-to-40-degree December weather in Mississippi and stepping out of a plane into the upper 80s was a bit of a shock, and the sweat poured on my walks back from town, carrying heavy bags of groceries. It would take a week or more to readapt to the tropics.

Sleep didn't come easy my last night in Rincon—partly because of the heat and humidity and the crashing surf, but mostly because of the excitement of anticipation. I stayed up late, marveling at the incredible beauty that surrounded me. Sixty-foot coconut palms leaned out over the water's edge, backlit in the soft white glow of a full moon that rose just after dark. The palms rattled in the light nighttime trade winds, and I walked the beach in nothing but shorts, thinking about friends and family back home bundled up for the cold, if they were outside at all. I felt lucky and blessed beyond measure to be able to live this experience. I had high hopes for the journey ahead, but I had learned from the first leg of the journey that one man's plans meant nothing in the face of wind, sea, and unforeseen manmade obstacles. Wiser now, my hopes and dreams were tempered with the reality that the key to successfully traveling these waters by kayak was flexibility and a willingness to change plans at a moment's notice.

I was up at 4:00 that first morning, breaking camp and preparing the kayak for a quick getaway in the predawn darkness, wanting to make as many miles as possible that first day. Just before I pushed off, a Puerto Rican vagrant I'd seen wandering the beaches every day I'd been in Rincon stopped by to see me off.

"*Buena suerte*," he called as I paddled away to the south.

I thanked him. I could certainly use some good luck. I paddled past the beach house that belonged to Elaine's parents and doubted I would ever see her again. I had not called to tell them I was back in Puerto Rico, as I had arrived so late at night it San Juan and left so early for Rincon.

Before dawn began to light the sky, I was reacquainted with the kayak and paddle and fell effortlessly back into my traveling stroke. South of Rincon, the shoreline of Puerto Rico's west coast curves inward in a huge indentation where the city of Mayaguez is located. Not wanting to paddle near the city, I maintained a southerly course, and the land to my port side receded into the distance until I was paralleling the shore from five miles out. I watched the sun rise over those same mountains I had seen it rise over the last time I had paddled my kayak, when I was heading north to Rincon from *Celebration*. That promise of a new day I'd been given had at last been fulfilled, ten months later.

My early start paid off, as I covered fifteen miles by noon and was soon near shore again, closely following the beach well south of Mayaguez. I stopped on a deserted strip of sand to eat lunch. The entire beach was littered with garbage, so I pushed on to search for a better place to camp. Two miles to the south was a tiny cay separated from the mainland by a half-mile-wide channel of clear, shallow water. As I approached it, skimming over coral reefs, I could see that it was a park of some kind. There were picnic tables and a bathroom, shaded by a grove of tall Australian pine trees. It looked like an ideal campsite, but my old friend, the "NO CAMPING" sign, was nailed to a tree, though here, of course, it was printed in Spanish. As I walked around the beautiful cay, wishing I could enjoy a night there, three well-dressed businessmen in a powerboat came out to the island to have lunch on one of the picnic tables. One of them showed me where we were on my map, which did not indicate the little cay. He also told me that just to the south I would find miles of nice beaches for camping, so after a brief rest, I slid back into the cockpit of the kayak and pushed on.

I soon reached a deserted strip of coastline, consisting mostly of mangrove swamps, but interspersed with scattered pocket beaches overgrown with coconut groves. The water off this coast was nearly transparent, and the reefs below suggested the possibility of fresh fish or lobster for dinner. I pulled into a quiet little cove and landed on a beach where the palms overhung the water. It was perfect, I thought, but I was dismayed when I walked into the palm grove and discovered a thatched hut that was well hidden from the open beach. The hut was of elaborate construction, the side walls woven from individual palm leaves and the roof thatched with plaited coconut fronds like those I'd seen in the Dominican Republic. It was a classic beachcomber's hideaway, like that of some castaway stranded on a South Pacific island. The owner's bare footprints were everywhere in the sand, and there were piles of coconut husks, fish bones, and other signs that someone was a full-time resident here. Whoever he was, it seemed obvious that he liked his privacy to live in such isolation. I began to wonder if perhaps the resident here was an illegal Dominican who had crossed the Mona Passage in a small boat and was hiding from immigration here. But why would a Dominican alien in the promised land of U.S. territory live in more primitive conditions than he had left behind? Then it dawned on me that whoever built this hideaway could be a fugitive from the law. The thought made my skin crawl as I realized my vulnerability, and I could almost feel eyes upon me, watching from somewhere in the dense underbrush. I lost no time in retreating to my kayak, leaving this lovely spot to the solitary man who had claimed it first.

About a mile farther south, I found a beachcomber's paradise for myself on a small point of land that jutted out from the surrounding mangrove swamp. There were numerous reefs with exposed coral heads scattered about that would make it difficult for any kind of large boat to approach. Coconut palms shaded the beach and extended back in a dense grove as far as I could see. The point was exposed enough to catch a good breeze that would keep insects away, so I landed and pulled my boat far enough into the palm grove to render it invisible from the water. When I explored farther inland on foot, I found that there was an old dirt road winding through the coconut plantation, but there were no signs of recent use.

This campsite was so peaceful that when I woke the following morning, I decided to stay another night. This was, after all, the sort of perfect tropical paradise I had come to the Caribbean in search of, and I was in no particular hurry to get anywhere. I spent the day snorkeling on the reefs and lying around in my hammock, thinking how glad I was to be missing the cold weather back home. The reefs were devoid of large game fish, as far as I could tell, but the coral formations were colorful and interesting to look at. I didn't really need fish anyway. There were more coconuts than I could eat in a lifetime hanging over my head, so I gathered some to go with the supplies I had bought in Rincon. I came up with a smarter (or lazier) method of getting them down from the trees than by climbing. A long piece of bamboo washed ashore at the high tide line gave me the idea. I split one end of it and lashed my machete into the slot, perpendicular to the shaft, the sharp edge of the blade facing downward. With this long razor-edged hook, I could reach up into the crowns of the shorter palms and cut loose all the nuts I wanted with a forceful downward slash. It may have been a more dangerous method than climbing, though, because as soon as I made the cut I had to dash out from under the tree to keep from getting clobbered by the falling ten-pound nuts. In addition to using the coconuts, I enjoyed a delicious dinner of sautéed hearts of palm that night, taken from one of hundreds of young palms sprouting up at random in the grove.

I expected my second night there to be as peaceful as the first, but I awoke after midnight to the sounds of footsteps and something crashing through the undergrowth towards my camp. Within seconds, a flashlight was shining into my tent and I could hear the voices of three men speaking in Spanish. Blinded by the light, I yelled: "HEY!" which was all I could think of as I struggled to get out of my sleeping bag. The men ran towards the beach where my kayak was hidden as I fumbled for my Beretta and took off after them, wearing only my underwear. I was relieved to find that they had kept going past the kayak, leaving it untouched. Apparently they had disappeared into the mangrove swamp north of my camp. Whether they had arrived by boat or on foot, I could not tell. Needless to say, I didn't sleep any more the rest of the night, wary that they might come back, and doubtful of their good intentions. But dawn broke at last with no more disturbances.

As I was breaking down my camp in the morning and loading the kayak, I noticed two fishermen swimming on the reef nearby, wearing dive masks and carrying homemade gigs. The men came over when they saw me stirring on the beach, and I saw that they had been hunting octopus, as each had several small ones in the net bags they carried as they swam. They asked questions in rapid Spanish, but I understood only enough to know that they thought I was a *Dominicano*, who had just crossed the Mona in my kayak. Though I could barely speak their language, they still seemed unconvinced when I insisted that I was a *Norteamericano*. As I left I began to wonder if the two fishermen were the ones who stumbled upon my camp in the darkness. Whoever it was, the encounter obviously scared them as much as it did me.

I paddled south on a dead calm sea to the next settlement, a waterfront town called Puerto Real. There were plenty of boats in Puerto Real, including several large sailing vessels, but no foreign flags were in evidence, and all the yachts had Puerto Rican registration numbers. I knew that Josephine and Frank had planned to stop at Boqueron, the next settlement to the south, so I headed there, hoping to find someone who might know their whereabouts or someone who might have heard of George Bouillon. I made a long side trip into the anchorage looking for familiar yachts but found none. One fellow I talked to on the radio said that *Winning Edge* had indeed been in Boqueron for several months but that George had sailed back to the Dominican Republic to get his wife, Millie. He said that *Celebration* had also been there, months before, and that they were last seen in Salinas, on the south coast of Puerto Rico, just two weeks ago. I had expected Josephine and Frank to be far down in the Leeward or Windward Islands by now, but knowing how they liked to linger in agreeable ports, I should not have been surprised. I checked my map. I could reach Salinas in about a week of paddling. Chances of seeing them again were good, so with a reunion to look forward to, I set that town as my goal and paddled out of the Boqueron anchorage after just a brief stop on the beach.

South of Boqueron, I passed long stretches of crowded beaches, where there were many Puerto Ricans camped out for the weekend and dozens of speedboats zipping back and forth just offshore. It was a party atmosphere, and I would have been welcome to camp there, but I was in no mood for crowds this early in my trip. I had visions of another secluded paradise like my last camp.

There was no such place, however, along the last few miles of the west coast of the island, so I decided to go ahead and round Cabo Rojo that day. This rugged cape of red cliffs that appeared to be more than a hundred feet high separates the west coast of Puerto Rico from the Caribbean shoreline of the island's south coast. As I paddled under these cliffs, I left the lee of the island, which was protecting me from the prevailing easterlies of the trade winds, and found myself instantly in a world of frothing whitecaps and twenty-five-knot breezes. Large swells rolled into the broken cliffs, creating rebounding breakers that met the incoming waves and sent their crests straight up. I had to brace constantly with the paddle to maintain my balance against capsizing. People on the overlook at the top of the cliff shouted and waved, their voices carried away in the wind. They must have thought I was crazy to be paddling in such chaotic seas, so close to the many rocks that protruded out of the water at the base of the cape. I waved back and kept going, until at last I was clear of the rebounding seas and heading for the beach just east of the cape.

I was ready to camp but, after landing, found that there was a dirt road connecting this beach to the road that led to the overlook at the cape. This was just the sort of place that would attract a lot of beer drinking, hell-raising teenagers and young adults, judging from the cans, cigarette butts, and used condoms that littered the area. A mile farther on, I found a better spot, a beach framed by sparse mangroves and thick bushes, affording a spot where I could hide my tent from the more open terrain farther inland, where there was also a dirt road. This part of the island was arid and desert-like, with cactus and thorn bushes and distant blue mountains that looked as desolate as those of Arizona.

No one disturbed me that night, but in the morning as I was packing to leave, a jeep approached from the road, driven by an ornithologist with a group of his graduate students. He explained that they were

doing an annual bird count all over the island. After asking many questions about my journey ahead and offering some advice, he gave me a
half dozen oranges to take with me.

My progress was pitifully slow that day, as I was not back in top
shape for paddling yet, and I was going headfirst into the trade winds,
which picked up to full force by 10 A.M. This area of the coast was
crowded with Sunday afternoon boaters. The attraction here is Bahia
Fosforoscente, a bay with an unusually high concentration of biolumi-
nescent marine organisms. I had hoped to camp near the bay so I
could do some night paddling and check out these sparkling waters,
but I pushed on a little east of the bay to find a more secluded spot to
spend the night.

After pitching the tent on a beach completely hidden by outlying
mangroves, I set out to do some hiking, climbing a rugged mountain
just inland of my camp. The slopes of this peak didn't appear to have
seen rain in a decade, and the dry grays and browns around me were a
striking contrast to the lush green of the mangrove swamp and the
sapphire blue of the Caribbean below. From my lofty perch at the summit, I could see dozens of boats zipping in circles around the scattered
cays I had just paddled through, but I was much too far away to hear
the buzz of their motors.

The following day I paddled mile after mile along the edge of a great
mangrove forest that formed an impenetrable green buffer between
the sea and the arid coastal hills. In the distance, I had an ever-changing
view of rugged blue mountains in the interior that formed the spine
of the island. Despite the fact that Puerto Rico is one of the most
crowded places in the world, this part of the coast is remarkably wild
and uninhabited. I longed to set off into the mountains on foot, but I
had not come equipped for serious backpacking, so I pushed on in the
kayak, visions of more perfect campsites luring me ever onward.

On this south coast of Puerto Rico, the wind became my number one
enemy. The trade winds here were stronger than any I had encountered

in the Bahamas the previous winter. When they reached their full strength at 10:00 each morning, my forward progress was reduced to a desperate crawl. I fought for every mile; soaked in steep, choppy white-caps not big enough to be dangerous but relentlessly trying to push me back to where I had come from. I decided that it was no use to try and fight such wind with stubborn, brute force. I would have to rearrange my schedule around it. I took to stopping around noon to set up camp, and left each morning at 3:00 to make my daily mileage before the wind started blowing. This seemed to be the only way to make my goal of fifteen to twenty miles per day, but it was frustrating stopping so early, often on hot, unshaded beaches. And paddling in the predawn darkness each morning made me more than a little nervous. I vividly remembered the aggressive sharks of the Bahamas, and I knew that nighttime was feeding time in the ocean.

Campsites were no problem to find along this coast, though they were often littered with garbage and populated by rats. I was to learn that camping is a popular diversion for Puerto Ricans, but unfortunately, many have not heard of low-impact camping and have little regard for the environment. It was not uncommon, at a good beach campsite, to find old couches and other cast-off furniture hauled out by some camper who wanted to bring all the luxuries of home. Many of these campsites were on little cays separated from the mainland. For security reasons, I always chose an island camp over a mainland site if it was available. Despite the garbage and junk, on this coast I enjoyed solitude once again. By taking the precaution to camp on little islands I avoided nocturnal visitors like those in the coconut grove.

Although I avoided the trade winds by paddling east in the early morning hours, I had the other difficulty of facing the glare of the rising tropical sun each day. The reflection off the glassy calm seas made it impossible to see where I was going. The only solution was to paddle at an angle, tacking far to the south and then back to the north of my course until the sun was high enough not to be in my line of vision.

South of Ponce, Puerto Rico's second largest city, I camped on a sandy cay that was one of many in a small group. That night the glittering lights of the city sparkled on the black slopes of the mountain, merging into millions of stars in the sky above the range. On the white sand of the beach, the reflected light from all those stars and man-made lights was almost bright enough to read by. To the southeast, five miles offshore, I could see the silhouette of Isla Caja de los Muertos, or "Coffin Island," so named because the hill in its center resembles the lid of a coffin when viewed at a certain angle.

In the light of day the next morning, however, Ponce did not look as enchanting as it had when seen at night from a distance of more than two miles. As I paddled past a seedy waterfront of docks designed for commercial shipping, a horrible and overpowering stench of dead fish drifted out from the Bumblebee Tuna factory. Canned tuna was a staple of my camp meals, usually mixed with rice or pasta, but after paddling through that odor for more than an hour, I wondered if I would ever buy another can of tuna. I put as many miles as possible between Ponce and me before ten, when the inevitable trade winds picked up, pitting me in an all-out battle to reach the next habitable campsite.

Nothing remotely resembling a good place to spend the night turned up, so I was forced to fight my way along an unprotected shoreline for eight miles. It seemed I was hardly making progress in the angry boiling whitecaps, but there was no place I could land to get out of it. The coastline here was rocky and unforgiving. Scattered reefs dotted the shallows for miles, forcing me to stay well offshore. I had already scraped the bottom of my hull several times in the past week since leaving Rincon, adding to the considerable damage that I had repaired with only duct tape. I couldn't risk landing on a questionable beach with waves this rough, as I was sure the boat could not take another really hard lick.

For five miserable, soaking-wet hours, I plowed on, until I finally reached the lee of a small point. There was a mangrove swamp surrounding this point, with a maze of channels leading in from the sea.

I didn't know exactly where I was, since I didn't have proper navigation charts, but I ducked into the nearest protected waterway leading into the labyrinth and got out my road map of Puerto Rico.

In most places, the road map was all I needed for kayaking. How could I get lost paddling around Puerto Rico as long as I kept the main island to my left? I couldn't afford to buy all the large-scale nautical charts most skippers of larger craft would require to navigate these islands, so the road map was all I carried. It actually contained more practical information for a kayaker than a marine chart, because it provided more detail of villages and cities, roads along the coast, and which areas were sparsely populated and might offer a potential camp-site. But in the mangrove areas such as this one, the map was vague on shoreline details, leaving me to wonder exactly where I was. I paddled on along the channel I'd selected at random, until I came to a hidden bay where I found a waterfront town with several yachts at anchor nearby. I assumed this must be Salinas and looked in vain for the familiar blue and white hull of *Celebration*. When I could not find it, I paddled to a dock and asked a small boy if this was Salinas.

He pointed east through the mangrove maze and assured me that Salinas was *mucho* kilometers farther that way. Dejected, I paddled on beyond the sight and sounds of the little town, the name of which I never learned, and found a perfectly hidden beach under a tunnel of mangroves. I had covered twenty miles that day, fifteen of those after the trade winds started blowing. I was ready for a secluded camp where I could get cleaned up and well rested. I took a saltwater bath and shaved, then cooked dinner and crawled into the tent before sunset. I would leave early in the morning to push on to Salinas. I still wasn't sure exactly where I was, due to the mangrove nature of this coastline that made it hard to define, but I knew I was surely within five miles of Salinas, despite the dock boy's exaggerations.

I paddled out of the mangroves in the darkness of early morning and by daybreak could see what appeared to be a town on the next point to the east. A cluster of little islands off the point corresponded in position to the Cayos de Ratones (Rat Keys) that my map showed to be south of Salinas. Even if *Celebration* was not there, I needed to stop and find a store to buy supplies, so I set a course for the distant buildings on the shore and began a two-hour crossing. Halfway across, a fishing boat changed course and came in my direction. The man at the helm offered me a tow to the harbor, feeling sorry for me because I had no motor and not understanding why I chose to paddle. I thanked him and he motored away with a bewildered look on his face.

From two miles out, I could make out a cluster of masts, a telltale indicator of the location of the anchorage within the encircling ring of mangroves that surrounded the harbor. I picked up the pace, growing more excited. Was *Celebration* there? Maybe even *Winning Edge*? It would be great to see George again, as well as Josephine and Frank. Somehow seeing them would connect this segment of the trip to my original journey, at least in my mind. I focused on the aluminum masts and closed the gap in less than an hour. On the far side of the anchorage was a tall mast with double spreaders, indicating a yacht the size of *Celebration*. I paddled through a narrow cut in the mangroves and into the anchorage. There were four boats anchored out and another dozen or so tied to the docks of the marina. The big one on the far side of the harbor with the double spreaders was a canoe-stern design, and yes, there was a broad blue strip just below the sheer line on the while hull. It was *Celebration*—the yacht I'd lived on for two months. I had never thought I would see her again.

I paddled up and tied my kayak alongside the dinghy, then climbed into it and rapped on the fiberglass hull. It was still early, about 7:00 in the morning.

"Who is it?" Josephine yelled from the forward cabin in a sleepy and irritated voice.

"Come see!" I yelled back.

A few moments later, Josephine climbed up the companionway ladder and nearly fell back with surprise when she saw me in the dinghy. "I thought I recognized the voice," she said. "Frank! Come see!"

"Who the hell is it? Whataya? Outta yer mind waking me up at this hour?" His voice was sleepy and irritable, until he joined her in the cockpit.

"Jesus Christ! You made it back to the islands! I thought your trip was finished."

I was invited aboard, and over coffee, Josephine and Frank filled me in on all the yachtie gossip I'd missed in my ten-month absence from the cruising life. They had only sailed a hundred miles in that period and explained that it was because they liked Puerto Rico so much they had lingered long in each port. Hurricane Hugo had not hit Salinas hard. *Celebration* had ridden out the storm with no damage, secured within the protective ring of mangroves surrounding the harbor with all the anchors they had aboard. Josephine and Frank had wisely taken no chances once the yacht was secured and had retreated to the safety of a hotel in the mountains until the danger was passed.

"George is in St. John, in the Virgin Islands," Josephine told me. "He married Millie, and after he finally got clearance for her to leave with him, they sailed out of Puerto Plata. She had never been on a boat before, and threw up the whole time. She was so miserable that George had to take her back, and now he's working to earn enough money to fly back and forth to see her."

Poor George. He just never could seem to get it right. All that longing and searching for a woman to accompany him; then he finds one and goes to the ultimate measure of marrying her, only to find out after the wedding that she can't stomach sailing. And poor Millie, the innocent young Dominican woman swept off her feet by a charming Frenchman with a sailboat and promises of a better life over the horizon, far from the poverty that was all she had ever known. I hoped the best for them, but I didn't see how it could ever work out.

Josephine and Frank also told me that *Texas Tumbleweed*, the yacht we'd last seen in the Caicos, had been blown ashore from an anchorage on the east side of the island by the storm. Stan and his family were living in an apartment while they undertook major repairs in a boatyard. Hundreds of yachts had been lost or severely damaged in Puerto

Rico and even more on the harder-hit islands of Culebra, Vieques, and St. Croix.

After a good long visit with Josephine and Frank, I left them to attend their other business of the morning and paddled over to an interesting marina dock that was built around the hung mangroves that bordered the shore. There was a bar at one end of the shaded dock and a spacious deck with tables and chairs that were deserted at this hour. Across the harbor beyond the green of the mangroves on the opposite shore, blue mountains in the distance provided a backdrop for the masts of *Celebration* and the other yachts in the anchorage. I was already taken with Salinas, even before I met the interesting people I would find there. But at the time, I had no intention of staying more than a few hours, so I made my way along the road that led from the marina to the main part of town, two miles away. I was looking for a grocery store, and after I found one I returned to the marina sweating under the load of supplies I'd bought. I washed my laundry in the automatic machines provided for marina guests and took a shower while I waited for the clothes to dry. This done, I sat in the cool of the shade on the deck and updated my journal, frequently interrupted by other boaters who were curious about my strange mode of travel.

Josephine and Frank came to the dock in the meantime, and as the afternoon slipped away in conversation I decided I might as well stay a day or two in Salinas. Josephine told me I had to meet Fred and Mary, a sailing couple who lived on their boat here, since they knew a lot about the Virgin Islands and could give me plenty of useful information.

When Fred and Mary showed up a little later as we were having a drink, Josephine introduced us, telling them I was from Mississippi.

"Mississippi! Are you *really* from there?" Mary asked. "You don't sound like a redneck."

Mary was from Connecticut, Fred explained.

I assured her that I was, switching to my best southern drawl in response to both questions. You would think that Mississippi was the most exotic, dangerous, and unknown Third World country on earth, the way Mary questioned me about my home state. She said that she had once passed through a portion of Mississippi, on the way to New Orleans with some college friends. She spoke of the trip as if she did not expect to make it through, actually surprised that she did not end up in a small town jail or victim of a lynching party.

Fred, a California native, was laid-back and much less outspoken than his partner. He and I hit it off from the start, due to our mutual interests in boats, the sea, and the islands—and our mutual dislike for mainstream society. Fred and Mary insisted that I come to their yacht, *Estrelita* (Spanish for "Little Star"), for dinner, and before we finished eating, Fred invited me to stay with them for as long as I liked. He said I could boost my travel funds by helping them with some work on *Estrelita*, which had been badly damaged by the recent hurricane while anchored in Coral Bay, in the Virgin Islands. Fred said he would pay me by the hour, and in addition, provide meals and a berth on *Estrelita*. Since he was an expert in fiberglass repair, he would also help me patch up the hull of my kayak in a more permanent manner than my duct tape job.

It was December 21. Christmas would be better spent in good company, I reasoned, and my kayak did need a better repair. I took Fred up on his offer, and he said we would start work in the morning.

Fred told me about his experiences in Hurricane Hugo, saying he had chained *Estrelita* to an immovable mooring in Coral Bay. He stayed aboard the yacht alone, while Mary went ashore for safe refuge. Fred said that he had to wear a diving mask to go on deck to adjust lines in the hundred-plus-knot storm winds. The damage to the yacht came not from the wind but from another sailboat that broke free of its anchors and was blown into *Estrelita*, breaking off a section of the bow and the bow pulpit, and ruining lifeline stanchions and a lot of paint. If Fred had not been on board to fend off the other yacht, he and Mary would have lost their boat, which was also their home.

Fred said that they owned land in St. John and normally anchor nearby in Coral Bay, but after the hurricane they brought the boat to Salinas for repairs because they needed a slip with electricity to run power tools. Parts and materials were also more readily available on this more industrialized island. Fred had been in Puerto Rico and the Virgin Islands for seventeen years, working as an engineer and a commercial diver. He learned to dive in the Navy and had been a SEAL operative in the Vietnam War. But Fred wasn't the kind of fellow to talk much about himself and shrugged off his experience as no big deal. He seemed more interested in helping me with my trip by giving me a job and repairing my boat than anything else.

I spent much of the next two days using an orbital sander to smooth down the teak toerails and other exterior deck trim that Mary was going to refinish with varnish. Though the sun was intense, the trade winds I had fought so hard against to get here blew constantly, providing refreshing relief that made the working conditions pleasant enough. Sleeping in the airless and confined space of Estrelita's cabin was more difficult than the work for me, since I was so accustomed to sleeping outside in my well-ventilated tent.

Our work started late each morning, as Fred and Mary liked to sleep until at least 10 A.M., giving me time to wander around the quiet streets of Salinas until they were ready to begin. Even when we were working, the pace was never fast, and by the time the sun "dropped below the yardarm" each day at 5 P.M., Fred figured it was time to make some margaritas. I was set up with the eating as well. If Mary didn't cook an elaborate dinner, Josephine did, or we would all go out to eat at a pizza restaurant near the marina.

During a break from our work on Estrelita, I unloaded my kayak and Fred and I lifted it up on the dock to access the hull damage. When we removed my duct tape, we saw that it was worse than I thought. Evidently I hit some rocks pretty hard even in the short trip from Rincon. There was a crack all the way through the hull in the well-worn section of the bow, and though I hadn't noticed any leaking, thanks to the tape, I wouldn't have gotten much farther in a boat with a hole in the bottom. Fred made a list of materials we would need and said that we would make a trip to the hardware stores in Ponce after Christmas.

We continued our work on *Estrelita* on Christmas Eve, and then on Christmas Day all the yachties in the harbor got together to produce a potluck dinner on the dock. The offerings included traditional Christmas favorites as well as island specialties, but it didn't seem like Christmas to me in these tropical surroundings. I called my family back home and learned that Mississippi was in the grip of an unusual deep-freeze, with a low temperature of 4 degrees above zero. I was wearing shorts and sandals. It was 85 in Salinas.

One unexpected opportunity came my way at the potluck when I met a single-handing cruiser who was planning to sail his boat across the Pacific Ocean after leaving Puerto Rico. When he learned that I had a portable, hand-operated desalinator, he offered to buy it for his life raft emergency kit. I didn't expect to need it in the islands ahead, now that I was past the arid Bahamas, and his offer of $450 sounded too good to pass up. I had bought it for less than $400, wholesale from the manufacturer. He came over to *Estrelita* with the cash the next day, and I gladly parted with the watermaker, hoping I wouldn't be sorry later by getting myself lost at sea with no water.

Fred and Mary had recently purchased twenty-five acres of rain forest high in the mountains north of Salinas, and Mary offered to take me to see it, since they recently hired a surveyor and she needed to check the boundaries. I doubted it would be a *real* jungle, despite Mary's insistence that I needed my long pants, insect repellent, and machete. Puerto Rico does have a tropical national forest called El Yunque, a pristine remnant of the original jungles that covered all of the larger Caribbean Islands, so I looked forward to going with her to see how it compared with the forests I found around Samana Bay.

It took an hour to get there, even with Mary driving at breakneck speed along the twisting mountain roads that were cratered with potholes. We passed scenery that could have been in the Dominican

Republic—crude shacks, chickens, dogs, pigs, and children lining the roadway, banana plantations, and wild breadfruit and mango trees. As the road climbed away from the sea, we passed through clouds of white mist that shrouded the green-cloaked mountains.

At the entrance to the property, on a steep dirt road that forced Mary to put the Nissan pickup into four-wheel-drive, we stopped at the house of eighty-seven-year-old Don Felix, who lived with his wife in a small house surrounded by an herb garden. Mary told me that people come from all over Puerto Rico to visit Don Felix, a man reputed to have great knowledge of medicinal plants and of the natural healing methods of the old shamans who were his ancestors.

Senor Felix greeted us before we got out of the truck. With a machete in hand and the agility of a man a fourth his age, he led us up the steep slope above his home to the wall of green where his fields ended and the jungle began. Near the edge of this forest there were dozens of citrus trees, and we paused long enough to sample softball-sized grapefruit. Don Felix then led the way downhill into the bush, following a steep ravine of slippery, mud-covered banks that forced us to grab branches and tree trunks for balance. I was amazed at his ability to move through such terrain, but I had no time to ponder it. If I slowed down to catch my breath, the old man would be out of sight in the thick foliage.

At the bottom of the ravine we reached a stream of clear, cold water and turned east to follow it into what was truly as legitimate a rain forest as any I had seen in the Dominican Republic or on television. Tall trees, whose species names I had no clue of, formed a solid canopy overhead. Interspersed among the varied hardwoods were lofty palms Mary said were sierra palms. These and the giant tree ferns that were everywhere lent a primeval feel to the scene. Vines, orchids, and bromeliads hung from every available space on trunks and branches, and ferns and other herbs covered the ground to waist level, making it impossible to see where we were putting our feet. I was glad to know there are no poisonous snakes in Puerto Rico. Don Felix pointed to countless plants, talking constantly in rapid Spanish, which I understood none of and Mary comprehended only parts of. She said he was explaining the medicinal uses of the various species, as well as reciting totally unrelated poetry as he walked.

We followed the orange surveyor's flagging that marked the edge of the property until Mary was satisfied that she knew where the boundaries were. Then we returned to Don Felix's house to drink coffee brewed from the beans that grew in his backyard. From his door, there was a magnificent view to the south of folded green ridges backed by the backdrop of the blue Caribbean Sea far below. Mary gave Senor Felix and his wife a bag of groceries she had picked up for them in Salinas; then we headed back to the coast. Once again, Mary drove as if she were running from the law. She pushed the tired old Nissan pickup to the limits of its braking and suspension system, and when we somehow made it back to the marina in one piece, I told her I'd rather walk than ride with her again.

The next day Fred and I collected the fiberglass repair materials we would need for my kayak as we drove all over Ponce, searching half a dozen hardware stores. Fred would need some of the stuff we had left over, so I only ended up paying for about twenty-five dollars' worth of materials. We spent another day actually making the repairs—sanding the damaged areas down to bare Kevlar, applying strips of fiberglass tape saturated in epoxy resin, waiting for it to cure, then sanding and fairing until it was ready to paint. Fred knew a lot about working with fiberglass, having built many small boats and repaired numerous larger ones. Little did I know that this first experience with epoxy resin would lead me to becoming a part-time boatbuilder and boat repair specialist. But at the time, I had little interest in any work-related pursuit. I just wanted to get on with the repair and get under way again as soon as possible with the extra money I had come across in Salinas.

When Fred was done, the repair was invisible except for slightly mismatched paint. My kayak was as good as new. I left it out of the water for a few more days at Fred's insistence, to give the resin and the paint time for a full cure. Finished with my boat, we continued our work on

*Estrelita*, replacing winches and other deck hardware, and then the mast stays and masthead lights. For these tasks I had to ascend the fifty-foot mast in the bosun's chair, hoisted aloft with the halyard winch by Fred.

On New Year's Eve, we took the day off to go sailing with Fred's Dutch friend, Balca, on his beautifully restored classic wooden ketch. Balca and some of his employees sailed the boat from Boqueron for the holidays, and we spent the last day of the year and the decade anchored near some islands south of Salinas, snorkeling among coral reefs and taking frequent breaks to sample fine wine and cheeses on deck. Back in Salinas that afternoon, I helped Fred and Mary finish off a bottle of tequila without the margaritas, and then we headed to the Salinas yacht club for the special party that was being held for all the boaters in the harbor. I didn't need anything else to drink after that tequila, but when a certain cute young Puerto Rican woman named Brenda, who was working at the bar, kept insisting on giving me free drinks, I found her hard to refuse. I didn't find my way back to *Estrelita* until sometime the next afternoon.

Despite all the fun, I was growing impatient to leave now that my kayak was fixed and the holidays were over. I paddled around the harbor to test the boat and started reorganizing and packing my gear. I made several trips to the grocery store in Salinas to stock up on supplies, and by January 3, I was ready to leave. I felt good about having the boat repaired, but even better was having a new supply of money. I had the $450 from selling the desalinator, Fred and Mary paid me $200 for the small amount of work I did for them, and I sold them my Beretta pistol for an additional $100. I knew I wouldn't be able to take firearms into most of the countries ahead on my route, and I planned to get rid of the rifle as well somewhere in the Virgin Islands. After buying all my supplies and making final preparations to leave, I had a total of $1,250, almost twice the amount I had come to Puerto Rico with four weeks before.

Fred and Mary treated me to a lobster dinner the night before I left, and the following day I ate lunch at the pizza place with them and Frank and Josephine. It was afternoon before I paddled out of the marina, and I knew I wouldn't get much of a start, but I could at least reach the islands we visited on Balca's sailboat and find a place to camp. I was ready for the freedom of the sea and my kayak. I couldn't bear to think of another night in the stuffy confines of a sailboat, with good company or not. Like my later passion for working with wood and fiberglass and building boats, little did I know that I would one day become an enthusiastic sailor and even live aboard a sailboat smaller than *Estrelita*.

# NINE

# INTO THE WIND

If a man is alive, there is always the danger he may die, though the danger
must be allowed to be less in proportion as he is dead-and-alive to begin with.
A man sits as many risks as he runs.

**—HENRY DAVID THOREAU**

The serenity of Salinas harbor was an illusion that made me temporarily forget my monumental struggle against the trade winds ever since rounding Cabo Rojo. As soon as I left the protection of the mangroves, I found myself battling a fierce headwind that threatened to tear the paddle from my hands. I was glad I did not have far to go that day. I stopped at 4:30 P.M., when I reached the string of cays where we had snorkeled on New Year's Eve. I paddled through a cut in the mangroves and found a small beach Fred told me about. Though it was more mud than sand, it was high enough to provide a campsite, and quite secluded as well, hidden as it was from both the open sea and the sound inside the islands. A few coconut palms shaded the beach, but none bore any nuts. I set up my tent and built a fire to roast one of the huge plantains I bought from a farmer in Salinas. As I was eating, a bold rat came out of the surrounding bushes to watch me from the other side of the fire, hoping for a handout. He had no fear and would not leave even when I threw rocks at him. Others joined him during the night, but they could not get at my food, as I learned long ago to keep my kayak sealed up tight at night.

Views of the rugged north shore of the Dominican Republic from several miles offshore

I was in the habit of getting up late after my lazy days in Salinas, so it was 8:00 before I was traveling the next morning. I stayed in the lee of the string of cays as long as possible, then took a winding channel that Fred had told me about that tunneled under the mangroves for half a mile before exiting in the open sea. Beyond these mangroves, I came to a barrier reef that he had not told me about and could find no opening to deep water. I followed it east from the inside for two miles until I came to a dead end where the reef met the curving beach of the main island. I could see a place to get out, but the powerful breakers cresting at the cut were as high as ten feet. I didn't relish the idea of tackling such breakers in rock-strewn waters, but I didn't want to back-track for miles to search for a safer way either.

I chose to take a chance in the surf and managed to make it through, drenched and charged with adrenalin, but by frantic bracing with the paddle, I avoided capsizing. My problems were not over once I was in the open. Around the next point I encountered wind so strong I could barely make headway against it. A rest of only a few seconds resulted in

precious lost ground as I was blown back almost as fast as I could paddle forward. I was paralleling a nice sandy beach off to my left but
couldn't think of landing there as it was pounded by crashing breakers.
I stayed two miles off, opting for the safety of deeper water, but there
were scattered shoals and reefs even that far out that caused the waves
to stack up and break. The situation was getting dangerous, as ten-
footers were not uncommon and some were even bigger. The wind
blew white crests of foam off every peak, and the sea was an opaque,
muddy brown rather than the clear emerald green I had come to
expect of the Caribbean.

One swell lifted me high above the rest, and I nearly panicked when
I saw what was coming. A brown wall of water at least fifteen feet high
and hundreds of yards wide was rolling my way, cresting and getting
ready to break. I strained to turn my bow to face this monster and succeeded just in time. Farther down the wave, to the left of where it
would overtake me, I could see the top curling to form a "pipeline." It
crested right under my hull rather than breaking on top of me as I
feared it would. For a moment, I was suspended in the air over fifteen
feet of nothingness until the kayak fell through the space the wave had
occupied and landed in the trough with a resounding splash. I paddled
on, shaken by the near wipeout and looking out to sea with dread for
similar killer waves.

I reached the lee of Punta Figuras by the end of the afternoon, so
exhausted I could barely wield the paddle. I found a pass through the
reef and landed on a brown sand beach. There was an old lighthouse
tower on the end of the point, accessible by a dirt road where a couple
stood by their parked car, making out and watching the sunset.
I wouldn't have cared if there were a shopping mall on the point.
I wasn't going any farther after what I had been through. I set up my
tent near the water's edge and cooked dinner. The last light of the setting
sun cast lovely shades of purple on the mountains beyond the beach,
framed by a surreal green foreground of coconut palms. I snapped several
pictures, unaware that the used Pentax 35 mm camera I had brought

back from Mississippi to replace my dead Minolta was not functioning at all. I would shoot dozens of rolls of film on this segment of the trip only to discover that none of them were properly exposed when I dropped them off for processing upon my return.

Taking a cue from my experience with the wind and waves the day before, I left well before daylight the next morning and paddled five miles to the next point of land, where I found a more secluded beach. Though it was still early in the morning when I got there, I went ahead and set up camp, far back in the bushes and hidden from the beach. I wanted to take a day off to study my maps of the east coast of Puerto Rico and the crossing to the Virgin Islands. There was a trail leading to the beach nearby, but my tent and kayak were so well-concealed by the palm fronds I draped over them that people walking by never knew I was there. My map showed no beaches on the southwest corner of the island that looked suitable for camping, so I knew I would have to make a long day when I left this campsite to get around to the eastern shore of the island. I turned in early and left two hours before daylight, making a wide detour back to the west to skirt a barrier reef that blocked the point from the open sea.

Just past the next headland to the east, I paddled in close to shore, paralleling a long sandy beach shaded with palms and sparsely settled with cool-looking bungalows. It looked like the perfect place to live, and I envied the lucky residents who woke up every morning to such an idyllic setting. There were big breakers dumping hard between me and the beach, but I felt I was far enough out to avoid them, even though I was close enough in to wave to the few people walking along the shore who noticed me paddling by. Preoccupied with these sights on land, I didn't notice until the last minute that a huge breaker was closing in on me from seaward with all the fury of the one that nearly wiped me out two days earlier. Once again, I was lucky. The wave crested just as it passed under me, lifting me fifteen feet straight up and then breaking in a roar of whitewater that probably would have smashed me into the beach if it had broken a few seconds sooner. What a way to wake up! I snapped out of my lazy, early-morning musings and quickly paddled well out until I was a mile off the beach. I learned my lesson about playing around too close to the surf zone.

A couple hours later, I rounded Punta Tuna and could suddenly see the blue outline of the island of Vieques, floating on the horizon to the east. I had at last conquered the south coast of Puerto Rico. Now the shoreline curved to the northeast. My plan was to follow it all the way to Fajardo, near the northeast corner of the island, and from there make my crossing to the Virgin Islands by way of Culebra, another Puerto Rican island similar to Vieques that lies about halfway to St. Thomas.

Near Punta Tuna, the coast offered nothing but inhospitable cliffs, so I had to paddle miles before I finally reached a place to stop for lunch on Punta Yeguas. The lovely crescent beach enclosed within a split in the point would have made a first-rate campsite, and I had already done ten miles that day, which was as good as each of the last two days of fighting the wind. But now I had the wind to my starboard beam as I was going more northward. I wanted to make progress while I could, so I left the point after taking time to eat and swim.

Early in the afternoon, I came to the ritzy marina at Palmas del Mar and turned into the channel to look for *Texas Tumbleweed*, since this is where Josephine said the yacht was undergoing repairs. The big ketch from Texas was there all right, propped up on jack stands in the boatyard, but I didn't see any sign of Stan or anyone else I knew. My inquiries among the other boaters resulted in no friendly conversation, so I headed back out to sea. The boatyard was a depressing place of wrecked and broken dreams, and the sailors there who were trying to rebuild their lives after Hurricane Hugo's devastating visit had no time for a free-spirited kayaker who escaped their misfortune.

The skies grew dark as an ominous-looking storm approached from the east, but after I left the marina and passed another headland to the north, the beach I found there was unapproachable due to a tremendous surf break. I was effectively trapped between the storm and the surf, so

I headed toward the storm, knowing after my experience with the two big waves that I would be safer in deeper water where breakers were less likely.

The wind increased steadily as the squall closed in, and I watched in fascination as dark clouds and the curtains of rain beneath them swallowed up Vieques, ten miles away, and kept coming my way. The heavy overcast took the light from the green water and turned it to gray, punctuated everywhere by whitecaps and blown foam. I wasn't too worried though, feeling sure I was well beyond the big breakers that closer inshore could do me harm. The worst I expected was to get drenched by rain and blowing spray. I kept paddling north, stretching out to make long, powerful strokes that I hoped would carry me out of the storm's path.

That's when I saw disaster coming. A wall of green water appeared inexplicably from seaward, dwarfing the surrounding seas. It was a rogue wave, and to my horror, I saw that it would crest at about twenty feet. There was nowhere to go and no way to outrun it. I was directly in the path of this monster, which was already curling at the top. This one would not pass under me like those others that had broken too late to be a problem. It was about to dump its full fury right on my head. I dug in frantically with the paddle to spin the kayak bow-first into the wave, but sea kayaks are long and narrow, designed for straight tracking rather than quick maneuvers. The best I could do was not good enough, and I was able to turn only partially into it. I took a deep breath to prepare for the inevitable dive I was about to take. In almost slow motion, a cascade of roaring white water tumbled down the near-vertical face of the wave, and the next thing I knew I was swallowed up and being rolled over and over in its fury like a rag in a washing machine. Though I managed to stay locked into the cockpit with my knees at first, the wave kept the boat under for so long that I had to pull the sprayskirt and swim for the surface before I ran out of air.

I came up in the midst of an angry gray sea under a sullen gray sky, out of my kayak, and treading water more than three miles from land.

It suddenly hit me how alone I really was, facing the open ocean in nothing but a seventeen-foot kayak. There was no time to ponder my predicament, however. I had to catch my boat before it was swept out of my reach. Somehow, I still had the paddle in one hand, but the nylon cord that I normally used to tether it to the deck snapped like a thread. The kayak was close by, thanks to the fact that it was both flooded and inverted, the only thing that kept it from being carried all the way to the beach by the big wave. I swam to it, righted it, and quickly got back in by climbing over the stern, straddling it like a horse until I could slide far enough forward to get my rear end down into the cockpit. The whole boat was half-submerged, with the cockpit completely full of water, but I rapidly pumped it out while scanning the horizon for more rogue waves. Thanks to my careful lashing of everything on deck and in the cockpit, no gear was lost, and no damage was done. I resealed the sprayskirt and finished the pumping until once again the kayak felt light and responsive to the paddle.

The seas around me averaged five to seven feet, so I could only assume the one that capsized me was a rogue that was big enough to break over some shelf of shallow water I had wandered unknowingly over. The darkest of the storm clouds were now passing well to the south of me, so I paddled north as fast as I could, hoping to miss the worst of the wind. I was soon overtaken by blinding rain but was able to navigate by keeping the sounds of the breaking surf far to my left, as I traveled up the coast.

The shoreline here was quite straight, with miles of beach exposed to the open sea. When the rain let up I could see that I was going to have to face the surf zone if I wanted to get to shore, and I *had* to get to shore; I was too exhausted to go much farther. I had already paddled twenty miles that day before the capsize, and there would only be a couple more hours of daylight. I had to get to shore to get all my gear out of the storage compartments and make sure water had not damaged it or my food supply.

I took my usual precaution in big surf of coming in stern first, back-paddling between wave sets, and keeping my bow to seaward so I could see and prepare for breakers. The waves breaking on this beach were seven to ten feet, but as there appeared to be nothing on the shore but soft sand, with no signs of rocks or reefs offshore, I decided to go for it and succeeded in getting through the surf. As the stern was swept onto the sand I leapt out of the cockpit and dragged the heavy-loaded boat beyond the reach of the next wave. Then I took a deep breath, grateful to be on dry land again, and looked around at the deserted beach where I had landed. There was nothing but sand and coconut palms for as far as I could see in either direction. The palms were so dense that I knew they had to belong to a commercial plantation, but there was no sign of a road leading to this part of the beach. I breathed a sigh of relief that I had found an uninhabited landing site where I could dry out and recover from my ordeal.

I quickly unloaded the kayak and spread my wet gear on the deck and about the beach. Some water had gotten into both the bow and stern storage compartments, but thankfully not enough to ruin anything. I pitched my tent and was about to prepare supper when I saw a lone man walking toward me from a mile down the beach to the north. When he reached my camp, he began talking excitedly in rapid Spanish, some of which I could understand. He was asking if I planned to camp here alone, and when I told him yes, he seemed more excited and jabbered and pointed into the forest of coconut palms behind my tent. I didn't catch everything he was trying to say, but I did hear the word for "murder" several times and got the impression that he was trying to warn me it was dangerous to camp here. But so be it. The thought of mere murderers could do nothing to convince me to face that surf zone and paddle back out to sea after what I'd been through that day. When I showed no intentions of leaving, the man continued on his way south, shaking his head and mumbling under his breath. I watched until he disappeared into the distance; then I assembled and loaded the AR-7 rifle and placed it close to my sleeping bag—just in case.

No visitors with homicidal intentions came in the night to my campsite in the coconut plantation. I slept soundly until dawn and then quickly broke camp to leave, only to be caught in a downpour before I could get the kayak loaded. Disgusted with my luck, I covered my stuff with the tent fly and huddled under the palms until it passed over. The surf was still heavy when I shoved off, but I plunged through it without capsizing and reached the relative calm of deeper water.

I headed for Cayo Santiago, a small island just a few miles offshore that was en route to the next headland to the northeast. Fred and Mary had told me that there was a colony of Rhesus monkeys and possibly baboons as well, on Cayo Santiago—like the ones I'd seen on Key Lewis in Florida. Fred said they had been put there by the government years past for research. As I approached the small cay from downwind, I could smell the monkeys long before I got close enough to see them. The place stank like a zoo. I approached close to shore, snapping pictures (with my worthless camera) as I drifted, of monkeys that watched me from the trees. I stopped to eat lunch on a dock someone had built on the island, keeping a wary eye out for the baboons Fred had warned me about. I didn't see any, but the monkeys watched from a distance until I left. (I later saw a television documentary about the monkeys of Cayo Santiago, and there was no mention of baboons on the island.)

Though it was almost noon when I left Cayo Santiago, the wind was relatively calm, and the seas were almost glassy—a dramatic change from the day before. The water was a lot clearer than any I'd seen on the south coast of Puerto Rico, and I could often see the bottom as I passed over coral reefs.

With my water supply running low, I hoped to find a house or some place to refill on the next headland, but the south side of it was deserted. I rounded the cliffs on the point to the north side and saw several house-sized buildings spread out along a steep hillside. It looked like a good place to stop and make a friendly request for water, but when I paddled closer, something was wrong with this idyllic picture. I could now see that a tall chain-link fence surrounded the whole settlement, and there were guard towers strategically placed in the corners of this perimeter. I was looking at a prison.

It was a perfect place for one. The hillside was steep and barren, devoid of vegetation for a hiding escapee, and the only route to freedom was down a rocky cliff pounded by surf. I was close enough to see the inmates working on the grounds in the compound when a voice on a P.A. system warned me in Spanish to get away. I headed north, leaving the headland to make a long crossing to the next one, though I knew from my map that it was part of the Roosevelt Roads Navy base, and I would not be welcome to camp or even stop there.

When I reached the waters off the base, I stayed well offshore as I paddled past fenced installations. I didn't want to get in trouble for getting too close—or worse, get blown out of the water for it. Near a series of rocky cays, I came across two young couples eating lunch in an anchored motorboat. The men were both officers on the base and were taking a day off with their wives for some scuba diving and spearfishing. They gave me a cold Pepsi and a tuna sandwich, which I ate as I held my kayak to the side of their boat and told them about my journey. The men showed me on my map the shortest route past the base and warned me not to stop on any of the deserted islands owned by the Navy, as they were used for SEAL training.

The wind remained calm, allowing me to make good time the rest of the afternoon, so I was past the government property by 3 P.M. I could see the high-rise condominiums of Fajardo ahead in the distance and could still see Vieques off to the southeast. Directly to my east, I could see Culebra, and the expanse of open water that separated me from it. I headed for tiny Cayo Ramone, just off the coast from Fajardo, planning to camp, but a man in a boat tied up to the beach told me that it was private and suggested another cay just outside the entrance to the marina at Fajardo.

The aftermath of Hurricane Hugo was obvious everywhere in the vicinity of Fajardo. On the little island where I set up my camp, the few coconut palms still standing had been stripped bare of their fronds and now stood as stark, dying poles. Debris of every description from wrecked boats and buildings littered the shore and was piled high in twisted stacks among the mangroves, the only vegetation seemingly unaffected by the storm. While I was unloading the kayak, the boater from Cayo Ramone stopped by on his way back to Fajardo and shared a lot of useful information about the crossing to Culebra. He pointed east to a cay barely visible six miles out and missing from my map, saying it was called Isleta Palominitas, and that it would be a good stopover to break up the twenty-mile passage.

The next morning I paddled into the modern marina at Fajardo, passing the protruding masts and wreckage of several sunken yachts. The docks and buildings in the marina were designed like those in a Florida harbor, and the town of Fajardo had a south Florida atmosphere. It reminded me of the mainland more than any place I had seen in the Caribbean.

I bought enough food for a week and refilled my water jugs, then left Puerto Rico astern and set out for Isleta Palominitas. The six-mile crossing against contrary wind took three hours. The cay turned out to be a rounded hump of sand with a clump of palms in the middle. Unlike the brown sand found on most of Puerto Rico's beaches, this sand was white and stood out in vivid contrast to the green of the coconut palms and their understory of sea grape trees. I landed on the triangular-shaped island and discovered that it was only about eighty yards in diameter. A half mile to the north lies its much larger neighbor, Isla Palominas, another private island where uninvited guests are not welcome.

I unloaded the kayak so I could reseal the leaking rear bulkhead with silicon and then pitched my tent in the shade of the coconuts. This was such a perfect campsite I also stretched my hammock between two of the palms, knowing I would stay more than one night. This done, I explored the nearby reefs with mask and snorkel but saw no fish big enough to be worth the effort of spearing. I would be eating tuna out of a can for dinner instead of fresh yellowtail snapper or grouper.

But that was fine. I spent the afternoon in the hammock, cooled by the twenty-knot trade winds, reading and listening to music on my

Walkman. The view from my hammock was spectacular at the end of the day. I watched the sky change colors over Puerto Rico until the sun set behind the distant peak of El Yunque, which at 3,700 feet, is Puerto Rico's second highest mountain.

Waking up on Isleta Palominitas was even better. It rained before daybreak, and the wind was still blowing hard. I walked around the little island drinking in the fresh smell of the rain and delighting in the feel of soft coral sand between my toes. It was the first true solitude I had found on this second segment of my trip, and it reminded me of the countless isolated cays I had visited the previous winter in the Bahamas.

But solitude on the little island ended around noon that second day, when a chartered powerboat anchored just off the beach to drop off a young couple and all their camping gear. They unloaded coolers, beach chairs, and duffel bags, and then the boat sped away, making it obvious that the couple intended to stay a while. Isleta Palominitas is not the kind of island where you can ignore your neighbors, as it is hardly big enough for privacy, so I climbed out of my hammock and went over to introduce myself.

Of course they were dismayed at first to see a bearded, long-haired kayaker walking out of the grove, since they had obviously planned on being romantically stranded on a deserted island for a few days. But a quick narrative of my trip broke the ice, and I helped them carry their gear up to the middle of the island. The couple lived in San Juan and had taken a couple of days off in the middle of the week to escape weekend crowds. Once we had all their stuff moved to a good spot on the island as far from my camp as possible, they discovered they had made a major blunder by leaving their tent poles at home. I helped them rig a lean-to with their tent fly that would keep the rain off, and, luckily for them, the wind was strong enough to keep the bugs away. For my help, they invited me to eat dinner with them, saying they had plenty of extra food, so that evening I cooked a potful of rice to go with the pork chops they grilled. My Tony Chachere's Creole seasoning and their beer topped the meal off to perfection, and I went to bed early to rest for the sixteen-mile crossing ahead.

I woke at 5 A.M. to check the weather. The wind was still fifteen knots, but the sky was clear, so I decided at least to paddle out and see if I could make headway toward Culebra. I was off the beach by seven, unable to say good-bye to my neighbors, since they were still asleep under their lean-to. Outside the reef, there were big swells, but not breaking seas, and the wind didn't seem to be impeding my progress too much. I decided to go ahead and go for Culebra. It didn't take long to drop Isleta Palominitas from sight astern, though even that far out I could still see the high-rises of Fajardo and the mountains of the main island. I set my course for Cayo Lobo, a small cay that my map showed to lie two miles west of Culebra. I was hoping I could camp there one night before going on to Culebra itself.

Two hours into the crossing, I could see Culebra clearly but still could not find the smaller Cayo Lobo. I drifted for a few minutes while eating a snack and noticed that the waves this far offshore were a lot bigger than I had thought. I was still shaken from my violent capsize and more than a little nervous about the possibility of rogue waves. I had less confidence in the seaworthiness of the kayak now, simply because I had seen so many firsthand examples of what the sea could do, such as the storm we had weathered in *Celebration*. When I first paddled out of Tampa over a year before, I had naively thought I could go anywhere and ride out any storm in my kayak. Now I knew the reality of the forces I was dealing with. The open ocean surrounding these Caribbean islands was a lot different than my familiar Gulf of Mexico. I also thought about sharks as my kayak bobbed up and down in the swell. I knew the reality of them now as well, and before starting out this morning, I stashed my loaded bang-stick on the deck where it would be readily accessible.

After eating to replenish my energy, I refastened the spray skirt and pumped out the water that had sloshed into the cockpit while I was digging around inside for my food bag. I paddled on to the east into growing swells, some breaking hard and forcing me to use bracing strokes with my paddle. In another hour I could see two islands that had to be Cayo Lobo and Cayo Lobito, but I couldn't tell which was closer. I pointed the kayak to a spot halfway in between them and continued on that course.

Four hours out from Isleta Palomintas, Cayo Lobo and Culebra didn't seem to be getting any closer, though when I looked back toward distant Puerto Rico, I could tell I was making progress. I was ready to put this crossing behind me, since it was getting scary as the seas continued to build. The worst thing about long open water crossings is that once you're out in the middle of one, you're committed to it. At this point I was a long way from any land, so it was as easy to go on as to go back, and I was exposed to whatever the sea decided to throw at me, as there was nowhere to go if bad weather suddenly approached.

As I paddled on, I heard an engine behind me and turned to see the Fajardo to Culebra ferry approaching fast, on its way to Culebra. The captain changed course to pass close by me, apparently to give his passengers a look at the crazy fool in the tiny kayak. The ferry slowed down as it came within about thirty yards, its bow crashing through the 8-to-10-foot breaking seas I was struggling to make headway against. The passengers lining the deck stared and waved, but I was too busy with the paddle to wave back. I can't imagine what they thought about someone so far from land in such conditions in a narrow splinter of a boat like mine.

Six hours into the crossing, I stopped for another snack, exhausted from the battle against wind and waves. I was now close enough to Cayo Lobito to see that it was nothing more than a chunk of rock with sheer walls perhaps a hundred feet high. Cayo Lobo seemed just as forbidding, but I still had hopes of finding a place to land on it. Beyond these off-lying cays, I could see white sandy beaches on the western shores of Culebra, but that was at least another three miles away, and I didn't want to go that far. It took another half hour to reach the lee of

Cayo Lobo, and I paddled into rocky shallows where I could see spectacular coral formations twenty feet below. I found a cove-like indentation among the cliffs of the west side on the desolate island, and there was a narrow beach made up mostly of bowling-ball-sized chunks of rock and coral. A strong surge washing in and out over these rocks made landing there risky, but I decided to try it anyway. To prevent the waves from smashing my kayak against the rocks, I jumped out of the cockpit just as it touched shore and quickly began throwing gear and water jugs up on high ground so I could lift the boat out of the water and carry it over the boulder field. The newly painted hull suffered some nicks and scratches in the process, but I managed to get it to a high shelf out of reach of the sea.

There was, of course, no place to camp on the rocky beach, so I found a way up a crumbled portion of the cliff and reached a grassy plateau on top. Cayo Lobo was one of the most desolate and forbidding islands I had ever seen. There was nothing tropical about it. The landscape was alien, yet beautiful in a strange way. There was not a single tree, and the only vegetation was knee-high brown grass that rippled in the trade wind like the blue sea below. Fat barrel cacti with red blooms stuck up above the grass here and there and grew in dense clusters on the rockier sections. Above the flat area where I was standing, the island rose to a peak on the eastern end and to an even higher summit on the north end. On this summit were two gray concrete buildings that looked like abandoned military bunkers.

Getting my camping gear up the steep cliff to the grassy meadow was a chore, but I succeeded and managed to set up camp and cook in time to explore the island before sunset. I hiked to the summit to inspect the bunkers, which were empty. There was a circular concrete pad nearby, obviously once used for helicopter landings, but now long abandoned and overgrown with grass that sprouted through its cracked surface. The sweeping, 360-degree view from the heliport was inspiring, and from my vantage point two hundred feet above the waves that were pounding the cliffs below, I could see Puerto Rico,

Vieques, and Culebra—to the west, south, and east, respectively. To the north was nothing but the open Atlantic. The summit of the strange island had a kind of magical feel, starkly exposed as it was to all the powerful elements of nature. I felt new energy while standing there, and I was glad I had stopped on Cayo Lobo.

In the morning I needed to get off Cayo Lobo and paddle to Culebra, since it was my mother's birthday and I wanted to call her. I had more difficulty getting the kayak back into the water than I had in landing. As I tried quickly to stuff all the gear into the open hatches, the surge slammed the boat into the rocks and splashed water into my dry storage compartments. I couldn't get into the cockpit in such conditions, so I had to swim the boat out to deep water and then climb over the stern and enter the cockpit. It was a maddening struggle, and I began my day wet and cursing. The magic of the sunset on the summit of Cayo Lobo had been washed away by this aggravating surge. I was sick of the sea. It seemed that it was personally fighting against me and had been every day since I had left Salinas. I was sick of hearing the sound of waves smashing against rock, and I longed for the serenity of a campsite on the banks of a gently flowing river like Black Creek. I had grown acutely aware like never before of the sea's constant movement. It simply never stops. It is relentless, cold, and indifferent to the feeble efforts of a mere human in a tiny kayak.

It took less than an hour to close the gap between Cayo Lobo and Culebra, and I pulled up on a soft sand beach on a small outlying key called Cayo Luis Pena, about a quarter mile off the main island. This beach would have made a lovely spot to return to and set up camp after my trip into town on Culebra to use the phone and buy supplies. There was shade over part of the beach and good reefs in the quiet, clear water just a few yards out. But to my dismay, there was also a huge sign: NO ACAMPAR, NO FUEGOS, NO MOLESTAR LA FLORA Y FAUNA. I took a bath in the waters off the beach and paddled on to Culebra.

A narrow channel cut through Culebra from the west side and led to the anchorage in the protected bay on the south end. Near the entrance to this channel was the ferry dock, and a sign welcoming visitors to Culebra. The channel to the anchorage was too small to be negotiated by anything other than a small boat like a dinghy or my kayak. I paddled through and was shocked at the sight of the destruction all around me. Though Hurricane Hugo had hit back in September, almost five months before, it looked as if the place had been bombed yesterday. Where houses once stood, there were slabs of concrete piled with debris. Hulls of upside-down boats and masts of sunken ones dotted the canal and harbor. A thirty-foot sailboat was resting right in the middle of what once had been a waterfront home. Scores of other boats of all descriptions were on the beach and in the streets. Apparently, efforts to clean up and rebuild were slow to start, though sporadic sounds of Skilsaws and hammers around town indicated that some work was taking place.

There was a dinghy dock just inside the anchorage, near the channel through which I'd entered, and I tied up there and walked into town to look around. I called my mother to wish her a happy birthday and ate a greasy hamburger in a café run by a woman from Florida. She told me that camping was illegal everywhere, especially on Culebrita, a small islet to the east of Culebra, where I wanted to stay before jumping off to St. Thomas. When I told her I had camped on Cayo Lobo the night before, she said I was lucky I did not get caught by the Department of Natural Resources. She also informed me that Cayo Lobo was full of unexploded mines from military training that took place there. If this was true, I had been lucky again, having spent two hours walking all over an island that was, in effect, a minefield.

I got the impression that this woman was some kind of hard-core, anti-human environmentalist who didn't want anyone on the beaches of Culebra, and I didn't believe her warnings about camping being illegal everywhere around Culebra. It seemed that it was her personal mission to keep people from camping there, but whether it was true or not, I was sick of being told I couldn't camp. The Puerto Rican couple on Isleta Palominitas told me that camping was prohibited in the U.S.

Virgin Islands, with the exception of two private campgrounds on St. John where you have to pay exorbitant fees to camp. I had nothing to look forward to there but more trouble, but I knew I could resort to the techniques I had perfected in Florida and camp without getting caught.

I paddled back through the channel to the west side of the island and headed for the white beaches I'd first seen before landing on Cayo Lobo. The coastline there was deserted—just a strip of sand beach backed by impenetrable scrub forest that covered the small mountain slopes that climbed to the island's interior. There weren't any "No Camping" signs in sight, and there was evidence that others had camped there. I pitched my tent in the shade of some sea grape trees and enjoyed an undisturbed afternoon and night.

Three Puerto Rican guys in two offshore powerboats arrived the next morning and pulled up to the beach just a hundred yards north of my camp. They unloaded a lot of gear, apparently planning to stay a while. They made no effort to acknowledge my presence, so I ignored them too. But later, after hearing them laughing and yelling all afternoon, I began to get nervous when they started firing a pistol. I couldn't tell which direction they were aiming but assumed they were shooting beer cans. But when they finally came over and introduced themselves as Hector, Jose, and Ralph, I realized they were nice guys, despite my first impression. They wanted to know all about my trip, and Ralph, especially, was interested, as he had spent an entire summer alone on Mona Island, living off the reef and hunting wild goats and iguanas, while searching for the pirate treasure that is supposed to be hidden somewhere in the labyrinth of caves there.

Ralph invited me to eat hamburgers with them, but I declined and went back to my camp to cook some rice. As I waited for the water to boil, sitting on the beach and watching the sunset, I noticed an emergency flare hit the top of its arc and then turn to plummet back down into the sea, where it was extinguished. It took a few seconds for my mind to click and realize what I'd just seen. Then I was up in a flash, racing down the beach to the other camp. There was nothing I could do with only a kayak. Ralph lit a lantern and placed it on the beach so we could find our way back in the dark, and the four of us piled into one of their twenty-five-foot center-console skiffs and sped out to sea. At fifty miles per hour, it didn't take long to cover three miles or so, where we spotted an open powerboat, maybe twenty feet long, with twin 150-horsepower outboards, the engine covers removed. A young couple in their twenties were sitting in the open boat, wearing nothing more than swimsuits, drifting hopelessly towards the open Atlantic. With the water hundreds of feet deep, they couldn't anchor, and their VHF radio wasn't working. They had no food for anything other than a picnic. The next stop on the route the current was taking them was probably Iceland or northern Europe.

There was a flurry of rapid Spanish I couldn't follow between Ralph and the young man, but I got the impression that Ralph was letting him have it for his stupidity. The couple had started out from Fajardo, and one of their twin engines had failed right away. Then they continued on, using one engine, planning to cruise the twenty-two miles over to Culebra for a picnic and return home that same day. Needless to say, the other engine also failed before they reached their destination, and the flare I had seen was the last one they had on board after firing the others to no avail.

Ralph tossed the man a rope and we towed them slowly toward the entrance to the anchorage, where we were met halfway by a rescue boat Ralph called for on his radio. The couple didn't seem particularly grateful for our help and probably had no real understanding of the extent of the danger they had been in.

The incident reinforced my already strong beliefs in the superiority of my kayak over most other boats. It amazes me how blindly people trust their lives to technology such as engines and radios. Give me a kayak any day. When I'm out at sea in my kayak, I'm already prepared for the worst. With the food and equipment I carry I can survive at least a few days, even if adrift in mid-ocean. The young couple wouldn't have lasted long out there exposed to the tropical sun with no real clothing and no water. But they just seemed to take it for granted someone would bail them out if they got in trouble.

Back on the beach, my rice was ruined, so at Ralph's insistence, I joined them for hamburgers. They had an ample supply of beer and Scotch whiskey, so after we had a respectable number of empties, Hector broke out the little .25 automatic pistol they had been firing earlier and tried to hit some bottles he lined up on a branch. Not wanting to be outdone, I ran and fetched my AR-7 and proceeded to show them how a Mississippi boy who grew up knocking squirrels out of one-hundred-foot white oaks can shoot. They all loved the rifle and took turns trying it until I had to put it away to conserve my ammo.

I left Ralph and his buddies on the beach the next morning after breakfast and paddled into town to buy a boatload of supplies for the crossing to St. Thomas. It was Saturday, and Ralph had said all the stores would be closed Sunday and Monday for Martin Luther King's birthday. Today though, it was my own birthday, my second one in the islands, and I hoped to get a decent meal in town, though I knew nothing could compare to the previous year, when I celebrated my birthday on the luxury yacht *Destiny*.

At the dinghy dock, I met an older gentleman from a sizable wooden ketch anchored close by. The man was at least in his sixties, but his crew consisted of his two much younger children, fourteen-year-old Thomas and five-year-old Carmen. When he introduced himself as Peter Tangvald, I didn't realize at the time that I was meeting one of the greatest legends of sailing in the world. Originally from Norway, Peter Tangvald had built his fifty-three-foot wooden boat in French Guiana and had sailed it without an engine twice around the world. Tangvald had lost two wives at sea, Thomas's mother to pirates that attacked the yacht in Indonesia, and Carmen's mother, who had gone overboard while alone on her watch during a passage across the Atlantic. His boat was one of the very few in the anchorage undamaged by the recent hurricane, and that was because he had left the harbor at the approach of the storm and boldly sailed five hundred miles across the Caribbean to South America.

Peter Tangvald was extremely interested in my kayak and my trip, and we talked for hours that afternoon about boats and the sea. When he found out that I was from Mississippi, he told me that they planned to sail to the Gulf of Mexico sometime in the coming year, to visit New Orleans. Thomas had never been hunting but wanted to try it, so I gave them my contact information and told them that if I were back in Mississippi when they arrived at New Orleans, I would take them deer hunting on my family's land.

I never heard from them and just assumed that Peter either forgot about me or sailed on to some other part of the globe, but a few years later I came across a book titled *Love, Life, and Death at Sea* by Peter Tangvald. Tragically, just months after our meeting in Culebra, Peter Tangvald had sailed his beautiful boat, *Le Artemis de Pytheas,* onto a reef off Curacao and had perished, along with little Carmen. Thomas survived and finished the story that became the book I found.

When I left Culebra I paddled out of the south end of the anchorage and headed east to Culebrita, a fair-sized uninhabited island just to the east of Culebra. Once outside the harbor at Culebra, I could clearly see the mountainous island of St. Thomas, looming hazy and blue out of the sea in the distance, surrounded by smaller islands and cays. It seemed so close that I considered paddling straight to it, but I would be fighting a headwind and the day was late, so I would not arrive until the next morning. I didn't relish a long night crossing in these open waters. I needed some time to camp on Culebrita, to plan my crossing and wait for the right weather, as I had done on Isleta Palominitas before coming here.

I paddled to the far eastern side of Culebrita, even though the best beaches and a protected harbor lie on the west side, facing Culebra. I wanted to have a campsite with a good view of St. Thomas while hopefully remaining out of sight of any Department of Natural Resources patrol boats. But on the east side of Culebrita, the sea was not peaceful. Big swells rolled in unimpeded off the open Atlantic and rebounded off the walls of cliffs, creating havoc. I was in danger of capsizing in these rebounding waves but made it past the cliffs to a deep cove that was backed by a long, curving sweep of lovely beach. There was heavy surf hitting the beach though, so I had a tricky landing, coming in backwards, slowly, while trying to keep the bow into the breakers. I rode one last wave in once I was clear of some outlying reefs and landed heavily on the sand. I felt sure I would not be bothered on this beach. The only approach was by water, and that surf would deter any boat other than a kayak. Behind the beach the terrain was steep and rocky, thick with cactus and desert scrub, and littered with impenetrable piles of hurricane debris. It was as if everything in the Virgin Islands had been blown there by Hugo.

I set up camp and picked my way through the brush to the summit of a steep hill south of the beach. From there I had an excellent view of St. Thomas and the Virgin Passage that lay between. This fifteen-mile crossing was a true blue-water passage, with no protection of reefs or small islands. Little did I know that this first day was to be my best opportunity to paddle across and that by waiting I would be stuck for more than two weeks while stronger-than-normal trade winds kept the passage whipped up into 15-to-18-foot seas.

It was on the following morning, my first on Culebrita, that the change in the weather became evident. I listened in disgust as the announcer on the NOAA weather radio station said that the winds would be twenty to thirty knots for the next few days and that there was a small craft advisory in effect. I was stuck. The open beach on Culebrita turned out to be miserably hot by midday. There was nowhere to go for shade, as the only two trees standing were palms that had been stripped of their fronds by the hurricane. I took to the water to cool off and managed to spear one small fish that was not much more than a snack after I dressed and fried it.

For the next two days I suffered the heat of Culebrita, studying maps, listening to discouraging weather reports, and a country music station broadcasting from St. Thomas that billed itself as the "only Country in the Caribbean." I had the island to myself, and only once had a visitor, in the form of a huge helicopter, probably U.S. Navy, that swooped down to hover less than a hundred feet over my camp in the middle of the night. I was wrenched out of a deep sleep by its tremendous rotor-wash that sent sand and my gear flying everywhere and the piercing searchlight that flooded my tent. I leapt outside, wearing nothing but my underwear, sleepy and pissed off enough to flip them the bird as I stood transfixed by the light and squinting to keep the sand out of my eyes.

By the morning after that incident, my water supply was getting low, so I decided to paddle back to the anchorage at Culebra rather than wait any longer for a chance to cross that didn't seem to be coming any time soon. There was no water on Culebrita, so I had to take my chances with the big breakers that were smashing into the beach. I packed the boat and left, clawing my way out through the surf zone through avalanches of whitewater that threatened to bury me, but I made it through, and once I reached the west side of the island, the seas were more manageable.

At the dinghy dock I was pleasantly surprised to see some friends from my days in the Dominican Republic: Jack and Veronica of the luxury motor yacht *English Jack*. They treated me to lunch in one of the cafés in town, and then we walked a couple of miles together to Flamenco Beach, one of Culebra's main attractions. Jack and Veronica were on their way back to Puerto Rico, after a short cruise of the Virgin Islands. I stocked up on food and water after saying goodbye to them, and paddled back to my original campsite on the west side of the island, which was deserted now that Ralph, Hector, and Jose had gone home.

Nine days passed with little change in wind conditions, and I spent my time reading novels in my hammock, snorkeling the reefs, and trying to hike in the thick bush behind my camp. I paddled to town every other day or so to break up the monotony and to get food and water, but I usually didn't stay long before returning to the solitude of the beach. I was sick of the waiting and the helplessness of being pinned down in one location because of the weather. I longed to be able to paddle my twenty miles again every day, but it was not possible here.

By the sixteenth day after I'd first landed on Culebra, the forecast called for a slight break in the wind, so I paddled back to the lonely beach on the east side of Culebrita. I was dismayed to find the sea conditions in the Virgin Passage as bad as ever and the forecast apparently wrong. St. Thomas was tantalizingly close, in plain view, so I made camp and resolved to paddle there the following morning. When I awoke at 3 A.M., however, with intentions of leaving, the wind was howling across the beach, blowing sand and threatening to carry my tent away. There was no way I was going to be able to paddle fifteen miles against wind like that, especially considering the seas that would result. I stayed there another night, then escaped the surf-bound beach once again to paddle back around to the protected side of the island, where I made camp for one more night before heading back to Culebra.

It was on the eighteenth day of being stuck there that I happened into conversation with some boaters from a couple of yachts in the anchorage as I tied up one more time to the dinghy dock. They told me that a skipper named Shaun, who was in the business of chartering his thirty-eight-foot sailboat, *had* to take his boat to St. Thomas that very night to meet his paying clients in the morning. I found Shaun a little later, and he assured me that he was definitely going to make the crossing, come hell or high water. The boat had a strong inboard diesel, so contrary wind and big seas would not stop him. He was alone, so he needed an extra hand and said he could fit my kayak on deck. I was fed up with waiting and out of patience. As much as I hated the thought of crewing on another sailboat, I was going to go crazy if I didn't get moving again. And besides, this was just for a few hours. Shaun assured me that I would be paddling again come tomorrow. I knew that once I reached the Virgin Islands I could travel despite the wind, as there are so many islands in the group that long crossings would not be necessary.

I unloaded my gear and lashed the kayak down to Shaun's deck that afternoon, then joined him and a couple dozen other boaters for a Friday night barbecue near the dinghy dock. We boarded the boat at 10:00 that night and hauled in the anchor. I was elated to be leaving Culebra at last, though I knew that we were going to be in for a rough night.

# TEN

# THE VIRGIN ISLANDS

I suspect that, if you should go to the end of the world, you would find somebody there going farther . . .

**—HENRY DAVID THOREAU**

My nearly forgotten memories of misery at sea on *Celebration* were brought back in vivid replay shortly after Shaun and I left the harbor at Culebra. The thirty-eight-foot yacht was violently pitched and rolled by the 12-to-15-foot breaking waves of the open water, reminding me of why I hadn't wanted to crew on any more yachts. This was sailing at its worst. No white sails silhouetted against blues skies while sipping margaritas in the cockpit—this was the hard reality of sailing most romantic dreamers never consider when they decide to buy a boat. It was pitch black, the wind was howling, salt spray was flying over the deck and stinging our faces, and rocks and reefs close by in the dark waves would tear the hull apart if we got off course and out of the channel. I began to feel that terrible queasiness that marks the onslaught of seasickness and knew that it was going to be an interminably long night. Fortunately, the sickness went from mild to worse quite quickly, and I went ahead and threw up over the rail, feeling much better afterward.

Although it was only fifteen miles from Culebrita to the closest shore on the island of St. Thomas, the overall passage for a deep draft sailboat was much longer, as we had to leave from the deep harbor at Culebra and sail past the westernmost reaches of St. Thomas to the harbor at Charlotte Amalie. The passage took all night, but we were able to make steady progress with the engine despite the sea conditions. Before dawn, we had a close call with an unlighted freighter that nearly ran us down, but Shaun managed to get us out of the way in the nick of time.

Near the entrance to the harbor at Charlotte Amalie, dozens of cruise ships were hove-to offshore, waiting their turn to get in to the busy docks. Small inter-island freighters and private yachts plied the surrounding waters in all directions, requiring us to keep a sharp look-out. City lights sparkled on the slopes of the island mountains, still black in the pre-dawn darkness.

By the time we reached the anchorage where Shaun had a mooring, day was breaking and dark clouds that promised imminent rain were rolling in from the east. We headed straight to the fuel docks so he could fill the yacht's tanks before tying up to the mooring. Even at 6 A.M., we had to wait in line behind two other boats before we could approach the pumps. St. Thomas had a different atmosphere than any harbor I'd seen in Puerto Rico. It was much more crowded, and the waterfront buildings were modern and expensive-looking, though many were dirty and damaged by the storm. I was anxious to walk around town and spend some time ashore, but there was no time for that now. Shaun was a busy man, and he had just a few hours to get the boat ready for his paying guests. I had to unload my kayak and get my gear out of his way. I decided to do it at the fuel dock, since it was choppy out in the anchorage and would be more difficult there. Loading the kayak in the water from another boat is always difficult, even in calm water.

Just as I had all my gear spread out in his dinghy and my hatches wide open, the clouds let loose a deluge that soaked everything before I could cram it into the storage compartments. I was sleepy and infuriated about being wet, but despite this, still enthusiastic about being in a new place. After I finished loading up, I tied my kayak to the stern of the yacht and rode out to the mooring with Shaun to help him get it

Paddling off the mangrove coast of Everglades National Park (Pete Hill)

secured. This done, we shook hands, and he wished me luck. Then I paddled back to the Yacht Haven Marina, tied up to the crowded dinghy dock, and set off to see some of Charlotte Amalie.

Traffic was so heavy on the street behind the marina that I had to wait several minutes for an opportunity to cross. The difference in culture between the Virgin Islands and Puerto Rico was immediately apparent, first of all by the fact that people drove on the opposite side of the road. This was the English-speaking, black Caribbean—though it was full of outsiders, both tourists and white mainlanders who had come here to live permanently. Everywhere was evidence of the gap between the rich white minority and the impoverished black majority. Rastafarian graffiti on the walls spoke of the dream of rising up and overcoming the "oppressors" to take control of all the islands. Somewhere in the middle of the spectrum, between the Rastas and the wealthy business owners and tourists, were the hundreds of full-time yachties—many of them truly boat-bums from the States, chasing the dream of the island life but with no money to do it. They hung out in the waterfront bars, washed up on this outpost of American territory with hopes of somehow finding the means to continue the lifestyle. Bulletin boards around the harbor carried notices posted by many of them, looking for crew positions if they had no boat, or paying work if they did so they could keep on sailing. Jobs were scarce, costs of living were astronomical, and prices on everything in the stores were inflated to reflect the tourist economy.

The tourists were the easiest of all to spot. These pale-skinned invaders from the cruise ships and jets were everywhere, walking the narrow streets wearing Hawaiian shirts, cameras dangling from their necks, eagerly snapping up thirty-dollar T-shirts in the boutiques near the docks.

Seeing all this was interesting, but I wasn't in the mood to hang around this sort of place for long, so I bought some groceries from a giant supermarket with the best variety I'd seen since Mayaguez and headed back to my kayak. I made my way across the harbor, dodging boat traffic until I reached the east side of Hassel Island, where I found a deserted, rocky beach and made a crash landing through the surge. The island was directly beneath the takeoff and landing routes of the airliners coming in and out of the St. Thomas airport, but I didn't care. I had been awake for more than thirty hours, and I fell asleep in my tent despite the hot sun and the screaming jets overhead. I stayed there for two nights, pondering what I would do next while I recovered from my exhaustion. The crossing in the yacht from Culebra had further convinced me of the futility of trying to paddle all the way to South America upwind. But now that I was in the Virgin Islands, I was eager to do some exploring. The U.S. and British Virgin Islands stretch some sixty miles east from St. Thomas, and there are dozens of small cays scattered among the main islands where I was sure I could find places to camp, even if it was illegal. At least there would be no long crossings, and most of the time I would be able to stay in the lee of some of the islands and avoid the worst of big seas and high winds.

When I left Hassel Island, I headed east along the south coast of St. Thomas. Aside from a few exclusive resorts and extravagant waterfront mansions, this south side of the island was relatively undeveloped. I saw few people other than a nude woman lying in the sun on a private beach. A few miles farther on, at Long Point, I found a small beach under a wooded hill and landed there to set up camp. On the hill above the beach, cattle were grazing and a seldom-used dirt road led away from the coast, but I spent the night with no human interruptions.

The next day I encountered a new danger in the Virgin Islands that I had not seen elsewhere, in the form of large ferryboats that run frequently back and forth between St. Thomas and St. John, cruising at speeds upwards of forty knots. These boats came upon me suddenly out of nowhere, and I had several near misses with them while I was making the crossing from Long Point to St. John. I'm sure the captains of these craft could not see me as my kayak was often awash in waves, and their radar probably couldn't detect me either. I took a long, circuitous route out of my way to stay out of what appeared to be the busiest lane of traffic between the two islands.

St. John is supposed to be the "nature island" of the Virgin Islands, with most of its land set aside in the Virgin Islands National Park. After the congestion of Charlotte Amalie, I looked forward to seeing such an island. I also hoped to find George Bouillon there, since that's where Josephine had heard he was working when I was back in Salinas. I paddled into Cruz Bay, on the island's western end, searching hopefully for *Winning Edge* among the many yachts anchored there. The Frenchman's Hunter 27 wasn't there though, so I paddled ashore and found my way to the park headquarters, where I hoped to get camping information. The brochure given to me by a ranger said that the only two camping areas on the island were on the north coast, privately operated and charging, at the time, seventy dollars per night for a spot to pitch a tent. Unbelievably, despite these prices, the sites were booked six months in advance. I would find my own campsites, hiding in the bush. Fred and Mary had told me that the backcountry here was full of half-wild "bush Rastas" that do the same, in spite of park regulations.

Near the waterfront, I spotted one of these true "roots Rastamen," with real dreadlocks, not the fashionable kind popular with some urban islanders and mainlanders. Real dreadlocks are massive tangles of hair, never groomed or washed, and smeared with cow dung for added repulsion. This Rastaman was whacking the tops off a pile of green coconuts and selling them to passing tourists. When an obviously affluent white couple approached him, the husband raising a camera to get a picture, the Rastaman spat at them and cursed. The Rastas are anti-materialistic, and these rich tourists had made it difficult for them to practice their simple existence due to the inflated prices outside investors had created here. How could a young black islander ever hope to own a house when outsiders had driven the price of land on St. John up to more than $100,000 an acre?

I would side with the Rastas and "lib in de bush" while I was touring this island. Let the Yuppie tourists have their seventy-dollar campsites and three-hundred-dollar hotel rooms. I liked the Rastas, the more I learned about them. Their philosophy advocated a return to nature and a rejection of the possessions most people spend their lives trying to acquire. I knew where they were coming from. Was that not why I sold everything I had and paddled off in a kayak in the first place? The Rastas also had good music. I could appreciate reggae, especially here in the islands that gave birth to it. My tape collection included several reggae groups, and of course music by the great prophet of Rastafarianism, Bob Marley.

As I prepared to leave Cruz Bay to go in search of a place to camp, I was surprised to see two kayaks cruising through the anchorage. I waved frantically at the occupants, holding up my paddle, and when they saw me, they turned and came to the beach. I had hoped that they were fellow sea kayak travelers, but the young man and his girlfriend were actually new residents of St. John and had just received their new kayaks by freight that day. The boats were not touring kayaks, but rather the open cockpit, sit-on-top design intended for day trips and wave surfing. The man explained to me that he had ordered several of the kayaks and intended to start a rental and day-touring service for tourists. When I told him I was thinking about heading out to Lovango Cay, a couple miles to the north, to find a campsite, he wanted to paddle along with me.

Once we left the lee of St. John, we encountered a stiff headwind and steep chop. I expected this guy to be able to paddle circles around me, considering that he had an unloaded boat and a body builder's physique that included a set of arms that made him look as though he had already paddled ten thousand miles. But surprisingly, he soon dropped hopelessly behind, complaining that his "arms were burning" from the paddling. Looks can be deceiving, I realized, and figured that all the upwind paddling I'd done over the past few months had done me more good than I'd realized. I couldn't wait for him, as it was getting near dark, so I waved and left him in my wake, continuing on my way to Lovango Cay.

The rocky coast of Lovango didn't look promising from the south, but surprisingly, on the north end, under a densely forested hillside, there was a broad, sandy beach. Someone had built a small table onto the trunk of a giant tree that shaded the beach, and a fire pit nearby indicated that the beach was occasionally used for camping. Just across a narrow channel of deep water were the rocky cliffs of Congo Cay, and on the west end of the beach beyond where I was camping, the sand ended at the foot of a vertical wall of black rock. On both islands there were numerous small palms of a species I had not seen before, but no coconut palms were in sight. A couple of powerboats anchored briefly for some fishing in the channel between the islands, but no one told me to leave or disturbed me. I got a good night's rest and woke up with new confidence that I would be able to camp discreetly throughout the Virgin Islands.

I crossed back to St. John the next morning, planning to circle it from the north and go on to Coral Bay, on the east side, where Fred and Mary normally stay when they're in the Virgin Islands, and where I hoped to find George. Along the way, I planned to stop off on the beach at Trunk Bay, reputed to be "one of the ten most beautiful beaches in the world," and take some pictures. As I neared this famous beach around 9 A.M., I noticed a line of buoys roped together, blocking my entrance to shore, each lettered with the warning: "No Boats." The beach beyond was beautiful, all right—a long gentle crescent of white sand, shaded by a grove of lush coconut palms that gave way to even greener hills rising inland to the interior of the national park. I wanted to get a closer look, despite the signs, so I paddled over the ropes and headed for the beach. There was already a crowd, even at this hour, and many of the beachgoers looked and waved as I paralleled the shore from two hundred yards out, taking pictures with my non-functioning camera. Then I noticed a female lifeguard running to the water's edge, waving wildly at me with both arms, motioning for me to go away, to get back out to sea, as if my presence in the swimming area was a threat to the life of every tourist there. I continued as I had been going, slowly dipping my paddle and watching the woman's antics with amusement. As the beach curved out ahead, I was drawing closer to the shore on my easterly course, and I could now hear some of the woman's shouts. I was amazed at the urgency and anger in her voice, as if she really thought I was going to run over the snorkelers, none of whom were anywhere near as far from shore as I was.

This was really funny, I thought, and I continued on, even more slowly, just to spite her. It was then that I noticed a male lifeguard throw a surfboard into the water and start swimming it in my direction on an intersecting course as if he were on a mission to save the world. I could have easily outdistanced him, but I eased along, waiting to hear what he had to say. He drew within twenty yards and screamed: "Get the hell out of the swimming area—NOW!"

This was where he crossed the line. After all I had been through, fighting the very ocean itself for the past few weeks just to get here, I was in no mood to be ordered to do *anything*, by *anyone*. Who was this young punk to think he could intimidate me? Just because I arrived by kayak and was not a tourist staying in a three-hundred-dollar-a-night resort, did that mean that I had no right to see this world-famous beach, which was part of a U.S. National Park, and therefore as much mine as his? His audacity put me in a fighting mood, but I outwardly maintained my cool and calmly replied: "I'm just checking out the beach, man. Taking some pictures." I kept paddling slowly, as I had been doing.

He made a move closer and yelled again. "I'm telling you to get that boat out of the swimming area, now!"

At that point I lost it, and retaliated with a piece of my mind about how silly it was to think my kayak was any threat to swimmers, especially on a calm, clear morning like this when the bay was like a lake. I told him I was going to continue on my course, holding both ends of the paddle clear of the water like a weapon so he could see that he would get whacked in the head if he came any closer. I was trembling with anger, and evidently the tone of my voice had an effect. He knew that he was at a great disadvantage if he tried to attack while lying flat on his surfboard. He wisely kept his distance, but made threats about all the trouble I was going to be in, saying he hoped I got arrested.

"I would go back to the beach, if I were you, buddy. This kayak is a cruising vessel on the high seas. Your coming out here like you're going to attack me could be construed as an act of piracy, and I have the right to defend my vessel." As I said this, I pointed to the bang-stick that was stowed under bungee cords on my foredeck.

At this he turned and started back to the beach, furious because he knew there was nothing he could do. "You can't have that in a national park. You're going to jail!"

I laughed out loud and continued my leisurely cruise along the beach as if nothing ever happened. People like him just couldn't understand that I didn't care about their stupid little petty rules. I couldn't understand how this guy could be so serious about enforcing such rules. What difference did it make if I passed by his beach in a kayak making all of two or three knots? I had been apart from society for so long now that all its frivolous little constraints and restrictions seemed ridiculous to me. I was living in a different world—a world subject foremost to the laws of Nature. All that mattered was survival: avoiding storms, sharks, and rogue waves, finding a place to sleep at night, and keeping an adequate supply of food and water. My life had been reduced to the basics just as I'd intended when I left. I had no intentions of hurting anyone or interfering with their chosen way of living, but I didn't want anyone to interfere with mine either.

Near the end of the beach at Trunk Bay, I pointed my bow back out to sea and crossed back over the ropes, rounding a rocky point and continuing on my way to the east. Just in case the lifeguard did send out some ranger in a powerboat, I stayed far enough offshore to be hard to spot from land.

I paddled past Cinnamon Bay and its exclusive campgrounds, then went through an aptly named pass called The Narrows, with St. John on my right and Great Thatch Island, one of the British Virgin Islands, just a couple hundred yards off to my left. I would wait and clear customs into the B.V.I. later, after I had visited Coral Bay. Great Thatch was uninhabited, with no port of entry, so I could have crossed over unnoticed, but I continued on around St. John, ducking into the many coves on the northeast side, searching for some hidden beach where I might set up camp.

I found what seemed to be the perfect place: a beach at the back of a cove that was inaccessible to most boats because of outlying reefs. But when I landed I noticed a smoldering fire back in the mangrove thicket. Roasting on the fire were several large hermit crabs, and I assumed this must be the camp of some "bush Rastas," since a person had to be serious about living off the land and sea to eat hermit crabs. I wanted to talk to some of these people, as I was certain that I could learn a lot from them, but though I called out, the surrounding forest answered with only silence. I was unable to follow the bare footprints that were everywhere, as they disappeared where they left the sand and entered the rocky terrain beyond the beach. They were watching me, of that I was sure. I could feel eyes upon me, and it made me a little nervous. They probably thought I was a park ranger trying to roust them out. Mary had told me that the rangers periodically comb the park trying to track down these squatters, but the vegetation of the island is dense, and the mountains, though not high, are quite rugged. The Rastas usually elude their pursuers.

I had a lot of respect for anyone who could live in the bush under these conditions. Fresh water would be difficult to find, available only as pockets of rainwater trapped in rock basins. There was no abundance of edible plants that I could see, and the reefs had been mostly fished out as far as I could tell from my snorkeling.

Not wanting to disturb these people and having respect for their privacy and secrecy, I shoved off and paddled on until I found a smaller and even more hidden beach in another cove. There was no trail leading into the mountains from behind the beach, so overland access to the cove would have been difficult. I felt secure there, after pitching my tent in the shadows and camouflaging it and the kayak with brush to hide them from the eyes of any rangers who might pass by in boats. I was in no great hurry to get to Coral Bay or anywhere else at this point, so I decided I would stay in this cove at least a couple of days.

The second day there, I forced my way up the mountain behind my camp, pushing through the tangles of brush and briars until I reached the road at the top of the island's spine. From there, I could see Coral Bay far below, on the other side of the narrow peninsula the road straddled. The scattered yachts in the anchorage were too far below for me to identify any of them. From my vantage point, I could see the route into the bay that would require me to paddle a few miles around the end of the peninsula from my camp. It would, at any rate, be much easier than walking there through the dense island scrub forest. I returned to my camp and spent most of the afternoon snorkeling. No one noticed me during my two-and-a-half-day stay there, though I saw hundreds of boats of all descriptions out in the Sir Francis Drake Channel that separates St. John from Tortola, the largest island of the B.V.I.

The trip to Coral Bay the next day took most of the morning, since I stopped in several interesting coves along the way. *Winning Edge* was not in the anchorage, but there was one small vessel I recognized, a twenty-foot Flicka sailboat named *Stay Up* that belonged to a couple from Norfolk, Virginia. I had met them the year before in Georgetown. They were not on board though, so I paddled to the beach, looking for a place to land among all the debris and junked cars that lined the shore. The Coral Bay area had a trashy appearance that didn't at all look to be the result of a hurricane, and this surprised me, since Fred and Mary had raved about Coral Bay. I went up to the small bar called Redbeard's and was surprised to see several people lined up there, already doing some serious drinking even though it was only 11 A.M. I inquired about Fred and Mary and learned that Mary just happened to be in the next room, having flown to St. John to visit friends for a few days.

She was, of course, surprised to see me there, and called Fred right away to let him know I was still alive and well. Later that day, I rode with her and some friends across the island to Cruz Bay, in the back of another Nissan pickup she and Fred kept in Coral Bay for use when they were on St. John. Just as she had done in Puerto Rico, she pushed the little truck to the limit of its suspension system on the twisting mountain roads, and it was all I could do to stay in the back of the truck with a terrified young hitchhiker we picked up along the way. Despite the reckless speed, though, the views from the ridgetop road were breathtaking, and we somehow arrived on the other side of the island intact.

Mary's friends needed to go to a hardware store to shop for some PVC pipe for the house they were building, and I wandered around town, stopping to buy groceries at outrageous prices, since there was no real store in Coral Bay. On the way back, Mary's friend Terry insisted on stopping at the island dump, which was located on the mountainside above Cruz Bay. He was looking for parts for some device he was making for his new house. Watching him reminded me of the eccentric main character in Paul Theroux's novel *The Mosquito Coast*, which I had recently read during my long stay on Culebra. Like the fictitious inventor in the story, Terry ranted and raved in disgust about all the "perfectly good stuff" people had thrown in the dump. He became angry as he sorted through piles of twisted washing machines and refrigerators, cursing the fools that had thrown them away for their senseless waste. There was a herd of feral hogs rooting through the heaps of fly-covered garbage in the dump, and Terry stalked close to them with hungry intent, yelling back to his wife that the little piglets would make fine eating and promising her that he would return to shoot one.

Back on the other side of the island, we drove Terry and his wife to their home, which they were living in despite its half-constructed state. From the piles of assorted junk that covered the yard and filled the small rooms, it was easy to assume that Terry's affection for garbage dumps was not something he'd developed that afternoon. Despite all this, the view from his front door out over Coral Bay was inspiring, though I wondered at the logic of paying $100,000 an acre for barren, rocky ground that was useless for anything but the view. This end of the island was so dry that residents of Coral Bay had to drive all the way to Cruz Bay just to buy water. The astronomical prices and inconveniences didn't deter Fred and Mary either, who had also bought a lot on this hillside with intentions to build on it someday.

Terry had a friend who owned an undeveloped waterfront lot near the anchorage, and since he was not on the island at the time and we couldn't ask his permission, Terry told me to go ahead and camp there for the night. Back at the bay, I accompanied Mary to Redbeard's bar to have a couple of beers. Inside, there was an even larger collection of unsavory characters drinking themselves into oblivion now that it was mid-afternoon. Most of them looked like modern-day pirates or perhaps drug-runners, hiding out in this backwater to avoid either the law or the IRS. But I wasn't one to pass judgment, considering how I looked after months of kayaking. To me, though, Redbeard's had a depressing air, and the patrons inside had little interest in anything other than drinking or smoking ganja. I left and paddled over to the beach Terry had directed me to and set up my camp early. There was a solo sailor named Mike anchored nearby on a trimaran that he had recently sailed across the Atlantic from England. He shared my impression of the Redbeard's crowd, preferring to stay alone on his boat, but wanting good conversation, he invited me aboard for dinner and gave me three gallons of water from his rain catchment system.

I broke camp early and paddled out of Coral Bay after having a cup of coffee with Mike. Around the peninsula again, I pulled into a different cove than the one I'd camped in before, where I had the luxury of a larger beach and a view of Tortola and the islands along my route to the east. That evening as I cooked dinner, a curious mongoose visited my camp, eyeing me from just a few yards away and eagerly accepting the chunks of tuna I tossed his way. I had read that the abundant mongooses on the island were brought there by the early Danish sugar cane growers in hopes of controlling the rats. The plan didn't work, however, as the animals worked different shifts, the rats being nocturnal and the mongooses feeding by day.

That night I studied my maps and made plans to cross in the morning to Road Town, the main settlement on Tortola and a port of entry to the B.V.I. I looked forward to reaching the British Virgins. As far as I could tell from the maps, they were less populated and developed than the U.S. islands.

The crossing the next day didn't take long, since I left early to beat the trade winds. Up close, Tortola was an impressively high, mountainous island. I paralleled the coast for two miles to get to the wide bay where Road Town is situated. I was a little nervous about clearing customs, as I was not sure I would be allowed in if the officials knew I was camping. I tied up to a dock at a marina, and as I was digging my passport out of the kayak, a man approached and called me by name. I didn't recognize him at first, but I vaguely remembered him when he introduced himself as Philip and said he had met me near Darby

Island, in the Exumas, when I was having coffee on his friend's boat. Once again, I was embarrassed by my lack of ability to remember all the names and faces of the people I had met in my travels. It was easier for them to remember me, I reasoned, as my mode of travel was both unusual and conspicuous.

Philip directed me to the customs office, a white building about a half mile away along the waterfront. I was glad I had docked my kayak where I did. Maybe the officers in customs and immigration wouldn't bother to come out and take a look at it since it would involve walking so far. Along the way to the building, I couldn't help but notice the difference between the streets of this town and those of Charlotte Amalie. Everything here was neat and clean, perhaps reflecting the British influence. The wood frame houses were painted in bright island colors, and the streets were far less cluttered with cars and pedestrians.

There was a long line at the customs desk, but when I finally had my turn to apply for entry, I was asked surprisingly few questions and given a two-week cruising permit for about four dollars. After taking care of this business, I set off to look for a grocery store where I could stock up for my tour of the B.V.I. I quickly found that the stores were a lot like those of the Bahamas—small and stocked with limited and overpriced items. But by shopping in three different ones, I found enough supplies to get me by for several days.

To the south of Tortola, across the five-mile-wide Sir Francis Drake Channel, lies a string of small islands that stretch from St. John to Virgin Gorda. The islands in this chain are the most pristine of all the Virgin Islands, and I looked forward to spending a few days there, hoping to find similar camping conditions as I had experienced in the Bahamas. Upon leaving Road Town, I crossed the channel on a heading for Dead Chest Island. Dead Chest is a tiny little cay, right next to Peter Island, which is one of the largest in this undeveloped group. There was no one on Dead Chest, so I set up camp on a beach with a view of Road Town in the distance.

Some yachts were anchored within view in a small cove on Peter Island, but no one came to Dead Chest or seemed to mind that I was there. The next day I paddled over to Peter Island and continued past the anchorage to the south shore, where I came to a long, deserted beach at the foot of a steep hill. A grove of coconut palms stretched from one end of the beach to the other, so I continued close inshore until I spotted a couple of palms that looked climbable. Most of the trees in the grove towered fifty feet or more, but these two leaned out at an angle and held clusters of green drinking nuts just twenty feet over the clear water at the edge of the beach. I opened two for breakfast and stripped the husks off several more to make them easier to carry with me. The beach would have been a lovely place to camp, but a short walk back into the palms revealed a dirt road with fresh tire tracks. I followed the road and discovered that it led to a dump, where there were several rusting Land Rovers, as well as the usual assortment of garbage. I figured someone would see me and ask me to leave if I stayed on the beach, so I paddled away, continuing my journey eastward, past Dead Chest to Salt Island, the next in line. There was supposed to be a good diving site near Salt Island—the wreck of the H.M.S. *Rhone*—a freighter that had broken apart and gone down in a storm. But I had read that it was too deep to reach without scuba gear, so I continued on to Cooper Island, where I still didn't see a likely campsite.

The next island over was Ginger Island, more isolated than the others in the chain and extremely rugged looking, with tall cliffs rising out of the sea to barren summits of cactus and scrub-covered peaks. I skirted the shore of this island on the south side, which consisted of nothing but sheer rocks smashed by heavy swells from the open Caribbean. There was one indention on this side of the island that couldn't really pass for a cove, and in it was a small pocket of beach big enough for a tent, but the surf pounding it discouraged me from attempting a landing. I paddled around to the east side, passing under a rocky headland and, to my surprise, discovered a gorgeous horseshoe-shaped bay, lined in the back with a long sweep of crescent beach. Halfway into this bay, barring the entrance to the beach to most boats, a reef stretched from one headland of the horseshoe to the other. It would be a perfect hideaway for a kayaker, so I headed for the reef, confident I could find a cut through the barrier of coral.

When I found a likely looking opening, I cautiously backed through the surf zone and suddenly found myself in the quiet, protected waters of the inner bay. But the apparent tranquility of the surface of this sheltered lagoon was an illusion. In the clear waters beneath my hull, I could see tens of thousands of fish, all of a single species and about one foot in length. They moved in undulating schools and frequently changed directions to dart away in panicked unison. Then I saw the reason for their erratic behavior as I paddled on toward the beach. First one, then three, four . . . no, *dozens* of 5-to-6-foot black-tipped sharks were working the schools of fish in a feeding frenzy. When I'd first seen the transparent waters of the bay, I had thought I would grab my mask and snorkel as soon as my kayak touched the beach, but the sight beneath my hull quickly changed my mind. I hurried on to the beach, certain that there were probably a lot more sharks than just the ones I saw and sure that some might be a lot bigger.

As I pulled up on shore and looked back over my shoulder, I saw that the schooling fish were not only under attack from below but that death came from above as well. Scores of brown pelicans cruised low over the water, each frequently folding its wings to pierce the surface in a sudden dive and take another of the rapidly dwindling school. I watched this spectacle in fascination as I walked the lonely beach, looking for the best spot to pitch my tent. Like most of the other beaches I'd seen east of Salinas, this one was littered with junk blown ashore by the hurricane. There was one short coconut palm with about ten drinking nuts hanging within my reach, and these were a welcome addition to my water supply, since I knew from first sight that I would stay here for more than one night. It was as near perfect a tropical beach as I could expect to find. It was doubtful that many people ever visited this beach, because of the reef, and since the cove faced the open Caribbean, I could see none of the other Virgin Islands, and consequently no signs of civilization. I put my tent on the opposite end of the beach from the lone palm, under some large sea grape trees that afforded some shade.

There was a steep cliff on the east side of Ginger Island that dropped vertically at least a hundred feet to the sea. I was able to get to the top of this escarpment by scrambling up the back way, over slopes of loose stones held together by scrub brush. From the cliff, I had an excellent view of Virgin Gorda, the last big island in the Virgin Islands group. East of Virgin Gorda, there was nothing but the treacherous eighty-mile Anegada Passage that separates the Virgins from St. Martin, in the Leeward Islands group.

I spent a lot of time during the next two days sitting atop that cliff, contemplating the future of my trip. In one way I wanted to go on, to see all the islands of the eastern Caribbean, but I knew that the way beyond Virgin Gorda would be dangerous to the point of suicidal. I would still be facing the full strength of the trade winds, which I now knew I could not paddle eighty miles against in one stint. The only option would be to once again crew aboard a yacht to cross that passage, but even then I would have many open ocean hops of more than thirty miles as I worked my way south toward Grenada. I was through with crewing on yachts. I didn't like being on someone else's schedule, and I didn't enjoy living aboard or even the sailing near as much as I liked kayaking. All I wanted to do was paddle and camp on wonderful islands like Ginger Island, which assured me that there are still some unspoiled places left in the Caribbean where Nature is still in control. The life-and-death struggle taking place in the lagoon beneath my rocky perch was ample proof of that.

I broke camp on Ginger Island after a three-day stay and paddled on over to Virgin Gorda. I would turn back from there, I had decided, but I had to at least go and look over the edge into the Anegada Passage. On the south end of Virgin Gorda, I stopped to see The Baths, a world-famous natural wonder and tourist attraction. The Baths is section of coastline dominated by strange, rounded boulders of pure granite.

These are no ordinary boulders—some are fifty feet or more in diameter—and they are jumbled up like gigantic pebbles along the shore, both in and out of the water, forming dark passageways between them and sunlit grottos filled with pools of crystalline water. The place is a natural playground for anyone interested in exploring, rock climbing, or snorkeling, and I spent hours there, along with many other visitors who arrived by yacht or overland by the road. The beaches in the vicinity of The Baths were the most beautiful I saw in all my travels, despite all the hype about those on St. John. Here the smooth granite boulders decorate soft white sand, and green coconut palms scattered about provide areas of shade. The waters around the rocks are as transparent as glass, and since spearfishing is not allowed, the reefs teem with life.

There was a large modern marina about a mile north of The Baths, and I stopped to visit the grocery stores and have a sandwich in one of the cafés. After leaving the marina, I paddled on along the coast of the island to the north end, where from a distance the steep mountains inland appeared to be covered in lush jungle. As I drew closer, however, what had looked like a cloak of forests on the hillsides was, in reality, just low scrub like all the forests I had seen in the Virgin Islands. I camped on uninhabited Little Dog Cay, a bit to the west of the main island, and the next morning paddled back to Virgin Gorda in a pouring rain. The rain passed quickly, and when the sun came back out, surreal mists steamed off the verdant slopes, making this unspoiled part of the island look like a pristine paradise.

My goal for the day was the North Sound of Virgin Gorda, which is an area protected from the open ocean by a group of little cays. The North Sound is the easternmost safe anchorage in the B.V.I. for yachts headed across the Anegada for the Leewards. I had heard that those sailing down-island often wait for a considerable time to find the right

conditions to make the crossing. The Anegada has a well-earned reputation for rough going because of its strong currents and unfavorable
winds.

Even inside the sound, the wind made it difficult for me to reach the
east end, but after several hours of paddling, I arrived at the anchorage.
I scanned the sterns of the yachts there for names I recognized, but
there were none there, so I paddled on up to the docks. A sign over the
waterfront read: The Bitter End Yacht Club. Though I knew the name
was an old sailor's term for the end of a bight of line, it could fit in
another way as well. This place marked the bitter end of easy sailing in
the closely-spaced Virgin Islands, and it marked the bitter end of one
long kayak jaunt that was about to come to a close. I liked the name of
the yacht club, and I was glad I had come to the edge of the North
Sound and looked over. I found a waterfront sandwich shop and had
lunch.

# AFTERWORD

I spent eight more days in the islands after reaching the Bitter End Yacht Club, leisurely retracing my route back past The Baths, Dead Chest Island, and Tortola. I paddled back into the U.S. Virgin Islands unnoticed, without bothering to officially clear out of the B.V.I. Back in Charlotte Amalie, a travel agent helped me arrange to have my kayak shipped to New Orleans by airfreight at a reasonable price. The day before my flight out of St. Thomas, someone I met at the marina told me that George Bouillon was working in Red Hook, a town on the eastern side of the island that I hadn't visited by kayak. I took a bus over to see him, and we cooked a celebratory feast on *Winning Edge* while he filled me in on his past few months of sailing. He was still married to Millie, but he had come to St. Thomas to find work and only saw her once a month when he could afford to fly to Puerto Plata. He still had plans to sail on to St. Martin, where he could legally work as a French chef and get a visa for his wife.

When I returned to Mississippi, I found that I was not ready to make the adjustment back to normal living after such a long period of free-spirited travel. I returned to Black Creek in my kayak and spent nearly a month living in the woods along its banks. I did not forget my longings for Black Creek's peaceful tranquility while camping on the surf-bound beaches of Culebra, but during this time plans for another long journey began to take shape in my mind. I wanted to do a kayak trip that would not be so dependant upon the cooperation of the wind and that would not require hitching rides on larger boats to make lengthy passages. Inspired by Lawrence Pitcairn's descriptions of Canada while visiting with him and his daughter, Laura, on board *Heron I* in the Bahamas, I turned my attention to the north.

After paddling out of the Black Creek woodlands, I went to work doing some free-lance house painting and quickly scraped up the funds for another voyage. In July, just four months after my return from St. Thomas, my brother Jeff drove me to the Canadian border at Crane Lake, Minnesota, where I launched my kayak for a journey back to Mississippi. My route took me northwest along the old fur-trade route to Lake of the Woods, down the Winnipeg River to Lake Winnipeg, and then up the Red River of the North to its headwaters on the border of South Dakota and Minnesota. From there I traveled overland to the headwaters of the Minnesota River, then paddled downstream to St. Paul, where I entered the Mississippi, which I followed back to my home state at Vicksburg. This trip took only 102 days, even though at 2,600 miles, it was much longer than my Caribbean voyage.

After that kayak trip, my interests turned to boat-building and eventually to sailing, and despite my dislike of crewing on yachts in the Caribbean, I am now passionate about sailing and have a small live-aboard cruiser of my own. Even so, I still think that sea kayaking is the most rewarding and efficient form of water travel, and I foresee no end to my interest in exploring in these wonderful, human-powered boats.